South Africa's Crisis of Constitutional Democracy

T0273230

South Africa's Crisis of Constitutional Democracy

Can the U.S. Constitution Help?

Edited by Robert A. Licht
and Bertus de Villiers

With Lawrence Schlemmer
and Dawid van Wyk

The AEI Press

Publisher for the American Enterprise Institute

Washington, D.C.

1994

To order call toll free 1-800-462-6420 or 1-717-794-3800. For all other inquiries please contact the AEI Press, 1150 Seventeenth Street, N.W., Washington, D.C. 20036 or call 1-800-862-5801.

Library of Congress Cataloging-in-Publication Data

South Africa's crisis of constitutional democracy : can the U.S. Constitution help? / edited by Robert A. Licht and Bertus de Villiers with Lawrence Schlemmer and Dawid van Wyk.
    p. cm.
  ISBN 0-8447-3835-2. — ISBN 978 0-8447-3834-5 (pbk.)
    1. South Africa—Politics and government—1989– 2. Civil rights-
-South Africa. 3. Democracy—South Africa. 4. United States-
-Constitutional history. 5. United States—Politics and government.
I. Licht, Robert A. II. American Enterprise Institute for Public
Policy Research.
JQ1911.S693 1994
320.468'09'048—dc20   93-43191
                                            CIP

Chapter 6, "American Democracy and the Acquisitive Spirit," was originally published in *How Capitalistic Is the Constitution?* (AEI Press, 1982).

The AEI Press
Publisher for the American Enterprise Institute
1150 17th Street, N.W., Washington, D.C. 20036

Contents

Editors and Authors

ROBERT A. LICHT has edited a number of volumes in the American Enterprise Institute's series on the United States Constitution. These include *The Framers and Fundamental Rights, Old Rights and New,* and *Is the Supreme Court the Guardian of the Constitution?* With Robert A. Goldwin, Mr. Licht has edited *Foreign Policy and the Constitution* and *The Spirit of the Constitution.* Mr. Licht has taught philosophy at Bucknell University and liberal arts at St. John's College in Annapolis.

BERTUS DE VILLIERS is the head of the Centre for Constitutional Analysis of the Human Sciences Research Council in Pretoria. He is an advocate of the Supreme Court and has a special interest in human rights and intergovernmental relations. Mr. de Villiers serves on the executive of the Federalism Research Committee of the International Political Science Association. He has traveled extensively and has undertaken research on constitutional and political development in various countries, publishing three books and various articles on constitutional matters such as regional and local government, electoral systems, and socioeconomic rights.

LAWRENCE SCHLEMMER is the vice president for research of the Human Sciences Research Council. He has written numerous scholarly and popular journal articles, and chapters in books as well as monographs and research reports on issues in political science and public policy. He has worked on various team projects with the Arnold Berstraesser Institute of the Federal Republic of Germany, as well as participated in study tours of the United States, United Kingdom, and the People's Republic of China.

DAWID VAN WYK holds a chair in the Department of Constitutional and Public International Law at the University of South Africa. He has published widely in the field of constitutional law, and he is the editor of the journal *SA Publiekreg/Public Law.* He has been active in the Kwazulu/Natal Indaba (1986–1989); the Technical Committee of Working Group 3 (Codesa, 1992); and the Technical Committee of the Transitional Executive Council of the Multiparty Negotiation Process (1993).

KADER ASMAL is a professor of human rights at the University of the Western Cape and is the author of two books and numerous other publications. He returned from a twenty-seven year exile in Dublin, where he taught law at Trinity College and was dean of the Faculty of Arts from 1980 to 1985. He has been a member of the Constitutional Committee of the African National Congress since its establishment in 1986 and was elected to the National Executive Committee of the ANC in 1991. In 1992 he was appointed to the ANC's National Commission for the Emancipation of Women. He has served as a delegate to Working Group I of Codesa, the Convention for a Democratic South Africa.

WALTER BERNS is John M. Olin University Professor at Georgetown University and adjunct scholar at the American Enterprise Institute. He serves on the Judicial Fellows Commission, has been a member of the Council of Scholars in the Library of Congress and of the National Council on the Humanities and has served as the alternate U.S. representative to the U.S. Commission on Human Rights. Mr. Berns's most recent book is *Taking the Constitution Seriously*.

GRETCHEN CARPENTER is a member of the Department of Constitutional Law at the University of South Africa in Pretoria. She holds degrees from the University of Pretoria (BA, LLB) and from the University of South Africa. Professor Carpenter has published widely in the field of constitutional and administrative law. She is the author of *Introduction to South African Constitutional Law* (1987) and the translator of Marinus Wiecher's *Administratiefreg* (1985).

JAMES W. CEASER is professor of government and foreign affairs at the University of Virginia. His books include *Presidential Selection; Reforming the Reforms; Political Science and Liberal Democracy;* and, with Andrew Busch, *Upside Down and Inside Out: The 1992 Elections and American Politics*. Professor Ceaser has served as a consultant to the American Bar Association on elections and political reform, and he is president of the Publius Institute, a nonprofit research center for the study of public policy in the American states.

DENNIS DAVIS is the director of the Centre for Applied Legal Studies, University of the Witwatersrand, where he is also a professor of law.

He teaches in the areas of jurisprudence, labor law, insurance, and income tax. He is a member of the Technical Committee to the Multiparty Forum on the Electoral Act.

JOHN DUGARD is a professor of law, University of the Witwatersrand. He received the LLB from the University of Stellenbosch, and an LLB, Diploma in International Law, and LLD from Cambridge University. He is the author of *The South West Africa / Namibia Dispute* (1973), *Introduction to Criminal Procedure* (1977), *Human Rights and the South African Legal Order* (1978), *Recognition and the United Nations* (1987), *The Last Years of Apartheid: Civil Liberties in South Africa* (1992), and *International Law: A South African Perspective* (1994).

DANIEL J. ELAZAR is professor of political science at Temple University in Philadelphia, where he directs the Center for the Study of Federalism, and president of the Jerusalem Center for Public Affairs, an independent institute. Professor Elazar also holds the Senator N. M. Paterson Professorship in Intergovernmental Relations at Bar Ilan University in Israel. He is the author of more than fifty books, including *The American Partnership: American Federalism, a View from the States.*

ROBERT A. GOLDWIN is resident scholar at the American Enterprise Institute and former director of constitutional studies. He has served in the White House as special consultant to the president and, concurrently, as adviser to the secretary of defense. He has taught at the University of Chicago and at Kenyon College and was dean of St. John's College in Annapolis. He is the editor of a score of books on American politics, coeditor of the AEI series of volumes on the Constitution, and author of numerous articles, many of which appear in the collection *Why Blacks, Women, and Jews Are Not Mentioned in the Constitution, and Other Unorthodox Views.*

PIERRE JOHANNES JEREMIA OLIVIER was born in Usakos, Namibia, in 1936. He was appointed as a judge to the South African Supreme Court in 1985 and later to the South African Law Commission, as a full-time member; he is at present its vice chairman. Judge Olivier has been a project leader of the Law Commission's Working Paper and Interim Report on Group and Human Rights. He has been particularly active in establishing contact with African countries, with a view to building a common approach to human rights protection.

THOMAS L. PANGLE is a professor of political science at the University of Toronto. He is the translator of *Plato's Laws* and of *The Roots of*

Political Philosophy: Ten Forgotten Socratic Dialogues. He is the author of *Montesquieu's Philosophy of Liberalism: A Commentary on "The Spirit of the Laws"* and *The Spirit of Modern Republicanism: The Moral Vision of the American Founders and the Philosophy of Locke*. Mr. Pangle's latest work (forthcoming from Johns Hopkins University Press) is *Ennobling Democracy: The Challenge of the Post-Modern Era*.

MARC F. PLATTNER is editor of the *Journal of Democracy*, a quarterly publication that addresses the problems and prospects of democracy around the world, and counselor at the National Endowment for Democracy, where he served as director of program from 1984 to 1989. He is the author of *Rousseau's State of Nature* (1979), the editor of *Human Rights in Our Time* (1984), and the coeditor (with Larry Diamond) of *The Global Resurgence of Democracy* (1993) and *Capitalism, Socialism, and Democracy Revisited* (1993).

DAVID WELSH is a Capetonian by birth and was educated at the Universities of Cape Town and Oxford. He holds the Chair of South African Studies at UCT. His publications include *The Roots of Segregation* (1971) and *South Africa's Options* (written with F. van Zyl Slabbert, 1979).

Acknowledgments

The conference on which the present volume is based would not have been possible without the generous assistance of various South African individuals, businesses, and institutions. In this connection, E. Peter Gush and Henry R. Slack must be mentioned, as well as Anglo-American Corporation of South Africa, Limited; South African Airways; and Liberty Life. The Human Sciences Research Council of Pretoria provided indispensable intellectual and logistical assistance, especially the vice president for Research, Professor Lawrence Schlemmer.

Richard R. Davis, an American gentleman and patriot and a friend of liberal democracy in South Africa, conceived of the project and was its moving spirit. He persuaded Chris DeMuth, the president of AEI, that the Institute's resources, particularly its Constitution Project, might contribute uniquely to the desired transformation of South Africa. Additional support in the United States for the project was received from the generosity of the Engelhard Corporation and from Minorco (U.S.A.) Inc.

The present volume could not have been published without a generous grant from the United States Institute of Peace in Washington, D.C., which the editors here gratefully acknowledge.

South Africa's Crisis of Constitutional Democracy

1

Introduction

Robert A. Licht and Bertus de Villiers

The world of liberal democracies awaits anxiously the outcome of the present political and constitutional crisis in South Africa. In the past few years there have occurred dramatic, even unimagined, changes in the political fortunes of those illiberal regimes that seemed most immune to change. But change does not, of itself, compel political progress; there is no inevitability that the collapse of illiberal regimes brings forth liberal, that self-government and liberty replace servility and repression.

The evidence of progress we now see ranges from disheartening to uncertain. The desired combination of free markets and constitutional self-government is proving extraordinarily difficult to achieve. At the same time the barbarism of ethnic, tribal, racial, and religious strife is reemerging under the conditions of political and social entropy. Is liberal democracy destined to be the rare experience of the favored few?

This self-concern of the liberal democracies must seem quite selfish. What, after all, about the fate of South Africa itself? What can the liberal democracies provide to South Africa to help bring about the desired goals? Capital investment and liberalized trade seem to be the most desired assistance. Such tangible assistance, however, must await the political developments that will justify it. In political developments, however, South Africans must forge their own destiny. The adoption in South Africa, as this book goes to press, of a transitional constitution that looks toward drafting a permanent Constitution is a hopeful sign of positive developments. The purpose of the present volume is, in some small way, to help bring about the profoundly wished for transition to liberal democracy in South Africa, particularly as the deliberations about and drafting of a permanent Constitution get underway.

Purpose of This Collaborative Effort

The origin of this volume was a conference held in July 1992 outside Johannesburg, called "Constitutionalism in South Africa and in the United States: A Dialogue." The purpose of the conference was to bring together a small group of American constitutional scholars with a larger group of South Africans, not limited to constitutional scholars, to engage in a political-philosophic conversation on the topic of constitutionalism. No agenda or plan for South Africa was brought to the conversation by the American scholars, but simply their reflections on the principles of the Constitution of the United States of America, and on why its design has worked so well for so long.

That this may not be thought a disingenuous conceit, we acknowledge at the outset that the Americans were not "impartial" observers of the South African scene. They were and are each partisans and promoters of liberal democracy, and they are especially partial to its constitutional republican and federal form as it exists in the United States. Nevertheless, they did not, nor do they now believe that the American Constitution is simply transferable to South Africa. James Ceaser observes in his chapter in this volume:

> The object of such an exercise is obviously not to suggest a transfer of American laws or institutions to South Africa. It is rather to encourage consideration of certain basic constitutional principles. If some of these principles should prove interesting, their implementation in a different context would necessarily assume a different institutional form. It is an axiom of comparative politics that general principles translate into different societies in quite dissimilar ways. Such was the starting point of the most perceptive of all foreign observers of America, Alexis de Tocqueville, when he undertook his famous study, *Democracy in America*. "Let us not turn to America," he counseled his French readers, "in order slavishly to copy the institutions she has fashioned for herself, but in order that we may better understand what suits us; let us look there for instruction rather than models."

It is in this spirit that their considered reflections on the American Constitution might be useful to South Africans now embarked on the most difficult, and urgent, of human tasks. The American authors hope that their contribution to the conversation would be to introduce a certain philosophic distance from the immediacy of political circumstance, an opportunity to step back and to view, as from a distance, those enduring principles of constitutional design of the framers of the American Constitution. If there is one message for South Africa common to all the American political scientists, it is that South Africa should not place all its faith in a Bill of Rights and an independent judiciary. Precisely because the protection of individual rights is so important, the most important consideration in constitutional design, in their view, is the means by which the institutions and practices of self-government may be self-limiting while being at the same time effective.

In the most general sense, however, the reflections of the American scholars had as their inspiration the thought that the wisdom of the American framers could, they hoped, take wing, and contribute in some way to the possibility of thoughtful statesmanship in South Africa at a time when the imperatives of action and partisanship hold natural dominion.

The attentive reader will note that the original purpose of the conference, to serve as a means to a "dialogue," is not fully present in the resulting book. The charge to the Americans was to write their chapters from a perspective of the principles of constitutional design and practice as viewed through the lens of the U.S. Constitution, taking into account what they may have learned from conversation with their South African colleagues. With the exception of Daniel Elazar, who is a student of the theory and practices of federalism worldwide, they do not claim direct and intimate knowledge of the complexities of South African history and life, and their thoughts on the particular details of constitutional design in South Africa are rightly diffident. Conversely, the South African contributors cannot call upon a particular compelling South African constitutional tradition for guidance to the future; they are struggling with the issue of constitutionalism on the front lines, as it were, and their chapters necessarily reflect their involvement with the deliberations of a particular time and place.

The summaries that follow reflect the parallel treatment of topics of the chapters of the book.

Constitutionalism, An Overview

Constitutional Traditions. In his chapter on constitutionalism in South Africa, Pierre Olivier analyzes the approach of various political formations to the meaning of constitutionalism. Although most of

3

the political organizations agree that a future constitution should be the ultimate authority in the country, there are serious differences regarding the meaning and consequences of constitutionalism. If these differences among the drafters of the constitution are not resolved, the inheritors of the constitution will have difficulty in interpreting the constitution uniformly.

Olivier proposes that the following elements should form the core of "constitutionalism":

• Government should be constrained by the constitution. That is, certain limits should be placed on what government on all levels may do.

• Legal and constitutional limitations should be placed on the way in which government power may be executed.

• Fundamental rights and liberties should be protected; that is, all government action should comply with the provisions of a justiciable bill of rights.

• A system of normative principles should determine governmental action.

• A balance should be struck between limited government and majority government.

Olivier analyzes what he calls the five models of constitutionalism, namely the Westminster, American, German, socialist, and African approaches. He discusses the approaches of some of the political formations in South Africa and concludes that all the main parties share the view that a new constitution should be written and entrenched, and that constitutionalism should be the basis for all governmental activities. He predicts that a combination of the American and German approaches will feature prominently in the unfolding South African debate.

The U.S. Constitution's Relevance for South Africa. Thomas Pangle, as is to be expected, does not discuss the variety of constitutional traditions, as does Olivier. Rather, he examines only those that are relevant to the U.S. Constitution.

The fundamental goals of the Constitution were "the securing of natural or human rights; the fostering of republican self-government; and the protection of a tolerant and enlightened Protestant Christianity." American constitutionalism seeks "to maximize, for each and all, the opportunity to accumulate ever-increasing material welfare through the competitive private enterprise system."

The principles of constitutionalism, popular sovereignty and majoritarianism, are self-protected in the U.S. Constitution by the design of a limited government through checks and balances, through decentralization, and through regional or federal structures. This system of self-limitation of government is also a rejection of the "mixed regime" model, which requires a subordination of party interest to an overriding idea of the common good. America rejects aristocracy, a royal family, or an established church.

This design results in a "competitive, interest-group politics" that renders "the formation of a uniform majority faction unlikely." Nevertheless, implicit in the American system is the tradition of civic republicanism harking back to the notion of man as a political animal, and the tradition that republican self-government is itself "a good whose value extends beyond the securing of individual rights." In addition, "Protestant Christianity may be said to have contributed to American political consciousness much of the fervor with which Americans embraced the idea of an elevated equality of all human beings."

Pangle has reservations about the prospects of American-style constitutionalism in South Africa:

> The unfortunate history of apartheid has rendered almost every one of the pillars of the American consensus suspect in the eyes of either the black majority or the white minority. It was the securing of basic rights of *individuals*, not groups, that was preeminent among the founders' constitutional concerns.

Nevertheless, Pangle hopes that in a transitional phase "the experience of free enterprise and of access to the opportunities and rewards of the free market" might recommend "the advantages of a free and vigorous private sector." Moreover, "the development of private associations of all kinds might begin to break citizens free from tribal, party, and gang allegiances." "A sense of patriotism and pride in nationhood might well take hold as South Africa assumed its rightful place as the economic and political leader of sub-Saharan Africa."

On Federalism

The National and the Democratic Parties. Kader Asmal examines the debate on federalism against the background of proposals made by two exponents of federalism. He summarizes the basic differences between a federal and a unitary dispensation:

• In a federal constitution the powers are divided between the national and regional legislatures, while under a unitary dispensation

5

the central parliament is supreme and has final authority over the whole of the country.

- In federations the constitution is the highest law, while in a union the will of parliament is supreme to all laws. The will of parliament can, however, be limited by means of constitutional provisions such as a bill of rights.
- Federations normally provide for two houses of parliament, with one of the houses representing regional interests. Although some unions have bicameral legislatures, this is not a basic feature of or requirement for a union.
- In the final instance, federations provide for separate regional institutions and governmental bodies with original powers, while the powers, if any, of regions in a union are not original but decentralized.

Asmal stresses that regions within a federal dispensation do not necessarily have more powers or autonomy than those in a unitary dispensation. Some decentralization programs in traditional unitary countries are quite extensive and provide for more actual autonomy than exists in many federal-type constitutions.

The author argues that the federal option in some political ranks has become a serious matter only since the normalization of the political process in South Africa. The National party has since 1989 supported federalism as a way to protect minorities through veto powers vested in racial groups. It was only in 1991 that the National party actually started using the word "federal" to describe their aims.

The Democratic party is also a strong supporter of the federal ideal, but this should be seen in the context of the party's proposed "drastic restrictions on majority rule." As in the case of the National party and the Inkatha Freedom party, Asmal questions the motive for the somewhat sudden support for federalism.

Asmal then turns to the powers of the different levels of government. In the allocation of powers in South Africa, the need for reconstruction and the role that the center has to fulfill in that process will have to be borne in mind. The National party is endeavoring to place certain socioeconomic matters, such as housing, security, education, and welfare, beyond the reach of the center by allocating them to regional and local governments. Similar criticism is expressed against the proposals of the Democratic party, and Asmal concludes that "the depressing aspect about the Democratic party proposal is not simply its suspicions of a central parliament but its refusal to acknowledge the inherent dangers in denuding the central government of authority by constitutionally limiting its powers."

Asmal raises a number of arguments against federalism, such as the unitary nature of the South African state since 1910; the misuse of federalism to limit the access of people to government; the frustration of a national majority on a regional level; the retaining of resources in the richer regions; and the inability of the center to address historical injustices in order to bring about social and economic transformation.

The response of the African National Congress (ANC) to the federal debate is that it has always been in favor of a unitary form of government. This does not mean that provision cannot be made for regional governments. Such regions should, however, not render the national government powerless to implement its policies. The constitution should protect regions in order to prevent their abolition, as happened in 1986 with the provincial councils. Their powers should be concurrent; this would allow the national legislature to override regional laws, to set policy guidelines, and to ensure minimum standards.

Federalism in South Africa. Daniel J. Elazar argues that what both South Africa and the United States "have in common is that both need, each for its own reasons, federal solutions" to their political problems. "Federal countries need federal polities, and South Africa . . . is a federal country."

The American republic, of course, is thoroughly federal and has been since its inception. Its federalism is territorial, not ethnic or tribal—even though its homogeneity was overstated by the American founders.

> The United States was founded by uniting separate states that felt themselves to be akin to one another and that had conducted a revolution against the mother country together. The question before South Africa is, Can a unitary, highly centralized state be transformed into a federation?

Although "the record is not unambiguous," Elazar believes that it can and should be done. He discusses the elements of constitutional design that would have to be the elements of a transition to federalism in South Africa.

For Elazar, the benefits to South Africa of federalism are compelling:

> Federal democracy addresses the great questions of political sovereignty and the distribution of powers (competences), the relationships between power and law or right, and the great issues of centralization and decentralization. It does so

by vesting political sovereignty in the people who constitute the body politic rather than in states and requiring them to allocate competences or powers constitutionally among the governments of their creation. They must do so in a way that encourages multiple centers of power and in a manner that provides for both centralization and decentralization as needed, but always within a noncentralized framework whereby all exercise of powers is governed by law and related to the rights of the constituents.

On the Economic Foundations of Constitutionalism

Liberty, Commerce, and Prosperity. Dennis Davis argues that it is not a matter of choosing between a centrally planned state on the one hand and absolute capitalism on the other. It is generally agreed that some form of state intervention is required in fields such as education, infrastructure, and welfare. He refers to the unequal distribution of resources along racial lines and stresses that such inequality threatens the social equilibrium of the total population. He warns that a new constitutional dispensation could be stillborn if adequate consideration is not given to the linkage between economic and political inequality.

The author considers the recommendations of the South African Law Commission and analyzes some of its provisions, including those dealing with property and with social and economic rights. He questions the arguments of the commission that social and economic rights impose an economic cost that cannot be enforced by a court, and also the absence of consensus that such rights be included in a new constitution.

After analyzing the debate on property rights, Davis concludes that any new constitution that entrenches present property relations will reinforce the patterns of inequality and constitute a major obstacle to popular political participation. A constitution born of the economic inequality of present-day South Africa cannot ignore the international trend to incorporate second- and third-generation rights. He argues that to exclude social and economic rights on the basis of their complexity would be to promote a distorted view of equality.

The Acquisitive Spirit. Marc Plattner observes that "more and more critics nowadays contend that there is a fundamental tension—or even contradiction—between America's capitalist economic order and its democratic political order." These critics "seem to deny . . . that there is any intrinsic connection between the political system whose

protection of equal rights and liberties they applaud and the economic system whose inegalitarian outcomes they deplore." But a
study of *The Federalist*, especially No. 10, "reveals that the framers of
the Constitution recognized that an economic system that permitted
material inequalities was not merely compatible with but was an
essential aspect of the political structure they sought to establish."

The writers of *The Federalist* held the view "that men should be
encouraged to exercise to the full extent their 'different and unequal
faculties of acquiring property,' despite the inequality this inevitably
produces." Unlike the small republics of antiquity, which sought to
produce "the greatest possible unity among the citizens," the American framers "chose precisely the opposite course, of encouraging
multiplicity and disunity." They preferred, therefore, the large, extended republic to the small. "It is critical to *The Federalist's* concept
of the large republic . . . that the population be divided into a
considerable diversity of *economic* interests. This, in turn, requires a
relatively advanced and complex economy."

But how can the pursuit of the spirit of acquisitiveness "redound
to the public good"? Again, it is precisely "the division of society into
a multiplicity of interests" that brings about "what virtue cannot be
trusted to accomplish." "Such a division impedes the formation of
oppressive majority factions." Moreover, "the avarice stimulated by
commerce, though undeniably a selfish passion, is nonetheless conducive to habits of industry, prudence, and sobriety—in short, to
regularity of morals."

But a permanent division of the wealthy and the poor would also
be destructive of republican liberty. The poor, always a majority,
would tend to "unite to defraud or despoil the wealthy." This
possibility is countered by the large republic with its multiplicity and
diversity of interests. Further, the tendency of wealth to accumulate
in a few families was an equally great danger to economic opportunity
for all: "The principal instrument advocated by Jefferson (and others)
for preventing inequality of fortune sufficient to threaten republicanism was laws encouraging the equal partition of inheritances."

Four economic principles of the framers' political theory may be
discerned: (1) industry and the pursuit of gain should be encouraged;
(2) superior industry and skill justly merit the greater material rewards they naturally tend to reap; (3) the rights of private property
must be secured, both on the grounds of justice and as a necessary
condition for promoting industry; (4) the laws should favor the free
and rapid circulation of property, so that all may have a chance to
become rich and so that distinct and permanent classes of either the
very rich or the very poor are unlikely to form.

On a Bill of Rights

Human Rights and the Rule of Law. John Dugard expresses his belief that the U.S. experience will continue to influence the human rights debate in South Africa. The apparent failure of the Westminster system to provide adequate protection for individual rights and freedoms, as well as general distrust of the system, has led to a search for new models. In the process, care should be taken against oversimplification, especially given the different backgrounds and circumstances of the two countries.

The current debate has witnessed a shift in approach to the protection of human rights by both the National party and the African National Congress. Politicians, in their search for consensus, have refused to become too closely involved in the debate on a bill of rights. Attention has been focused more on matters such as federalism and the composition of parliament. The dilemma is that agreement on a bill of rights may be more apparent than real. Serious differences remain as to the content and purpose of a bill of rights.

The National party views a bill of rights as an instrument to protect individual and minority rights. The ANC expects much more of it. For them a bill of rights must signal an end to apartheid and a visible sign of the victory of the liberation movement. One major area of dispute is whether a bill of rights should create or declare rights. Other areas of dispute are

- the protection of minorities in a bill of rights
- private discrimination, and whether a bill of rights will be applicable to such discrimination
- economic policy and the principles of a free market and property rights
- affirmative action
- social and economic rights

Dugard also considers the formulation of a bill of rights and whether it should be short, couched in general terms, and phrased negatively or should be extensive, including positive rights regarding socioeconomic matters. The role and composition of the judiciary are also addressed.

The Use of a Bill of Rights. "What use . . . can a bill of rights serve in popular government?" James Madison asked in a letter to Thomas Jefferson in 1788. Robert A. Goldwin pursues the answer to this question as Madison understood it. He also shows the genius of

Madison's statesmanship as he recounts the story of the formulation and adoption of the Bill of Rights.

Madison "saw a bill of rights as problematic . . . and complained that the bills of rights of his time . . . were least effective when they were most needed." Modern political thought has given unprecedented freedom of action to individuals. One consequence of this, however, "is that individuals and groups within the political society are more at the mercy of other individuals and groups. . . . The right to do whatever is not forbidden gives us more freedom to benefit ourselves . . . but it also leaves others more free to harm us . . . unless they are restrained. And to the extent that the government is called on to restrain them, the intrusive power of government increases, and our realm of privacy potentially diminishes." How then to moderate the behavior of citizens? "The connection between moderation and the security of rights is vital."

One of the "great facts of modern political life" is the persistence of "small-group loyalty," a cause "almost everywhere" of hostility and violence. From this perspective it is possible to "appreciate the daring of the American constitutional attempt to combat it almost entirely by silence." "Protections under the Constitution of the United States are for individual persons, and all persons are considered equally." Nowhere in the Constitution are group rights mentioned. "The purpose seems to have been to combat the power of small-group loyalties and animosities by refusing to give them constitutional standing."

For Madison, the answer to the question of what truly protects rights "follows from the principles of a properly constituted free society: that rights are primary and that the public good is best served by the habits developed by citizens exercising their rights in opposition to other citizens doing the same thing." This favors a multiplicity of interests and religious sects. The institutions established by the Constitution make that possible by the multiplying of a diversity of interests. "The scheme of representation . . . gives voice to a tremendous diversity of interests. . . . The federal structure . . . makes it possible to have republican government over an extended territory . . . which also adds to the multiplicity of economic interests."

Thus Americans do not rely upon "disinterested self-restraint," but on "the energetic pursuit of self-interest by others." Ambition counteracts ambition, and "the private interest of every individual may be a sentinel over the public rights."

Goldwin concludes his chapter with an account of the masterful statesmanship of Madison in having a Bill of Rights adopted that did not alter in any way the fundamental design of the institutions of the

Constitution, on which the security of individual rights has its true foundation.

On Limited but Effective Government

The Westminster System. Gretchen Carpenter examines the experiences of some of the former British colonies in functioning according to Westminster institutions and value systems. (The Westminster system was transplanted, with some variations, in most of these colonies when they became independent.) In most cases the majoritarian nature of the system, coupled with the dominant role of the central parliament, has not been conducive to the development of democracy. Although majoritarianism took root, the nuances and conventions associated with Westminster were often ignored.

Carpenter argues that strong government is not irreconcilable with limited government, provided that the limitations ensure the proper exercise of government power. There are a number of ways of limiting such power:

• the establishment of a representative legislature based on universal suffrage
• the separation of legislative, executive, and judicial powers
• federalism and devolution of power to regional and local tiers of government
• the protection of individual rights and freedoms

The author considers whether powers should be separated, and she summarizes what this implies: the formal division of state authority among the legislative, executive, and judicial branches; the separation of personnel so that one person or organ does not perform simultaneously in more than one branch of government; the separation of functions so that one branch of government does not usurp the functions and powers of another; and the application of the principle of checks and balances so that each branch of government can restrain the other branches and thus achieve the desired equilibrium among the three components of governmental authority.

In the discussion of the relationship between the legislature and executive, the following points are highlighted:

• that in the Westminster system, members of the legislature may also be members of the executive
• the importance of ensuring that members of the legislature be elected
• the phenomenon of delegated legislation, which enables subordinate officials to draft legislation

Carpenter expresses concern at the proliferation of measures whereby legislative powers are conferred on the executive in South Africa.

Other issues discussed include the relationship among the legislature, executive, and judiciary; the question of unicameral or bicameral legislation; and the powers of the executive. The argument is raised that should provision be made for a bicameral legislature, the body should serve a real purpose and not be an expensive luxury. Some of the matters concerning a second chamber are its composition, powers, and relation with the first chamber.

Carpenter concludes that the legitimacy of the new constitution will be a crucial issue that may well determine the structure of the legislature, executive, and judiciary. The ethnically divided nature of the South African population also has to be taken into account when institutions and the way they relate to each other are considered. Some systems may encourage rather than discourage conflict, and this may influence the choices that have to be made. The author argues that whatever system is eventually adopted, an extensive system of checks and balances will be essential.

The Necessary Circumstances for Democracy. Walter Berns makes clear regarding the American founding "how much its success is the product of the favorable circumstances that attended its birth." The country is geographically united and blessed with waterways and natural resources. More significantly, as Publius observes in *The Federalist*, the colonists were "one united people . . . speaking the same language, professing the same religion, attached to the same principles of government." Moreover, the Americans were fortunate that they had one common *foreign* enemy, Great Britain. And the Americans had a chance given to few other nations, of making a fresh beginning, there being no *ancien régime*. In the words of Tocqueville, "They arrived at a state of democracy without having to endure a democratic revolution, and . . . were born equal instead of becoming so." Nonetheless, "the framers . . . had no illusion that their task was an easy one."

"There was no question but that the government would have to be republican in form." But no previous republican form "could serve as a model for America." But a new science of politics, according to *The Federalist*, "had devised models of a more perfect structure . . . which were either not known at all, or imperfectly known to the ancients." The "new forms of government" serve as the means by which democracy is constitutionalized."

Foremost among the political scientists "to whom the framers were indebted" was John Locke. Locke "requires men to hand over their natural rights not to a leviathan but rather to the community with the understanding that the community be governed by laws made by a legislative body." "It is not by chance that Article I of the Constitution of the United States establishes the legislative power." Locke also laid the foundations "for a separation of powers, one of the features of the 'more perfect structure' that Publius speaks of." This in fact is "the central feature, because it serves both 'to control the governed' and to oblige the government 'to control itself.' " The separation of powers certainly is the most well-known means by which, in the words of *The Federalist*, "the accumulation of all powers . . . in the same hands . . . the very definition of tyranny"—is avoided. But this device also allows the government to "control the governed."

The independence of the executive is one of the most important innovations in the Constitution. The executive, of course, is subordinate to the legislative for the execution of the laws. Locke, however, understood that "the safety of the commonwealth cannot be assured by laws alone." The requirement of statesmanship in foreign or domestic emergencies, in Locke's words, "is to act according to discretion for the public good, without the prescription of the law and sometimes even against it." According to Publius, "this power to deal with emergencies is given a place in the Constitution" as part of the executive power of the presidency. The executive is "not chosen by the legislature," and thus "he can act without its consent." Nevertheless, "it is easy to fix responsibility for what he does."

This account of the separation of powers reflects the framers' view of the matter. The widespread modern assumption, however, is "that the most effective means of limiting government is the power exercised by the independent judiciary, the power of judicial review." But an examination of the history of the Court's activities does not uniformly bear this out. Where the judiciary "has made a difference . . . [is] in those cases where the states and localities have abridged rights." "But enforcing an order against the president or Congress . . . , while technically no different, is another matter, and sometimes proves to be impossible."

It is remarkable, given the limitations placed on direct popular involvement in the national government, that the people consented to it. "The people were left in no doubt about the essential characteristics of the Constitution." It was intensely and minutely debated. It is clear to Berns that given another opportunity to ratify the Constitution, the people probably (and much academic political science definitely) would not, finding it wanting in democracy. "Indeed,

14

there seems to be something about political scientists that leads them to favor efficient majority-rule government and to be oblivious of the forms (in Tocqueville's sense) that make it safe." But the framers did not have to contend with academic political scientists: "They were not on the scene in 1787–1788, and their absence must be counted among those circumstances that favored the adoption of the Constitution. Without them, the framers were able to . . . ratify a Constitution that establishes a government of the people and for the people but not immediately by the people." "By any fair reckoning, however, the people have not been excluded from its benefits."

Parties and Government

Ethnic Divisions and Shifting Majorities. David Welsh addresses the issue of parties and the government under a new constitutional dispensation. As a point of departure he proposes that any democratic dispensation should be based on

- universal suffrage, with the right to participate in free, fair, and frequent elections
- the protection of fundamental rights and freedoms of individuals
- an independent judiciary

The author discusses the unique problems experienced by ethnically divided societies in their efforts to achieve and uphold democratic norms and systems of government. Major problems experienced by countries with circumstances similar to those of South Africa are creating and sustaining a feeling of nationhood and an overarching patriotism, protecting political and ethnic minorities, and ensuring effective political participation to all.

Welsh emphasizes the importance of what he calls "shifting" majorities, which means that no single party should form a permanent majority because of its ethnic support base. Welsh argues that to sustain a democratic form of government, opposition parties should have the real possibility of becoming the governing party, while the governing party should face the possibility of being replaced in an election. He refers to the problems faced in this regard in countries such as Sri Lanka and Northern Ireland.

The author also considers the implications of international experience for South Africa. He illustrates how some parties have a zero-sum approach to the political process, which could lead to a win-lose rather than a win-win outcome. A dilemma facing South Africans is that the respective political parties have a fairly fixed support base, which means that the average voter may not choose a party on the basis of its policy but because of historical and ethnic considerations. The prospects for nonethnic parties do not look favorable at this stage.

The Semiparty System. James Ceaser addresses the link between political process and constitutionalism in the American republic. "Without an understanding of the connection between the political process and constitutionalism in America, the American political process is unlikely to hold much interest for South Africans engaged in the task of constitution making. . . . But when the link . . . is made clear, the American case might help to promote fruitful reflection on some of the constitutional issues that face South Africa."

The conventional wisdom about "the American model" links "American constitutionalism with the related concepts of a written constitution and judicial review." But "there is a danger in identifying these features as the core of the U.S. Constitution or the essence of the American model of constitutionalism." Ceaser turns then to "revisit the American understanding of constitutionalism."

"Virtually all agree that the fundamental aim of the American constitutional system is the protection of basic rights under a government that is democratic and effective." But when we examine how rights have actually been protected in the American system, "we find that—contrary to the view implied by purveyors of the American model—the protection of basic rights has not been conceived in America as the exclusive . . . domain of judges interpreting constitutional provisions." Rather, the framers understood the inherent weaknesses and limitations of the judiciary. They "argued that it was necessary for the political process to be so arranged as to make a violation of rights less likely."

> Summarizing the founders' argument . . . we can say that while courts relying on bills of rights can do much to protect basic rights, a major part of the responsibility . . . lies with the political process. . . . The identification of rights with things that courts alone deal with . . . perpetuates the false notion that the political process is concerned with mere interests, while only courts and judges deal in the sacred realm of protecting rights.

Ceaser turns from a consideration of the Constitution to an empirical examination of the political process of representation, and he investigates how America has come to have what he calls a "semiparty" system. "The concept of the political party is neither absent from the American system nor dominant, as it is in a parliamentary system. This fact accounts for the oddity of American elections." "A semiparty system rests on a pluridimensional view of representation." That is, it embraces what Ceaser calls the "classical view" of representation, which has two vital elements: first, representatives are chosen to act for "the good of the nation," and second, "to promote the interests of his geographic constituency." He contrasts this with "the modern party view," where "the representative . . . represents the positions of a national party."

Ceaser asks, "What are the causes for the existence of the semiparty system in the United States?" First, it is part of the continuing "spirit of the Constitution." Then there is the "structure of the government itself": that is, the separation of powers. Finally, it is the system of nomination within the parties themselves. "Although the parties loosely nominate the candidates, in fact it is the citizens in each state or district who identify with the party that made this decision." Thus "there is no central party control over the nomination of the candidates."

The function of the semiparty system is reflected in the nature of majorities in the American political process. "In America, no group of representatives are virtually bound to vote together or to function as a unified team." "*Majorities must be built on each issue, each question, and each policy.*" Thus "power is remarkably dispersed on domestic issues in the United States."

Turning to the constitutional question in South Africa, "It may be wondered . . . to what extent it is wise today to lock a particular idea of representation into an entrenched constitution." "Observation of the American political process indicates that it matters greatly whether immediate, effective power is in the hands of a tiny handful of persons, even if they are subject ultimately to some kind of democratic check, or whether it is placed into scores of hands."

"To a far greater extent than is commonly realized . . . the genius of the American system lies in its political process and not exclusively in the legal mode of judicial review."

2

Constitutionalism in the New South Africa

Pierre J. J. Olivier

The laws of inevitability dictate that South Africa will soon have a new constitution. In terms of the Constitution, Act 110 of 1983, the life of the present tricameral Parliament expires on February 1, 1995. No future election that excludes the majority of South African citizens from voting for an all–South African Parliament can or will take place under the present constitution. Before that date, therefore, we shall have to adopt a new constitution, whether interim or final.

Some of the major parties involved in the now suspended negotiations for a new constitution have committed themselves to establishing a regime based on constitutionalism. The question is whether they agree on the meaning and scope of this vital concept and, further, whether there is, even in relative terms, a general and broad consensus on "fundamentals" or guiding normative political ideas or values. I agree with Willie Esterhuyse's description of the South African problem, namely, that:

> The issue of *institutionalized participation* presents an extremely important normative dimension, involving a whole range of political ideas, values and principles, including ideas on human rights; the value of a multiparty system; equality before the law; the political independence of the judiciary; freedom of association; the distribution of power; sources of authority; forms of representation, etc. In the final analysis it entails consensus on a definition of democ-

racy. This will prove to be the bottom line of the negotiating process.[1]

To many South Africans, a consensus on definitions of democracy and constitutionalism by the major political parties appears to be improbable, if not illusionary. The reasons for this negative perception are manifold, but I shall mention only a few.

First, we have never had a full, all-embracing democracy in our country. Since our first constitution of 1909, on which the new state was founded on May 31, 1910, white minority rule has been exercised and justified, explicitly or otherwise, on the basis of a fundamentalist absolutism—racism. What is now required is a rather dramatic about-face by some 3.5 million whites to accept a policy diametrically opposed to that which they have espoused and defended for more than eighty years. As far as our black citizens are concerned, they have not had any meaningful experience in practicing an all-embracing democracy. Democratic constitutions were adopted by the four homeland states, but in three of the four cases they have evolved into military dictatorships. Outside the homelands, the political scene is dominated by both the rhetoric of democracy and the brutalities of power politics. Indeed, consensus on the political meaning and dimensions of democracy seems to be a remote prospect.

Second, there are fundamental differences on the meaning and scope of constitutionalism among various groups and parties. This disparity raises some difficult questions: What is constitutionalism? Is there only one correct model of constitutionalism, and how fatal, for negotiations toward a new constitution in South Africa, are the different perspectives held by the various groups and parties? What are these differences, and are they reconcilable? In what follows, I shall deal with various aspects of constitutionalism insofar as they appear to be relevant to our present situation in South Africa.

Is Definition of Constitutionalism Possible and Necessary?

As a point of departure, we can accept, as Louis Henkin does, that constitutionalism means "that the government to be instituted shall be constrained by the constitution and shall govern only according to its terms and subject to its limitations, only with agreed powers and for agreed purposes."[2] But constitutionalism means much more. It is "a wonderfully complex and rich theory of political organization."[3] It is, moreover, capable of change and capable also of supporting multiple understandings, all of which share certain elements but may differ in others: "Constitutionalism is therefore a composite of different historical practices and philosophical traditions, some cultural, some ideational."[4] A useful and relevant account of constitutionalism in our country would therefore appear to be less a matter of deft definition and more a matter of analyzing the main elements thereof and identifying, in our context, the different historical practices and philosophical traditions.

Constitutionalism as Limited Government. Most constitutional lawyers accept as the main principle of constitutionalism that of "limitations upon governmental power that cannot be altered by the ordinary means of legislation. In a constitutional government, there are substantive objectives, structural limitations, and procedural guarantees that limit the exercise of state power. Indeed, the concept of limited power, of restraints upon not only the exercise but also the proper objects of power is central to any understanding of constitutionalism."[5] This view is shared by many constitutional experts.[6]

The basic reason for the emergence of the notion of government limited by substantive and procedural restraints must lie in mankind's painful experience of man's capacity for inhumanity toward his fellow man. This capacity is directly related to the power of man—whether king or parliament—over others. Constitutionalism signals the success of the revolution of the powerless, the oppressed, persecuted minorities, and individuals. Limiting power affords one way of limiting the potential abuse of power. Many factors limit the power of all rulers—economic factors, the degree of its support, the physical means of exercising power and overcoming opposition, and the like. But constitutionalism signifies the *legal* and *constitutional* limitations of the powers of a government:

> The idea of constitutionalism is very old, far older than the institutions that ultimately came to embody it. It means, in a single phrase immortalized in 1656 by James Harrington in his *Commonwealth of Oceana*, "a government of laws and not of men." Or, as a leading scholar of constitutionalism has defined the term: "It is a legal limitation on government; it is the antithesis of arbitrary rule; its opposite is despotic government, the government of will instead of law."[7]

One of the most important arguments for constitutionalism is the sovereignty of the rights and freedoms of the individual citizen. This sovereignty requires that the power of a ruler or government be limited in purpose and scope: its purpose is merely to represent the citizenry in protecting and enhancing the fundamental rights; the scope of what it can do is limited by the extent of such fundamental rights. John Locke voiced this idea succinctly:

Their [the legislature's] power in the utmost bounds of it is limited to the public good of the society. It is a power that hath no other end but preservation, and therefore can never have a right to destroy, enslave, or designedly to impoverish the subjects; the obligations of the Law of Nature cease not in society, but only in many cases are drawn closer, and have, by human laws, known penalties annexed to them to enforce their observation. Thus the Law of Nature stands as an eternal rule to all men, legislators as well as others.[8]

Louis Henkin therefore quite correctly states that modern constitutionalism reflects the notion of the liberal state, of minimal government: "Free men instituted government and agreed to be governed by it only for the purpose of securing their life, liberty, and property and other rights. The individual retains these rights even against the people's representatives in government."[9]

Constitutionalism as a System of Normative Principles. Modern constitutionalism entails much more than merely limited government. It finds its *raison d'être* in certain normative principles. Graham Walker states:

The first thing to be noticed is that all the important arguments in the field of constitutional theory are normative. . . . When it comes to constitutional matters, the stakes are high, and serious thought thus moves readily into the normative, prescriptive mode. . . . Normative theory necessarily implicates, or stands upon, some kind of foundation in morality.[10]

Modern students of constitutional theory share Walker's view—Ronald Dworkin, for example.[11]

But what are these normative principles? One school of thought finds the normative principle behind constitutionalism in the "fixed principles of right reasons." The father of this school is perhaps Cicero, who stated the principle so clearly in *De Republica*:

True law is right reason, harmonious with nature, diffused among all, constant, eternal; a law which calls to duty by its commands and restrains from evil by its prohibitions. . . . It is a sacred obligation not to attempt to legislate in contradiction to this law; nor may it be derogated from nor abrogated. Indeed, by neither the Senate nor the people can we be released from this law; nor does it require any but ourself to be its expositor or interpreter. Nor is it one Law at Rome and another at Athens; one now and another at a later time; but one eternal and unchangeable law binding all nations through all times.

Although Cicero's hopes were too idealistic, many scholars still find his basic theme unassailable—that true law is right reason; that constitutionalism is "the empire of reason."[12] Let it be conceded that reference to constitutive principles or principles of right reason abounds with definitional imprecision. But that is no reason to dismiss these ideas. "No less than other forms of political organization, such as liberalism and democratic theory," John E. Finn states, "constitutionalism is a living tradition capable of change and capable also of supporting multiple understandings all of which share certain elements but may differ in others."[13] Still, one has to meet the challenge of describing the "principles of right reason" underlying constitutionalism. Some find it in the public welfare or public good; some find it in articulated reason; others, in the consent of the citizenry, in reflection and choice, or in moral belief.

Carl J. Friedrich teaches that the origins of constitutionalism must be understood as embedded in the belief system of Western Christianity and the political thought that expresses its implications for the secular order.[14] Finn is of the view that human dignity is the touchstone of Western constitutionalism.[15] And although the concept of dignity "has about it a teasing imprecision that promises comfort to all suitors and satisfies none,"[16] the challenge to apply it in concrete cases demands a "great imagination as well as huge measures of technical legal knowledge, historical lore, political wisdom, and skill in human relations."[17]

Constitutionalism and the Will of the Majority

A question of great practical importance to the immediate process of constitutional reform in South Africa is how to reconcile constitutionalism as, among other things, limited government with the will of the majority of citizens. If sovereignty lies in the will of the majority of citizens, how can its representative organ, Parliament, be bound by norms and principles not supported by the said majority?

On the one hand, there is the viewpoint that limited sovereignty is a contradiction in terms, as stated by Austin and Dicey.[18] And in the judgment of the Appellate Division of the South African Supreme Court in *Ndlwana v. Hofmeyer*, it was stated that "it is obviously senseless to speak of an act of a sovereign body as *ultra vires*. There can be no exceeding of power if that power is limitless."[19]

On the other hand, the modern view is that the sovereignty of the will of the majority is precisely the notion that has been rejected by contemplative civilization. This view is stated forcefully by the French philosopher Benjamin Constant (1767–1830) as follows:

When one assumes that the sovereignty of the people is unlimited, one is setting up and throwing into human society in haphazard fashion a degree of power too great in itself, and which is an evil regardless of in whose hands it is lodged. It is the degree of power which is at fault, not those who wield it. One must act against the weapon, not against the arm which brandishes it. Some bodies are too heavy for the hands of men to bear their weight. . . . Of necessity there is some part of human existence which remains individual and independent, and which by right falls outside all social competencies. Sovereignty exists only in a limited and relative manner.

No authority on earth is unlimited, neither that of the people, nor that of those who claim to represent it, nor that of kings, under whatever title they reign, nor even that of the law, which being only the expression of the will of the people or of the kings, according to the kind of government, must be circumscribed within the same limitations as those of the authority which issues it. . . . No duty can bind us . . . to those laws which not only restrict our legitimate liberties but order us to act in ways which run counter to those eternal principles of justice and pity which no man can cease to observe without degrading or denying his very nature. . . . The will of a whole people cannot make just what is unjust.[20]

Laurence J. Boulle also points out that the liberal-democratic tradition has always experienced a tension between the principles of majoritarian democracy, based on the rights of popular majorities, and constitutionalism, founded on the fear of an abuse of power.[21] Thus it is asked, If majority rule is the essence of democracy, does this entail unlimited power for a bare majority? And conversely, if constitutionalism involves limitations on the exercise of power, can it also limit the popular will? Boulle shows that constitutionalists tend to answer the latter question in the affirmative and are able to draw on a long, somewhat diverse, intellectual tradition in support of the view that popular majorities should be constitutionally restrained—for example, Locke, Rousseau, Madison, Burke, Tocqueville, Mill, Hayek, Finer, Rawls, Dahl, and Friedrich.

Constitutionalism, Constitutional Emergencies, and Political Violence

The viewpoint that popular majorities should be constitutionally restrained is put to the test in the case of constitutional emergencies and political violence. In these cases, limits on the exercise of power seem most implausible and unwelcome.[22]

Perhaps the answer to this problem is that we can speak of genuine constitutionalism only if the majority realizes that behind and beyond the outward limitation of power lie a long intellectual tradition, a wealth of experience, and a world of reason, requiring that even in case of emergency and public violence certain rules remain valid and inviolable, whether they suit the majority at that particular time or not. It is "the institutional embodiment of a national aspiration to rise above accident and force by governing ourselves by the claim of reason."[23] It keeps in mind that the basis of justice is the recognition and respect of and protection of human dignity at all times.

Particularly pertinent to the process of constitutional transformation in South Africa at present are Finn's wise observations:

> Widespread domestic violence can present constitutional governments with a situation in which part of the citizenry no longer consents to and indeed rejects the current constitutional order. In these circumstances, political prudence alone, as well as a commitment to constitutional maintenance, demands not the restoration of a constitution whose legitimacy is in dispute but rather establishment of conditions that allow better reasoning about the proper reconstruction of the constitutional order. The responsibility of constitutional governments is to make possible conditions in which constitutional principles can be affirmed. . . . Constitutional maintenance in such cases requires not the restoration of a constitution in dispute, but rather the restoration of conditions in which all parties can reason fairly and honestly about the proper reconstruction of the constitutional order. Not restoration but reconciliation is the ultimate constitutional necessity.[24]

Also:

> I hope it is clear, therefore, that I am *not* arguing that constitutional democracies must meekly suffer violence. (Feebleness is no guarantee of constitutionalism) and if those who reject constitutionalism refuse to reason, government may—indeed must—take steps to protect the community. Political violence offends the dignity and security of all citizens, and the project of constitutional maintenance requires that governments seek to prevent this affront. There is little point in reasoning with those who refuse to accept reasoned discourse as a method of settling political disputes. I *do* argue, however, that in formulating responses to politi-

cal violence, states that aspire to constitutional status must not act in ways that deny or ignore constitutional values in the name of defending them.[25]

Models for Constitutionalism in South Africa

Having read the constitutional proposals of all the major potential constitution makers and having had the benefit of hearing much debate by their spokesmen and supporters on this subject, I see five main models of constitutionalism that could influence our constitution-making process:

- the British or Westminster model
- the American system
- the European or Germanic Rechtstaat idea
- the socialist approach
- African constitutionalism

For present purposes, it is not really necessary to discuss all the fundamentals or intricacies of each of the five systems. I shall attempt to describe, albeit in general and perhaps in imprecise terms, the main features of each:

The British or Westminster System. This system, which has dominated our own constitutional history to the exclusion of all others, is based on parliamentary and legislative supremacy, absence of an enforceable or justiciable bill of rights, with resultant powerlessness of the courts to test and invalidate duly enacted laws. It is also characterized by a weak system of separation of powers, in that the legislature is dominated by the executive and the executive in turn by the bureaucratic administration, and the relative majority system, according to which candidates contend in single-member constituencies so that the one who gains at least one vote more than any other candidate becomes the duly elected member of Parliament. The notion of the rule of law, which has existed since the nineteenth century, implies a number of unwritten requirements for laws and their enforcement: they must be clear, duly promulgated, general in their application, and impartially enforced by the courts. The truth is that the rule of law has been ineffective in guaranteeing fundamental human rights or placing effective, practical limitations on the power of Parliament in the modern context.[26] This is the system adopted in South Africa in 1910, which allowed apartheid to flourish.

The American System. This system is based on separation of powers, checks and balances, a justiciable bill of rights, federalism, and presidential rule. The difference between the American and the British systems is succinctly defined by Boulle, Harris, and Hoexter as follows:

> With the backing of the courts' review powers the American Constitution takes on the nature of a higher law. This means that the provisions of the Constitution will prevail over all other legal or political actions of government which are inconsistent with it: they become null and void on the basis that there was no legal authority for them. This may be contrasted with the English doctrine of parliamentary sovereignty: in the English context Acts of Parliament are legally supreme and the constitution is subordinate, while in the American context the Constitution is supreme.[27]

For the purposes of our discussion, it must be kept in mind that the Bill of Rights and the review powers of the courts are part and parcel of the U.S. Constitution.

The Rechtstaat Idea. The concept of Rechtstaat (for want of a better word, I shall translate it as *law state*) is a Germanic one but has influenced continental thinking and a number of South African scholars. D. H. Van Wyk's description of the Rechtstaat[28] has been summarized as follows:

> The characteristic of a material Law State is that it is a state in which government authority is inherently bound by (certain higher) legal values and consequently the exercise of government authority must result in a materially just legal situation. Among the legal values which have to be recognized in this way are human dignity, freedom and equality (legal values founded on the libertarian tradition). This approach prevents the relationship between state and subject being seen as divorced from the "ought to" element (normative element) so that it is accordingly a legal relationship governed by the law (as the bearer of these legal values).[29]

Superficially, this looks like the rule of law under another name, but Dion Basson and Henning Viljoen show that the two concepts differ in an important way:

> At first glance the doctrines of the Rule of Law and the Law State principle seem almost similar. This would, however, be an over-generalization when one remembers that these concepts developed from two different sources and are also supported by two different approaches to the law. The doctrine of the Rule of Law developed out of a positivist-oriented system in which the fundamental concept is the

sovereignty of Parliament. The result of this is that the doctrine is espoused widely and idealistically but as soon as a value judgement is demanded in a concrete case, its supporters have to fall back on the law in force, or positive constitutional law. In contrast the Law State idea is a principle-oriented approach to constitutional law which accepts that the law cannot be law without taking into account the multi-disciplinary reality in which it exists.[30]

Socialist Constitutionalism. Although there is no single model of socialist constitutionalism, the general pattern is that the institutions of the state are dictated by economic needs. It is said that only socialism and ultimately communism can eliminate the conflict between economic classes, so that in the end there will be no need for the ideas of law and of the state, and they will wither away. The object of the constitution is to protect the power and authority of the working class and the masses against capitalism. Socialist constitutions are, therefore, much more programmatic than liberal constitutions, because they postulate and entrench socioeconomic aims or standards as the very foundation of the constitutional order:

> In this context constitutionalism has an essentially different purpose. Whereas liberal constitutionalism emphasizes the need for limiting power and restraining rulers, socialist constitutionalism is concerned with creating the conditions for socialist society.[31]

The emphasis on the economic interests of society as a whole explains the absence in socialist systems of enforceable and justiciable fundamental individual rights, or meaningful separation of powers and, in contrast, the existence and implementation of the sovereign power of the party.[32]

African Constitutionalism. Despite colonization by Western countries, constitutionalism was never part of the colonial political, legal, or administrative order. In fact, the opposite applied. African people were not predisposed to concepts such as individual rights or separation of powers. The idea of a multiparty state, electioneering, competition for power, and limited government was therefore, after liberation, seen as a threat to national unity, effective government, or development. In the end, what remained were authoritarian, neocolonial states—and this is widely acknowledged today, especially by leading African thinkers.

As late as 1979, Sir Richard Luyt, principal and vice-chancellor of the University of Cape Town at the time and an acknowledged expert on African affairs, wrote the following:

The plurality of political parties in the Western model has always had rather a difficult ride in Africa, and it may well be that the right of an organization of subjects not merely to criticize the established authority but to strive to get it out of power and to replace it is too far removed from African experience and African concepts to be an acceptable import from the West. In African society differences of opinion were traditionally voiced, often vehemently, in their various councils, but this did not include the legitimate aspiration of a dissatisfied person or group to displace and replace in power those whom birth, custom or tribal decision had put there. As the Nigerian scholar S A Akintoye, emphasizes in his book *Emergent African States*, "The aim of inter-party rivalry [within the imported Western democratic constitutional system] became the destruction and not merely the defeat of one's opponents." I will have more to say about one-party systems later, but on my recent visit to Kenya and Zambia less than three months ago, I found objective observers, Black and White, becoming increasingly persuaded that the kind of rivalry and ambitions that exist between and in political parties in the Western White world are not consistent with peace on the African political scene, and that this is not merely because of a lack of political maturity or sophistication, but has at least some relevance to the traditional African view of rights and relationships as between rulers and ruled.[33]

African constitutionalism is now developing, however, at least in theory, and the essence of the new concept has been described by Issa G. Shivji:

The new concept of constitutionalism should rest on an accountable/responsive state and collective rights/freedoms. The proposed concept is structured around four major foundations which, using the discourse of rights, may be described as "rights of peoples and nations to self-determination"; "right to democratic self-governance"; "right to organise" and "right to the integrity of the person." All these four rights are, as a matter of fact, composite names of several other traditionally recognizable rights, whether in liberal democratic or "socialist" constitutions. What is new in our proposition therefore is not so much an invention of *new* rights as such but rather (1) attributing a broader and deeper meaning to them based specifically on the historical experience of Africa (2) seeing them as integral rather than hierarchical and (3) recognizing both their programmatic (or ideological) as well as normative (or regulatory) value.[34]

What the Parties Say about Constitutionalism

The question then remains, What form of constitutionalism will be the matrix of the new South African constitutional regime? The answer to this question will be determined, not by intellectual and dispassionate academic debate, but either by hard bargaining by politicians or by more or less revolutionary change. The outcome of both processes is unpredictable, but let us survey the present policy positions of the major contestants.

The Governing National Party. In the latest summary of this party's constitutional principles by Tertius Delport, the deputy minister of constitutional development, in June 1992 in Parliament, we find strong influences of the Rechtstaat idea.[35] The first principles stated are that an entrenched constitution should be the supreme law, that it will have a higher legal status than all other legislation, and that the constitution and the law in general will restrict arbitrary action by government. While accepting the idea of an entrenched charter of fundamental rights, the deputy minister stated, however, that the introduction of such a charter would come into conflict with the doctrine of parliamentary sovereignty. He then went on to say: "This matter will have to be handled carefully and with circumspection during the transitional phase." Furthermore, unspecified "structural means" for protecting "group or minority rights" are envisaged, as are separation of powers, a collegial executive council, and established autonomy of regions. Finally, it was stated that "there must be a healthy balance between socioeconomic development and the social responsibility of the state." The boundaries of each, however, are left undefined. The electoral system opted for is that of proportional representation coupled with regional representation in the central Parliament. Perhaps one can best describe this system as a combination of the American model and the Rechtstaat idea—definitely not Westminster, despite the ominous homage paid to the sovereignty of Parliament.

The ANC. In this analysis, I refer to the ANC Policy Guidelines for a Democratic South Africa as adopted at the National Conference of May 28–31, 1992. The ANC envisages a democratic, written constitution. It states that sovereignty vests in the people of South Africa; they will elect representatives to adopt a constitution that shall be the highest law of the land guaranteeing their basic rights.[36] The voters will have the right to remove any government through periodic elections.[37] Popular participation and accountability and responsibility to the people are fundamentals, the aim being to prevent the abuse or oppression of anyone.[38] Government will be divided among central, regional, and local structures, and there will be an executive president and a prime minister. A central place is given to a justiciable bill of rights enforced by an independent judiciary.[39] Special reference is made to the protection of the rule of law.[40] These guidelines also contain a copious discussion of socioeconomic policies to be enshrined in the constitution, such as land reform, housing, health, social welfare, education, the development of human resources, and the like.

Without doubt, the ANC's guidelines envisage a mixed model of constitutionalism. Despite its problematic foundations, it is decidedly modeled on the American and Rechtstaat concepts of the continued existence of the state, multiparty competition, the supremacy of the constitution, and the protection of human rights.

The Democratic Party. This party has consistently been the champion of liberal democracy, the protection of individual rights, and the limitation of governmental power—in a word, of constitutionalism. It will continue to play an important role in enhancing these values in South Africa.

The Inkatha Freedom Party. According to the 1990 Inkatha Declaration, individual rights are to be protected above all else. Starting out in 1990 by favoring a Westminster-type political model, Inkatha has more recently adopted a federal-regional model, with emphasis on local autonomy and the protection of minorities. Inkatha is, therefore, also shaping its ideas on the American and Rechtstaat models.

The Pan-Africanist Congress. The Pan-Africanist Congress cannot be said to have developed any model of constitutionalism. In its manifesto, it merely affirms the "inalienable right to self-determination by the indigenous African majority."[41] The manifesto continues:

> The African people will not tolerate the existence of the other national groups within the confines of one nation. For the healthy growth and development of the African nation it is imperative that all individuals identify themselves materially, intellectually and spiritually with the African nation.

The Conservative Party. The Conservative party is in favor of partition and the right to self-determination for Afrikaners in their own state. It has accepted the idea of a homeland but rejects power sharing, believing that to share power is to lose power. Its policy remains that of separate development. It is said that South Africa is a country of different nations and each must have its own geographic territory in which it can rule. The party is in favor of a confederation of states. It supports the National party's idea of group rights but rejects a unitary state based on the principle of one man, one vote.

The Labour Party. The Labour party favors a federation. At the central level, it favors an enforceable bill of rights, proportional representation, and separation and limitation of powers.

Some Conclusions

Having sketched the position of the more important parties, I shall attempt to make some deductions: First, with the exception of the Pan-Africanist Congress and the Conservative party, all parties favor one or another form of constitutionalism. The chances that the Pan-Africanist Congress or the Conservative party could impose its ideas on the rest of the population appear at this stage to be slim. It can, therefore, safely be predicted that our future constitutional regime will be based on constitutionalism, in its broadest meaning.

Second, there seems to be a strong convergence of views regarding the particular form of constitutionalism to be implemented in South Africa. The British model—with its system of parliamentary and legislative sovereignty, the absence of a justiciable bill of rights, its reliance on vague notions of the rule of law and government by the cabinet—enjoys no support. The main players favor, at least ostensibly, something resembling a composite American-Rechtstaat model. Although the ANC's guidelines are strongly programmatic, they are not modeled on African constitutionalism or the socialist model to the exclusion of Western concepts: in fact, Western concepts serve as the matrix.

Last, however, the harsh realities of political life in South Africa at present seem to contradict the policy position of those parties committed to democracy and constitutionalism. Although it is believed, by the government as well, that the solution to the present constitutional crisis is not constitutional restoration or reform but reconstruction—as Finn explains—the process of reconstruction is too laborious, too slow, and too aimless. Many citizens have lost faith and interest in the process. Furthermore, the conflict between Inkatha and ANC supporters has been allowed to escalate to such an extent that it seems out of control. Law and order appear to have broken down, as few arrests are made in response to the killing of many thousands of citizens. The result of all this is an emergent cynicism about democracy, human rights, or constitutionalism.

Bertus de Villiers, head of the Centre for Constitutional Analysis of the Human Sciences Research Council in Pretoria, as recently as October 1992 wrote the following:

> The verbal commitment of various organizations to democracy, and the way in which the very same organizations and their leadership handle differences of opinion, both internally and externally, could be questioned. In most cases it is the exception rather than the rule to tolerate competition, political conflict, mobilization of support, freedom of speech and differences of opinion. Laudable political ideals and principles are communicated in public while at the same time very little evidence is given of tangible commitments to uphold such ideals in practice.
>
> The lack of tangible commitment to uphold democratic norms inevitably leads to distrust and antagonism among supporters on grassroots level. This distrust is reflected in the following opinion surveys conducted by the HSRC: 52% of white respondents believed in January 1992 that blacks and whites do not have sufficient common interest to create a new South Africa, 88% of white respondents indicated that they do not believe the ANC when it promises that it would not tolerate black domination over whites, 67% of white respondents believed in January 1992 that the government has no control over the violence which plagues the country. Black respondents, on the other hand, show similar distrust when it comes to their perception of whites: 68% of the respondents in a March 1990 survey indicated that whites "gained" from the violence, while 31% of black respondents indicated in a November 1991 survey that the NP/SAP were "mainly" responsible for the violence in the country.[42]

It is clear, therefore, that we cannot allow ourselves to be complacent about whether we will have a constitutional regime in South Africa and how constitutional theory and political realities can be reconciled here.

3

South Africa, Viewed through the Eyes of the American Constitution

Thomas L. Pangle

When one looks from the vantage point of the American founders' constitutionalism to the present South African constitutional crisis, one cannot help but be overwhelmed by the enormous differences between the two founding situations. Among Americans at the time of the founding, a deep and broad consensus prevailed as to the goals of government and the best means to attain those goals. This consensus rested on a remarkable degree of homogeneity among at least the white population.

The founders' constitutionalism is defined by its threefold principled aim: the securing of natural or human rights; the fostering of republican self-government; and the protection of a tolerant and enlightened Protestant Christianity. The unfortunate history of apartheid has rendered almost every one of the pillars of the American consensus suspect in the eyes of either the black majority or the white minority.

It was the securing of basic rights of *individuals*, not groups, that was preeminent among the founders' constitutional concerns. In speaking of fundamental rights, the founders spoke of rights "by nature," or of "natural rights." By this they meant that they conceived of the human being as having essential, fundamental, and inextirpable needs, the pursuit of whose satisfaction entailed the inevitable demand and quest for specific freedoms. These unavoidable demands for specific freedoms were seen to manifest themselves as claims to "unalienable rights." It was argued that all humans, being reasonable, can come readily to recognize that the same needs and claims they find essential in themselves are also essential in others; in order to become secure, these aims must be mutually respected by all within a community of rules established by common consent. First among these needs, claims, or rights are those affirmed in the Declaration of Independence: life, liberty, and the pursuit of happiness.

More particularly and elaborately, the originating purpose of government is to provide as much security as possible for each person and to maximize, for each and all, the opportunity to accumulate ever-increasing material welfare through the competitive private enterprise system fueled by the profit motive. This system, conceived as the surest means to create general prosperity, is intended when the founders speak—as they do constantly and passionately—of the importance of property rights.

It is doubtful whether either of the major parties in South Africa has a firm and well-thought-out commitment to the protection of property rights. The African National Congress (ANC) has a strongly Marxist ideological genealogy; the white governing party has systematically infringed on the property rights of the majority and has run, for the privileged minority, a highly centralized and managed economy for most of the past generation. In other words, both sides to the current negotiations are used to conceiving of economic power as concentrated in the hands of government or government-guided private bureaucracies.

As regards the American conception of property rights and the free enterprise system, two observations are in order. First, the American founders were by no means categorically opposed to government regulation or even governmental ownership, to a limited extent. The great theorists who developed capitalist political economy—John Locke above all, followed by Adam Smith, David Hume, and Montesquieu—pointed emphatically to the need for legislation and other forms of government intervention with a view to the breakup and prevention of monopolies and the removal or erosion of hereditary privileges, starting with primogeniture. What is more, Montesquieu, especially, had argued for government stimulus and management of the economy, for redistribution of wealth through taxation, and for major governmental welfare supports for the unemployed, the sick, the orphaned, and the otherwise unfortunate.

Among the American founders themselves there was sharp and hotly contested disagreement over both the degree and the kind of federal as well as state government intervention in the economy.

Alexander Hamilton championed an extensive role for the national government, a role that would include not only the chartering of a national bank and an extensive public works policy, but the direct participation of government capital and planning in the setting up of vast industrial parks and the protection of fledgling industry. The Jeffersonians, who firmly and successfully opposed most of Hamilton's ambitious plans, were nonetheless advocates of a different kind of federal intervention, aimed at the support of cottage industry as well as of agriculture—the twin pillars, in the Jeffersonian outlook, of the American economy.

But here we come to the second observation: Americans across the political and economic spectrum at the time of the founding were, with a few exceptions, united in their vision of a society whose equality would be one of opportunity rather than of outcome or results. This is to say, Americans were inclined to suppose that in a free society, equality of opportunity would produce a social outcome in which the differences of wealth and way of life were narrower or at any rate less exploitative and grating than in any previous political system. The Americans of the founding generation were convinced that the considerable inequalities of outcome inevitable in the free enterprise system would be viewed by all, including the working class, as justified or just and hence acceptable. The raising of the economic standard of living for all, including especially the working class, was understood to require the incentive of profitable reward for the enterprising or lucky few.

From First Principles to Constitutionalism

For the American founders, the principles of human equality—that is, of equality in liberty or in rights—and of participation in self-government point clearly toward a democratic form of government. The founders were unanimous in their conviction that all governmental authority derives its legitimacy solely from the consent of the governed, expressed through majority rule. Majoritarianism, rooted in an original unanimous agreement—the social compact—by which all agree to abide by majority rule, is the sheet anchor of American republicanism.

But majoritarianism in itself is only the foundation for the structure of constitutional democracy. The American founders were grimly aware of what they saw to be the dismal historical record of all previous democratic experiments, including the greatest or most successful—the Greco-Roman city-republics, or the great republics of the Italian and German Middle Ages. In almost every known case, the attempt to rest governmental authority on majority rule or popular sovereignty had led to a mob mentality whipped up by demagogic leadership, provoking vicious oligarchic reaction and culminating in suicidal class warfare. No democracy, so far as the founders could discover, had ever done well at protecting human rights, either personal or economic. Monarchies and aristocracies—especially the modern English system, as celebrated by Montesquieu and Hume and Smith—had a record that put to shame anything visible in the history of democracies.

Yet the founders refused to abandon the cause of democratic republicanism. They determined, indeed, to save that cause by forging a new kind of democracy. They set out to create a democracy tempered, limited, checked, and balanced: a democracy that would be self-protected or self-insulated from its own worst vices. This project is the heart of American constitutionalism, or of constitutional democracy as conceived by the founders.

Once again, the contrast between the American and the South African outlooks is sharp. The Americans could agree on majoritarianism as the ultimate ground of all legitimate government, while also agreeing on the grave dangers of majority tyranny, precisely in a fundamentally democratic society. In South Africa, it is extraordinarily difficult to speak of the dangers of majority oppression without appearing to be masking a defense of the entrenched interests of the dominant white minority.

Decentralization of governmental power through regional or federal structures has come to be associated, for the ANC, with the failed and hypocritical attempt by the white government to create supposedly independent native states. The white national government has indeed showed little respect for white state and local government whenever it found such government an obstacle. Only the Inkatha party seems passionately committed to powerful regional government, and this stand appears to be in the interest of the preservation of tribal Zulu authority rather than being a principled defense of federalism as such.

American versus Traditional Constitutionalism

To appreciate the radically innovative character of American constitutionalism, we must keep in view at least the outlines of tradition of constitutionalism rooted in Aristotle and in classical constitutional thought. Traditional constitutionalism begins from the premise that every political society will inevitably be riven by class conflict, especially between the rich minority and the poor majority. The conflict is not adequately understood as merely an economic conflict; it is a much broader and deeper dispute among competing conceptions of justice, of the good life, and of human happiness. For the different classes are composed of human beings brought together in antagonistic groups by their distinct and often antagonistic ways of life. The rich, the poor, and the middle class are defined not simply by the relative amount but also by the character of their property and means of livelihood.

The major parties to the conflict—classes distinguished not only by economics but also by military, religious, ethnic, and geographic diversity—can all be shown to have biased and selfish conceptions of the common good and the human virtues. All can be shown to see a part, but only a part, of a truly comprehensive and humanly enriching shared communal way of life. It is the supreme task of the political philosopher to rise above partisanship in the attempt to articulate, as umpire, a dialogue leading to a higher and broader vision of the common good, a vision embodying fundamental compromises informed by a critical philosophic meditation on the "best regime" and on the human virtues, including the philosophic virtues themselves.

The practical political outcome or reflection of this conception of the problem and task of political theory is the famous notion of the mixed regime. In the construction of a mixed regime, the vision of the common good held by each of the competing classes or groups within a society is elaborated with a view to uncovering what is defensible and what is indefensible or dubious in the implicit vision of each. Then the attempt is made to create institutions, procedures, and mores, including educational mores, that define a political system in which each party plays a role calculated to restrain or suppress its most evil or dangerous proclivities and to awaken and empower its most beneficial and noble tendencies.

This approach to the problem of constitution making requires, of course, that each principal party be brought to acknowledge its own grave imperfections and its need to be restrained by competing parties with differing and in some respects superior insights into the common good. Each class or party must recognize that the common good in its totality transcends the interests and even the vision of any one party—before the party's becoming elevated and enlightened by joining the constitutional mixture. But first of all, the theory of the mixed regime presupposes the ingredients for a mixture: it presupposes that the consensus must emerge out of the fair-minded argument and ensuing mutual moderation of originally differing constitutional goals or visions. These fundamental differences begin as dangerous sources of instability and civil strife, but, properly woven together, they become the sinews of a dynamic and therefore fragile dialectical balance.

For Americans of the founding era, perhaps the most vivid example of a successful mixed regime was the English monarchy. Its underlying principles had been elaborated and celebrated (and somewhat embellished) by Montesquieu in *The Spirit of the Laws*. For Montesquieu, England represents a limited monarchy where the rule of one—the hereditary monarch—is checked and balanced by rival centers of power: by an established church hierarchy; by deeply rooted and geographically diverse hierarchies of noble families with enormous patronage networks grounded in hereditary authority; and by strong local magistracies in numerous cities, who answer to powerful commercial or bourgeois interests. The general populace was divided into subordinate groupings in some measure protected but also exploited by the competing hierarchical centers of power. But through its House of Commons, England mitigated the more traditional and stricter hierarchies inherited from feudalism by giving the ultimate sovereign power to a substantial portion of the common populace—not directly, but through the indirect means of representation.

Although Americans continued to look with admiration and even some nostalgia to the English system against which they had successfully revolted, they were firmly convinced that such a mixed regime was not viable or even, in the final analysis, desirable in the American context. Americans would not submit to an established religion, and the new nation lacked and would not tolerate the establishment of a landed, hereditary aristocracy or a royal family. America was infused with a radically democratic spirit that reflected the egalitarian conditions of its frontier society. Race slavery persisted in the South, but the founders generally supposed it persisted as an ever more obvious contradiction to the underlying ethos and future direction of the nation. America must then, the founders argued, abandon the mixed regime and create a substitute.

That substitute makes great use of three major features of Montesquieu's constitutionalism—confederalism, representative government, and the separation of powers. But these features are grounded on a new type of regime, based on a drastically limited conception of the scope and goals of politics and of the common good that can be achieved through politics. The new conception of politics follows from the new conception of human nature and natural rights that we sketched at the outset. In this perspective, government should no longer concern itself with promoting a specific set of virtues, a specific religious truth, or a specific way of life that aspires to provide human beings with fulfillment of happiness through civic participation. Instead, government and political participation should be viewed as a means, as a tool or instrument, for securing more important goods than active involvement in government and the civic virtues thereby realized.

The goal of government or the public sphere is mainly the protection of the private sphere—of individual, familial, economic, and social life, in which human beings are liberated from governmental interference and thus freed to "pursue happiness" in many diverse and competing ways. This limited or, as it came to be called, "liberal" definition of the nature and purpose of government had by the time of the founding become the overwhelming consensus among politically self-conscious Americans.

In South Africa today, although constitutionalism is weak and constitutional consensus difficult, party loyalty and party politics—of a kind closer to that associated with the mixed-regime perspective— are dangerously strong. May not some version of the mixed-regime perspective abandoned by the American founders actually fit the present situation better than the type of constitutionalism the Americans found suitable for their new country? Must we not begin by recognizing that at the bargaining table we find three distinct and competing visions of what kind of country, what way of life, South Africa ought to be and to follow? Is it possible in these circumstances to frame a constitution of the sort the Americans forged? Before any such constitution can be framed, must there not first be forged, through argument, experiment, action, and above all compromise, a middle ground of shared agreement on the nature of the economic system, the redistribution of wealth and influence and opportunity, the character of civic life, the goals of education, and the place for and protection of religion? In short, may South Africa at this juncture need not a permanent constitution but an interim government formed by coalition and power sharing—perhaps with a plural executive and proportional representation, based partly on national and partly on regional party lists?

There are, no doubt, dangers associated with such a course. South Africa would find itself in the anomalous position of lacking a constitution in the strict sense of the word for the foreseeable future. Among other costs, the attendant uncertainty might discourage investment. An interim government that lasted for years could become the vehicle for the white minority's entrenching something close to the status quo, or the interim arrangement could easily be perceived as such a vehicle.

But the lack of a constitution would permit experimentation, allow for jockeying and change in the constitutional views and proposals of the various parties, and in the best case foster an increase in trust as well as mutual understanding of each party's fears and hopes. Fear and suspicion are now rampant on every side. Each party is reluctant to elaborate honestly and openly its own vision of what the country should become and to express candidly its fears about what might be its fate. Constitutional provisions and proposals are viewed in an extraordinarily defensive perspective: each party warily eyes the constitution not so much as the structure of a successful government but rather as the fence that will prevent usurpation or oppression by the opponent party. All parties find themselves peering, baffled, into an unlighted future, where no one can do better than guess what any given institution will look like in practice, because no one has any experience of a truly multiracial and multiparty democracy at work.

For the American founders, who did not face anything like the dilemmas of contemporary South Africa, the agenda of the new constitutionalism was to create a democratic system that would rest ultimately on the will of the majority but with channels and checks that would prevent government from becoming oppressive of minorities and from excessively interfering in the lives of individuals. This system would still have to provide government with sufficient energy and power to perform the economic and peace-keeping tasks that were its proper business.

What are the chief features of the new liberal democratic constitutionalism of the American founders?

The Outlines of American Constitutionalism

First is the competitive, interest-group politics of a large, diverse commercial society, as characterized in James Madison's famous *Federalist* 10. It is true that such a society renders impossible the classical goals of extensive civic participation in sovereign decision making; that the ideal of fraternity grounded in shared religious and moral ideals must be drastically curtailed; that such a society lacks the permanent, clear, and deeply rooted class divisions that moderate and animate the classical mixed regime. But this new society allows and fosters a vast manifold of more petty and mutable competing groups—religious, ethnic, geographic, but especially economic. The heterogeneity and instability of the economic divisions make the formation of a uniform majority faction unlikely and create instead the likelihood of shifting majority coalitions, promoting compromise and accommodation among competing interests.

This process can work well, however, only if it is facilitated and channeled through appropriate governmental institutions of representative government. Through elected delegates, the people, or the majority, retains control over the government without becoming directly involved in potentially moblike collective action. Representative government can filter and refine public opinion: the men chosen by a mixture of direct and indirect elections are likely to be better educated, more articulate, more experienced, and more farsighted than the average citizen. The relative rarity of election days will make the public's judgment on these occasions more solemn and thoughtful. In other words, the system continues to presuppose and attempts to elicit some measure of civic spirit, moderation, and thoughtfulness on the part of many, if not all, citizens.

Yet this mass of petty competing interests filtered through representatives is still insufficient to guarantee personal liberty, security, and prosperity—unless the representatives are in addition divided into competing institutions governed by legal regulations that provoke and constructively channel continuing political controversy among alternative centers of power.

The first and historically most deeply rooted such institution is federalism. The division of powers between state and national government is the most obvious way in which federalism checks and balances government. Less obvious but perhaps more important is the barrier provided by the states against the national government's excessive interference in local government, the home of direct participation and hence of an attenuated but crucial continuation of the classical ideal of active citizenship. Last but not least, federalism contributes to the separation of powers within the national government, especially by way of the Senate, where representation is by states and not simply by population.

It is indeed the separation and competition among the branches of the national government that the founders looked to as the most important barrier against majoritarian tyranny or elite governmental oppression. In the old mixed-regime scheme, the divisions and competition between different branches of government—between, for instance, Lords and Commons, king and parliament, church and state—reflected the division and competition among distinct classes or estates of the realm. In the new American scheme, all the branches of government have much more similar constituencies: all are either elected by popular majorities or appointed and elected by officers who have themselves been popularly elected.

But each branch or subbranch is given a part of the popular constituency, divided by region and by time and mode of election.

The hope is that different segments of the populace, or the same segment expressing its will at different times in the choice of different representatives, will choose representatives who differ and compete. Moreover, the terms and scope of the various representative offices are so arranged as to foment competition by appealing to the ambitions and economic advantages of the representatives. Finally, an independent and substantially insulated judiciary armed with the power of judicial review stands as an umpire for the whole system and as a guardian of individuals who may find themselves otherwise overwhelmed by the awesome power and authority of the elected representatives and their subordinates in either the executive or the legislative branches.

Republican Self-Government

Self-government is conceived by the American founders as an essential means to and protection of the enjoyment of all other human rights. But it is also viewed as a good whose value extends beyond the securing of individual rights. The predominant philosophic influence on the Americans was that of the Enlightenment, with its stress on the primacy of the individual and on the need to educe all valid moral obligation from the originally free and independent individual. Nevertheless, Americans also continued to be influenced, if somewhat inconsistently, by an older and radically different way of conceiving the dignity of man and of self-government.

The classical republican tradition, rooted in Greco-Roman political philosophy and history, viewed man as "the political animal" rather than as a being whose essence was revealed in a state of independence and prepolitical anarchy (the state of nature). According to this older view, which played a powerful if subordinate and obscured role in the American outlook, human beings are fulfilled and their nature is flourishing only when they dwell in a society that compels them to participate directly and to a significant extent in the collective deliberations and actions by which men can together shape their own destiny.

In America, this way of conceiving human nature and the importance of politics lent a major additional impetus to the demand for decentralization of governmental authority, through strong reserved powers for state and local government. Especially in the realms of education, the maintenance of law and order, and local public works, the founding generation was jealous of any governmental administration that might take from local citizens the power directly to regulate their own lives.

In addition, what is today called by the Hegelian term "civil society"—the vigorous realm of voluntary associations for religious, economic, political, artistic, recreational, and other personal ends—was presumed by the founders to be the lifeblood and the foundation of free society. As Tocqueville was later to stress, this dimension of the American idea of freedom—the insistence on the need to keep governmental authority from interfering in the spontaneous flux and motion of associations—poses perhaps the most powerful counter-weight to the modern tendency for government to erode all rival centers of power and independence. This emphasis on the limitation of government and the freedom of associations inhibits the demo-cratic or egalitarian syndrome, which threatens to reduce humans to the status of adult children tied to the leading strings of paternalistic "soft despotism."

A vigorous civil society, animated by the formation and activism of lively private associations that would often impede or embarrass a powerful central government, does not easily fit into the statist outlook of either the ANC or the governing white party. Inkatha's rule over its own territory in Natal has not shown a favorable attitude toward dissenting or stubborn local associations.

As for the separation of powers, the tradition in South Africa as throughout Africa has been the parliamentary rather than the presi-dential and bicameral system. There is a wide consensus on the need for an independent judiciary, empowered to enforce a written consti-tution that includes a strict bill of rights. But perhaps too much burden is placed on the capacity of the judiciary to maintain the rule of law and protection of individual rights in the face of the coales-cence of executive and legislative power made possible by the parlia-mentary system. Insofar as the parliamentary system has, especially in Europe, maintained political and civil liberty and a political life where a loyal opposition has been permitted to contest elections and power in a meaningful way, its success can be attributed to the party system.

The party system has also played, of course, a major role in American constitutionalism. Yet the parties are nowhere mentioned in the Constitution, and the party system is the most massive feature of the Constitution that seems to have been largely unforeseen by the founders. Parties in America have represented the continuing pres-ence of something like the mixed regime within American constitu-tionalism. Except at moments of great crisis in the constitutional system, the major parties in America have not represented truly distinct visions of the common good or the way of life of the society. Yet within narrow bounds set by the overwhelming consensus that has usually characterized American politics, the two parties have offered different if closely kindred visions of the meaning of that consensus and the way it is to be implemented. The parties thus manifest a faint echo of the grander divisions and contests envisaged in the idea of the mixed regime.

Protestant Christianity

As Tocqueville again shrewdly observes, the role of religion in America has from the beginning been crucial. For no human associations deal with matters of so supreme and urgent importance as do religious associations, where human beings uniquely come to terms with the implications of death and the possibility of redemption. Therefore, so long as powerful, active religious organizations flourish outside the scope of governmental power, government cannot and should not try to provide the answers to the most important needs and questions. But religious associations not only afford an unmistakable barrier to the excessive pretensions of government; they can serve, and in America they always have served, as the nucleus and catalyst for charitable, educational, civic, and artistic associations. Religious associations are the inspiration and training ground of nongovernmental communal initiative.

Among the basic natural rights is one whose ground is to be found not only in human nature but in that dimension of the human condition that transcends the natural. Freedom of religion, as conceived by most of the founders and certainly by the bulk of the ordinary citizens at the time of the founding, was intended to protect and foster the Protestant Christian faith. The separation of church and state, the disestablishment of religion, and even the religious neutrality of the government, at least with regard to religions that did not threaten republicanism, were all broadly shared aims of Americans at the time of the founding.

But it is doubtful whether most Americans supposed that their new government should be neutral as regards irreligion or atheism. The shared Protestant faith was one of the firmest bonds uniting Americans in the founding era, and Protestant Christianity may be said to have contributed to American political consciousness much of the fervor with which Americans embraced the idea of an elevated equality of all human beings—viewed as created by and in the image of God, the father of all. This notion of mankind as deriving from and reflecting a higher being lent dignity and spirituality to the conception of the nature shared by all men; it also entailed a powerful sense of individual responsibility. The idea that human beings can and must assume the major share of responsibility for what they make of themselves and their lives—economically, politically, personally, and spiritually—has been a mighty engine of endeavor and labor throughout most of American history.

Conclusion

If we attempt to view South Africa in the light afforded by the experience of the American constitutional tradition, what are the general contours of the compromises and learning that we might hope would emerge and that we should try to promote in the course of coalition politics in an interim regime? Regarding the economy, we might hope that the experience of free enterprise and of access to the opportunities and rewards of the free market, fueled in part by outside investment, might convince both the ANC and the present government party of the advantages of a free and vigorous private sector. No small advantage to be gained in the actual experience of a society of truly open opportunity might be the diminution, in the populace at large, of ideologically inspired false hopes and fears concerning the outcome of capitalist enterprise. A weaning away from dependence on and fear of government bureaucracy—as regards the police, the military, the economy, the welfare state, and education—might be accompanied by a healthy development of individual and private group initiative.

Indeed, during an interim government, the development of private associations of all kinds might begin to break citizens free from tribal, party, and gang allegiances, for more constructive sorts of affiliation linked closely to the dynamics of a capitalist economy. Trade union leadership might be forced to respond more to the economic demands of the membership and to enter into collective bargaining and job action with less ideological, more sensible economic agendas. Business, no longer coddled or restricted by governmental, racial, and ideological imperatives, would likely focus more exclusively on economic efficiency. While it seems inevitable that the level of education for whites will suffer, education for black youths might recover markedly, and the general level of capacity for economic productivity and civility might rise dramatically in the turbulent population of black youths.

A sense of patriotism and pride in nationhood might well take hold as South Africa assumed its rightful place as the economic and political leader of sub-Saharan Africa. For those belonging to a South Africa that could finally participate without shame at the international table, the consciousness of being part of a great experiment in multiracial democracy—which just might create the model for the twenty-first century—could help to compensate for the disappointments inevitable in struggling to build a genuinely open society, where the dream of general prosperity ceases to seem a mirage.

A black middle class and a black economic and political leadership could emerge that would recognize how deep a stake it has in preventing the country's slide into fratricidal strife. White racism might well abate as the white populace begins to conceive of itself as a welcome and still leading part of a truly African nation. This source of dignity might well help compensate for the inevitable decline in the relative living standards of the privileged white elite.

This is a list of wishes and hopes, but I do not think it is pie in the sky. If South Africa is to succeed, it must allow itself dreams and aspirations of a sort that can guide concrete action. The United States is old, as nations go; South Africa is being born. The United States in its youth was blessed with a fervor for freedom, a fraternity, and a love of country that sustains it still. If South Africa is to find its way to the greatness that shimmers as a distant possibility, then its citizens and its leaders must surmount resentment and indignation and place before their minds' eyes something like this agenda of transformation.

4

Federalism and the Proposals of the National and Democratic Parties

Kader Asmal

Traditionally, constitutions may be classified according to the methods by which powers are distributed between the country's central government and the local governments that exercise authority over its parts. One may therefore choose between a federal government and a unitary one.

In a federal constitution, the powers of government, or sovereignty, are divided in such a way that each government is legally independent within its own sphere. The federal government is sovereign in some matters, and the state, provincial, or regional governments in others. Within its own sphere, each exercises its powers without control from the other, and neither is subordinate to the other. In other words, the parliament for the whole country has limited powers. Power is diffused, and the center and the states are coordinated in their authority and independent in their status. Under a unitary constitution, the parliament of the whole country is the supreme lawmaking body. Final authority vests with the central government.

The vast majority of countries have written constitutions that are described as the supreme law of the land. In a unitary state, the constitution recognizes limitations on the power of the central parliament to pass laws through devices such as a bill of rights. These laws are justiciable before a constitutional court, as in Portugal, Italy, and Spain, or before a supreme court. But what distinguishes a federal constitution from a unitary one in relation to the competence of government is that the allocation of power between a federal and a provincial government is delineated in a federal constitution. The basic terms cannot be amended at the discretion of the central parliament, or of a region or combination of regions. Changes in the allocation of functions may occur only through procedures laid down in the constitution.

Federations normally have two houses of parliament, the upper house representing regional interests. Disputes between the center and the periphery are resolved ultimately by the courts. Disputes concerning authority are bitter and contentious. In the United States and Nigeria, they have led to violent civil wars.

Federal arrangements are based on the inherent rights of separate governmental bodies. They usually provide for financial resources to be divided between the federal and provincial governments to match their respective responsibilities. In Germany and the United States—the two major federations—personal income tax is collected by the central government; so is the value added tax in Germany, and a formula regulates its distribution to the constitutional units with a special "equalization" procedure for the poorer regions. Germany, unlike the United States, offers no independent taxation power for the provinces.

Each state or region is an independent source of governmental power, with its own legislature, its own executive, its own bureaucracy, and its own ordinary and supreme courts. In some federations, the central government has offices to carry out the functions allocated to it in each of the states, resulting in a parallel central and local bureaucracy. In Germany, the central functions are administered by regional bureaucracies.

Studies have shown that the formal picture of separate and independent governments may not be reflected in practice. The control of the central government in a federation may be so great—as in Mexico, Venezuela, Australia, and the former USSR—that the states are little more than its administrative agencies. This may arise because of the greater resources of the center, emerging national needs, or the political culture of the country.

Conversely, the class of unitary constitutions is also wide and varied: the vast majority of states are formally unitary. Decentralization in practice may be so diverse that constitutions which are highly centralized on paper may be federal in practice. This is arguably the case in the regional devolution of unitary states such as Italy, Portugal, and Spain.

Proposals for South Africa

Proposals for a federal constitution in South Africa have been revived only recently. The Progressive party, through the Molteno Commission, supported the system in the early 1960s. It could therefore be argued that the Democratic party, as the lineal successor to the Progressive party, has been the only consistent supporter of some form of federalism. The revival of the concept arose in recent years among those who desired to protect minorities and who supported limited government. The Kwa Natal Indaba proposals of the mid-1980s for Natal/KwaZulu presaged a federalist option based on regional governments with their own special compositions, although the Inkatha Freedom party's (IFP) enthusiasm for federalism was never so strong. Only since the Convention for a Democratic South Africa (CODESA) balance of forces became evident has there been strong support by the IFP for federalism, veering toward confederalism.

The Declaration of Intent adopted by CODESA in December 1991 accepted that South Africa was to be a united state. Subsequently, because of pressure from the Inkatha Freedom party, it was agreed that the use of the term "united" did not predetermine the future structure of the government, which could be unitary or federal. The federal card was first played when the National party foresaw that its 1989 proposals for the protection of crude group rights and for veto powers to be vested in the legislature for racial minorities were doomed to failure, as they were unacceptable to national or international opinion. This federalist alternative had been rejected when the Kwa Natal Indaba proposals were turned down by the regime. In August 1990, Roelf Meyer became the first leading personality in the National party to call for support for a federal state of nine regions, each with its own government. Subsequently, a National party spokesperson referred to the need for the maximum devolution of decision-making processes—which can be achieved in a unitary country—and "three fully fledged" levels of government.

The National party proposals of September 4, 1991, do not use the dreaded word "federal" to describe their constitutional proposals. But words, especially as used by the National party, have lost their technical qualities. The real effect of these proposals is to impose a unique, tightly drawn, and inflexible version of federalism onto the South African body politic.

Under the guise of participatory democracy, the proposals suggest that political parties must participate in "power sharing." It is proposed that this concept, which has nothing to do with the democratic concept of the individual citizen participating in decision making and influencing governmental activity, will be implemented in such a way that "political power may be divided among various authorities. Most important here is the distribution of power among the different tiers of government. This is normally referred to as the principle of devolution of power."[1]

It is, of course, no such thing. Devolution of power may take place under a unitary state where the central government decentralizes functions either for more efficient administration or for political reasons. Such decentralization does not affect the authority of the central government to legislate in the area devolved or to supersede the authority of the central entity.

The National party proposes in addition to allocate functions among the different tiers of government "in such a way that the constitution confers autonomous authority on every tier. (That is, original and entrenched authority, with which the other tiers of government may not interfere.)"

The National party proposes there should be nine regions and local authorities with "autonomous powers." The constitution will determine which tier of government can perform a particular function in the most appropriate and effective manner. It is left strikingly vague as to which tier will perform which function, but the proposals state that while a given function may be allocated to one of the three tiers, it will be appropriate to spread functions among all three tiers.[2] This procedure would allocate to each tier that aspect of a function which can be handled most effectively in the interest of the community.

These proposals for the structure of a federal government must be seen in the context of power sharing. Consensus is necessary in decision making, and the regional executive and local authorities must be elected on the same basis as the president—that is, three to five persons represent the major actors. Majority rule even at the regional level has to be discarded in favor of the veto by a party which has a predetermined minimum representation in the Legislative Council.

In September 1991, the government called together supporting organizations to a conference on "a regional dispensation," and a technical report was presented. The philosophy behind it is spare to the point of minimalism. But it follows the approach of the earlier National party document, with a number of refinements and additions. The constitution shall provide for entrenched powers that could not be amended without the "consent of the regional legislature." It is not clear whether all or the majority have to agree. The central government will have no powers of taxation at all, and its actual powers will be limited to defense, national security, foreign affairs, and constitution planning. All other competences will be constitutionally allocated to the regions.

The Democratic party discussion paper of August 23, 1991, is more detailed in its case for federalism and in the way it is to be implemented. The party's case is as follows:

- federalism will distribute power and enable more people to take part in the process of power
- federalism will provide a variety of sites of power and a defense against tyranny, therefore making the need for central government power less important
- federalism will assist in accommodating the linguistic, geographic, and political pluralism of South Africa

Like the National party, the Democratic party insists that the power of the regional authority should be written into the constitution and entrenched. A central tenet of its policy is that the central parliament will enjoy coordinate sovereignty with the state parliaments.

The Democratic party favors having eight to twelve states, subject to negotiation. The powers of the federal government are all those powers essential to the national interest. All other powers will be exercised by the state governments. The Democratic party, rather than beginning with the powers of the central government, instead lists those of the state governments, which will include health, local government, licensing, town planning, local taxation, nature conservation, tourism promotion, roads, education, *police, prisons, and land settlements* (my emphasis). The federal list, which will be a closed one in the constitution, is limited to foreign relations, economic affairs, water affairs, labor, citizenship, currency, interstate commerce, defense, borrowing on the credit of the government, emigration, foreign trade, customs and excise, national transportation, and mineral and energy affairs.

In October 1992, the Democratic party produced a more comprehensive discussion paper on constitutional proposals. It reiterates the rationale for federalism found in the earlier document and again refers to "a central tenet of DP policy that the central parliament will enjoy co-ordinate sovereignty with state parliaments." This document lists the powers of the center and the regions. "The federal government will exercise those powers essential to the national interest." This list of powers is similar to the earlier one. All other powers will be exercised by the state governments. Although paragraph 2.6.1 states that "it is accepted that provision will have to be made for coordinate sovereignty to be exercised in respect of" these powers and "provision may have to be made for certain exceptions in respect of designated powers," it is not clear exactly what "coordinate sovereignty" means. Paragraph 2.6.4 provides for "coordinate management" of bodies that may operate at central and state levels, but coordinate sovereignty does not mean that where the states and the center have concurrent legislation the central authority will prevail in the event of conflict. Paragraph 2.6.5 provides for states' rights supremacy, as the state assemblies can amend central legislation in matters "over which the states have control."

Like the National party proposals, the Democratic party proposals should be evaluated in the context of the party's other proposed drastic restrictions on majority rule. Local government must be established on a first- and second-tier basis. The question of majorities, entrenched sections, and applicable vetoes should be contained in the constitutions of all levels of government.[3]

Which Powers Should Go to the Center?

The battles for the constitutional allocation of authority to the center or to the regions have been acute. Successful federations arose from a coalescence of existing units, each of which guarded its powers strenuously.

The allocation concerns the designation of those respective spheres in which the government of the whole country and the government of the constituent parts have authority. It puts limitations on the central legislature, and so the constitution may require elaborate provisions in relation to the exercise of the legislative area. The reconstruction of South Africa would require a political evaluation of what competences that central government should have, to what extent it should have access to resources, and what the needs of the country are. It is estimated that under the National party proposals, half of the national budget would be locked into the regions, beyond the reach of the central government.

The National party was coy about the allocation of powers in its original proposals. But President F. W. de Klerk stated on September 4, 1991, that his proposals offered the possibility of reasonable self-determination by communities in matters of intimate concern. This provides some insight into the kind of competences to be allocated to the regions and local authorities. The Democratic party list is broad enough to be acceptable to the National party. In addition, the Neighbourhood Council, the only authority that can decide by majority vote, would have broad powers over housing, security, education, and welfare under the National party proposals. These functions would be beyond the reach of the central legislature under the National party version of "federalism."

The Democratic party approach severely restricts the power of the central government, whose powers will be enumerated. All other powers will vest in the region. A contrasting approach, such as Canada's, is to enumerate the functions of the regions and to allocate the remainder to the center. A third approach is to provide two lists, one with exclusive powers for the center and the other exclusive to the regions. Finally, a number of jurisdictions provide a concurrent list, in which the center and the regions are allowed to legislate on some issues but in cases of conflict the central legislature prevails. Which approach is chosen depends on the end to be achieved: a weak or a strong central government.

The depressing aspect about the Democratic party proposal is not simply its suspicions of a central parliament but its refusal to acknowledge the inherent dangers in denuding the central government of authority by constitutionally limiting its powers. Experience has shown that it is impossible to foresee when important subjects may arise that the central legislature should control. It is a recipe for constitutional immobility and constitutional warfare to undermine the center of authority.

The U.S. government, through its offers to South Africans to visit the United States and observe how federalism works, and through the statements of the assistant secretary for Africa, Herman Cohen, has been attempting to induce a federal solution for South Africa. Significantly, the National party's proposal evoked a sharp response from the assistant secretary, in his testimony to the U.S. Congress on September 23, 1992:

> [I have] urged South Africans to consider seriously the degrees to which federalism might address many of the tensions inherent in their society. Subsequent debate has revealed that some South Africans portray federalism as a facade for stripping the central government of most significant authority. It is just such efforts to corrupt the purposes of federalism and turn it to the defense of the *status quo* that have earned it the enmity of so many in the disenfranchised majority and stifled debate. All South Africans should understand that effective federalism is a framework fully con-

sistent with strong responsive government at the national, regional, and local levels, with power and responsibility reserved to those levels most responsive to citizens' needs and desires.

In South Africa, the issues at the heart of the debate should be

- the fragmentation of our society, or the way we were forced to live apart, by land, urban, and group areas
- the division of our country into so-called white areas and Bantustans, with their myriad bureaucracies
- the separation of governmental functions into own affairs and general affairs
- the unequal apportionment of our life chances and opportunities and the need for redress, reconstruction, and affirmative action
- the polarization of our people, so that we cannot share the same symbols and owe allegiance to the same institutions, with a common sense of national unity

These issues can be tackled by a government that takes into account the concrete reality of South Africa, not some abstract model of good government developed by foreign think tanks or those who are insensitive or oblivious to the needs of the majority.

Constitutional Amendment

Constitutional amendment is much more complex in a federal state than in a unitary state. Formerly, the constitution of South Africa could with two exceptions be amended by a simple majority. In other unitary states, the constitution could provide for a special majority in one house or two houses—such as a two-thirds majority together with a referendum—if this were considered necessary for amending the constitution.

In a federation, it is a principle that powers are divided between a government for the whole country and for its parts and that these governments are independent of each other within their own spheres. It follows that the amending process must be so devised that neither the central government nor parliament acting alone nor the constitutional parts alone are able to alter the division of power in the constitution. Therefore, to amend federal constitutions, joint action between the central government or parliament and constituent units is necessary. In the United States, a two-thirds majority of Congress must pass the amendment, which then must be supported by three-quarters of the legislatures of states. In Switzerland, a two-thirds majority in parliament must be followed by electoral majorities in the majority of the cantons.

Such complex constitutional amending procedures may not raise difficulties for those who are committed to vetoes and special arrangements that may affect the composition of the regional parliament and executives. But in the context of South Africa, a rigid amending procedure would be part of the excessive protectionism, which can result only in resentment and instability.

In CODESA, it was accepted that there would be special majorities for adopting the constitution in a constitution-making body. In addition, a special majority would be required for dealing with the powers and status of regions, the specific majority in this area coming from those elected on the regional list.

The Arguments against Federalism

South Africa has been administered as a unitary state since 1910, when the federal approach was rejected by the all-white National Convention. The system of administration, supervision, and control and the division of functions have become part of its culture. Proposals for political federalism in a nonracist future can be perceived only cynically when considered within the highly centralized system under white minority rule.

Proposals that modify the present structure have nothing to do with participatory democracy or bringing the government to the people. Some of the most bureaucratic and impersonal governments are federal. The proposals of the National party and the Democratic party for coequal sovereign regions and autonomy down to the level of towns and neighborhoods could be the result of a rational, planned, and organized system of devolution. It is a method of locking wealth and resources into smaller units of government, where consensus decision making enables a veto to be used or where inordinately large majorities at the provincial executive level result in constitutionally protected walls of privilege—a recipe for the entrenchment of segregation and privilege.

The diffusion of constitutionally entrenched power enables parties representing ethnochauvinist interests, that have no hope of victory in national elections, to control regions where their interests may be paramount. Federalism may therefore be the only way for these parties to impede the reconstruction of the country, as the reconstruction approach requires macropolicies and national programs.

Under apartheid, South Africa has been fragmented to a degree unknown elsewhere, although ultimately power has been centralized in Pretoria. South Africa also has a highly centralized economy, controlled by a handful of companies. Such fragmentation is not the result of a policy of economic development and social uplift, but it does maintain the political power of the minority. The status quo can be maintained by ensuring that existing patterns of government, amended to avoid equating the four provinces with units of government, serve as the basis for regions. Proposals for a geographical federation fail to address the need for a recognition of the political and economic unity of South Africa. This is not simply a matter of sentiment or aspiration. Unity is important for an effective role in international relations, and it is crucial for the central management of the economy and for the redistribution of resources in favor of the less prosperous parts of South Africa.

In the context of a written constitutional order embracing a bill of rights that imposes severe constraints on governmental action and provides for determined protection of citizens' rights, it is vital that a democratic government in a free South Africa have the competence and authority to embark on the reconstruction of society. It must therefore have the constitutional competence to shift resources, to take commanding decisions that could be implemented by regions and local government, and to adopt national policies that would disrupt the established patterns of discrimination in housing, education, health care, and employment.

The federal option uses language to conceal its real meaning. Under this system, the central government will be constrained by constitutional restrictions of one kind or another from tackling the injustices of the past. The result would be to entrench these injustices, a sure recipe for ungovernability or civil war.

The function of economic management in a country where the economy has been operated for the minority imposes a severe challenge on the government. Any major changes to the constitutional order or to present arrangements have to be reconciled with a uniform approach in South Africa to the allocation of resources, to taxation arrangements, and to the management of the economy. If taxation raised in a region is locked into that region, or if the central government can allocate only 50 percent of total revenue for its purposes, then the need to "develop industrial policies aimed at transforming imbalances that exist between black and white, between urban and rural areas, and between regions," as envisaged by the Confederations of South African Trade Unions (COSATU)–African National Congress document of June 1990, will be totally frustrated. Each region will take autonomous and independent decisions. This document also urged the need for a recognition of rural industrialization, "with well-developed linkages with the local region." The argument for social justice depends for its effective application on the capacity of a government to control and use resources in order to ensure a larger measure of equality in public services and general standards of living.

It would be difficult, if not impossible, under a federal system to bring about social and economic transformation. This may give rise to serious problems concerning the implementation of aspects of the bill of rights, especially in relation to social and economic rights. Control over resources is vital in a democracy. Federations have been successful under conditions of approximate parity in economic resources among the federal units and a consensus about the goals to be achieved. But in neither area is there consensus in South Africa, and it is not difficult to envisage a rich and powerful region denying access to "its" resources and "its" taxable income, as has happened in other countries. Disparities in size and economic strength, reflected in the overwhelming economic and political power of the Pretoria, Witwatersrand, Verceniging (PWV), Durban, and Cape Town areas, would make a federation so "imbalanced as to be unworkable."[4] Such a system of disparities contains no equilibrium. In the Nigerian civil war of 1968, the north claimed that since its population was the largest, it should obtain the greatest resources.

The result of the artificial formation of a large number of statelets to provide credence to the federal idea would be disastrous because of the objective material facts in South Africa.

The fundamental objection to the federal idea is that it is based entirely on ahistorical premises by its proponents in South Africa. As the British Royal Commission on the Constitution pointed out, "Federalism was designed and is appropriate for states coming together to form a single unit, and not for a state breaking up into smaller units."[5]

Many of the National party's proposals are eclectic potpourris of examples that ignore the historical and political traumas of their evolution. Let us then look at some aspects of successful and unsuccessful experiments in federalism. In the United States, before the federation of 1789, the thirteen states that broke away from the British Empire regulated their common affairs from 1776 onward under the Articles of Confederation. They each had governments of their own and were agreed on the fundamentals of the new order: the maintenance of slavery and states' rights. In Germany, various states, with their Catholic and Protestant princes, fought each other vigorously and then came together. Under Bismarck they were brought together in 1871. That state became a federation in 1919—the Weimar Republic—on the basis of German interests. Although the 1949 Federal

Republic of Germany was not based on the historical states of 1871, the culture of federalism was quickly induced because of the totalitarianism of Nazism and the need to diffuse power. Its success lay on a material base—the capacity to provide for the needs of the people equally.

Similarly in Switzerland, over the centuries, a number of independent or quasi-independent statelets set up a confederation that evolved into a federation. The need to withstand pressures from its neighbors, especially France and Germany, was self-evident. Federalism was a device of convenience, bringing together units where religious or cultural groups were geographically discrete, in order to protect their interests against external intervention.

In the colonial territories of Australia and Canada, independence came to various Crown colonies, with their separate colonial authorities. These colonies then associated together, the better to organize their common endeavors. Even in India, which today can only be described as a quasi-federation, the units that came together were based on the colonial boundaries of the British Raj, complemented by the princely states that were coerced into what is described as the Union.

Theoretically, the USSR and Yugoslavia were federal states, based on the administrative divisions of the Russian and Ottoman empires respectively and supplemented by Stalin's and Tito's views on the national question. These views created so-called natural units of a federation; we know today that there was nothing natural about them.

Acting on the impetus of the U.S. example, a number of Latin American states, including Mexico, Venezuela, and Argentina, adopted a federal system. There was no material basis for these experiments in governance. They created a vast infrastructure of civil servants, governors, and legislators, but they were not able to grapple with the problems of poverty, illiteracy, and exploitation. The provinces became, in effect, the private possessions of warlords until the modernization process of the 1920s and 1930s.

The most dramatic example of the imposition of the federal option in Africa was the Central African Federation of the 1950s, uniting Nyasaland and the two Rhodesias. They were clearly meant to perpetuate the race rule of the small white minority of Southern Rhodesia and were doomed to failure. It was for this reason that Zimbabwe African People's Union (ZAPU) and Zimbabwe African National Union (ZANU) rejected a federal approach during the independence talks in 1979. The approach weakened national unity in a state already plagued by other problems. In Nigeria in 1960, the constitution established a federation bringing together the three units—north, west, and east—that had traditionally been administered separately by the British. The disparities in wealth, population, and levels of education, compounded by the discovery of oil in the 1960s, led to the success of centrifugal tendencies, with untold human suffering and loss of lives.

The Democratic Response

What the U.S. assistant secretary of Africa has described as the "disenfranchised majority" has traditionally been skeptical of the idea of separate sovereigns within the single territory of South Africa. But this support for a unitary state has not been motivated by promotion of a strong central government with a highly centralized bureaucracy. Neither has there been any desire to establish a *dirigiste* system to create a homogenized and artificial national identity.

The African National Congress, for example, has in its policy documents made it clear that its adherence to a unitary government presupposes commitment to a lively, participatory democracy. It is opposed to the overly centralized, impersonal, bureaucratic, and elitist concept of government that South Africa has had and to which the National party has been firmly attached. Throughout its history, the ANC has made its adherence to a unitary form of government a cardinal principle of policy. This has most recently been reflected in the discussion document on constitutional principles of April 1991. The "principles" document supports governmental structures and institutions that are based on "democratic principles, popular participation, accountability and accessibility." On this basis, the document comes out in support of "strong and effective central government to handle national tasks, strong and effective regional government to deal with the tasks of the region and strong and effective local government to ensure local government in handling local issues."

Federal systems in themselves are neither more nor less democratic than unitary systems, which range from the social democratic state of Sweden, with its decentralization, to the English model under Margaret Thatcher, with a powerful central government. Even a highly integrated state like France has in modern times set up a viable regional government. Conversely, the bureaucracies of federal government must not be confused with participatory democracy or with enabling more people to take part in the process of government, as the Democratic party claims. Unitary government can do this as well, if not better. History belies the supposed advantage of having a variety of sites of power, a claim made for federal government.

Racism and slavery in the United States show that discrimination was usually the local option. The development and encouragement of the organs of civil society, independent of the state, is a surer basis for the protection of individual and collective interests.

The claims made by the proponents of federalism are really arguments for a powerless central government. We reject a diffusion of power that would leave the central organization of people's power—the National Assembly—powerless in the face of artificially created units of governments that have neither a historical nor a rational basis. Instead we propose a constitutional order, with a strong regional and local authority component, that would provide appropriate, effective, and secure protection against oppression or domination. The strength of these proposals is that they are not specifically designed to protect the privileges of any group but intended to secure the fundamental rights and freedoms of all South Africans.

Accordingly, the February 1992 consultative document issued by the Constitutional Committee of the ANC entitled *Ten Proposed Regions for a United South Africa* makes a strong case for regional government. "The creation of vigorous regions is vital to the development of a united South Africa. [All the] problems of disunity and deprivation are to be found in every region. Within a framework of a national vision and policies, it is at the regional and local levels that practical day-to-day solutions will have to be found."

What has also emerged is the need to provide for constitutional protection of regions so that there can be no repetition of the frivolous manner in which the old provincial legislatures were abolished in 1986. In addition, the emerging consensus in CODESA, reflected in Working Group Two's steering committee report in May 1992 that "Government shall be structured at national, regional and local levels," provides a suitable point of departure.

It would also be acceptable that each level of government should have appropriate and adequate legislative and executive powers, duties, and functions and that these competences should be en-trenched in the future constitution. The fundamental point of depar-ture concerns the exercise of exclusive powers at "each level." In principle, functions such as education, health care, and physical planning can be exercised at different levels. But the central authority must have the power to insist that national policies are not vitiated by recalcitrant or obscurantist regions. After all, every citizen should be entitled to the same benefits throughout South Africa, and no one should be sacrificed at the altar of "states' rights."

For this reason, the ANC supports the idea that, apart from

powers exclusively vested in the central authority, *concurrent* powers should be exercised by all three levels. In the event of conflict between the center and a region, however, the "supremacy" clause would enable the central organs of government to have priority. Not every function would require a supremacy clause, and conventions could easily develop where regions and local authorities would have autonomy in their chosen areas.

Conclusion

The debate must not therefore be allowed to degenerate into a sterile discussion on the forms or structure of the governmental machinery. The struggle against apartheid has been concerned not only with the creation of democratic structures. It has also confronted the problem of redistribution of resources, which up to now have been used in a racist manner. The heart of the issue is the extent to which proposals for political change will assist or hinder the move toward the removal of apartheid and its effects on South African life. Put in another way, to what extent will federalism help in deracializing South Africa?

The details concerning the structure, powers, and finances of regions and their relationships with the central authorities must be matters for a Constituent Assembly. In its deliberations, the members of the constitution-making body could do worse than bear in mind Allister Sparks's words:

> The ending of apartheid and the prospect of a "new South Africa" are inevitably raising expectations in the black community. A system that paralyzes and prevents it from satisfying at least a minimum of those raised expectations will quickly result in the new regime being discredited. . . .
> That is why it is so important for whites to realize that excessive protectionism is not in their interest. It is a formula for resentment and instability.[6]

A democratic and united South Africa with a bill of rights, proportional representation for the election of all governmental structures, separation of powers, and an independent judiciary will provide a surer basis for the protection of the rights of all individuals and minorities.

5

Can American Federalism
Help South Africa?

Daniel J. Elazar

When attempting to compare and learn from the United States, one must begin by noting how different the conceptions and the experiences of Americans and many other peoples are. This problem of understanding can hardly be minimized. It is difficult for Americans to understand how politics is conducted in other countries because the latter are grounded upon the kind of permanent primordial or intergenerational groups with territorial bases or at least aspirations for territorial bases that are absent even from American ethnic politics.

Americans do have an ethnic politics, but it is an ethnic politics that runs counter, in most respects, to the territorial politics of the United States. Indeed, the great political change of the twentieth-century United States has been a movement from a territorially based politics, from the smallest precinct and township up through the federal government to a politics that mixes territorial and ethnic elements. Sometimes both sets of elements benefit one from the other. Sometimes they work at cross-purposes.

Understanding the U.S. Political System
in Light of South Africa

How different the situation is in South Africa, where ethnic politics is so closely connected with territory and with disputes over territory.

Moreover, this ethnicity is permanent. Unlike the United States, where people can change identities, in South Africa people see themselves tied to their ethnic group organically, fundamentally, primordially, from generation to generation. No matter where they are, no matter where they might go, no matter what the conditions of their political life or their degree of independence or subordination, these differences are truly great and will not be underestimated. What the United States and South Africa have in common is that both need, each for its own reasons, federal solutions. Federal countries need federal polities, and South Africa for its reasons, like the United States for its, is a federal country.

While the original confederation of the United States may simply have grown out of American experience, the American federal Constitution of 1787 was the product of political theory and thought as much as of experience. On the one hand, I think that is important precisely because the American experience is not transplantable per se. On the other hand, American political thought is worth studying and exploring by all.

Every political society, every polity, has to develop its own system of self-government through some combination of its experience and reflection and choice based on that experience. In *Federalist* 1, Publius (in this case, Alexander Hamilton) comments that it is given to few peoples of this world to choose their form of government not by force or by accident but through reflection and choice. And it is that critical factor, reflection and choice, that involves the combination of experience and thought. We cannot control our experiences. They are part of our heritage. We can only try to direct and control their effects after they occur.

South Africa has had its own historical experience. Its peoples have also had their collective historical experiences, in many cases forced on them. These have already had a tremendous impact on what its polity is likely to become in the future.

The Two Faces of Politics

Human, and hence scholarly, concern with politics focuses on three general themes: (1) the pursuit of political justice to achieve the good political order, (2) the search for understanding the empirical reality of political power and its exercise, and (3) the creation of an appropriate civic environment through civil society and civil community, capable of integrating the first two to produce a good political life. Political science as a discipline was founded and has developed in pursuit of those three concerns. In the course of that pursuit, political scientists have uncovered or identified certain architectonic principles, seminal ideas, and plain political truths that capture the reality of political life or some significant segment of it, and relate that reality to the larger principles of justice and political order and to practical yet normative civic purposes.

Politics has two faces. One is the face of power; the other is the face of justice. Politics, as the pursuit and organization of power, is concerned (in the words of Harold Lasswell) with "who gets what, when and how." Politics is equally a matter of justice, however, or the determination of who *should* get what, when, how—and why. Power is the means by which people organize themselves and shape their environment in order to live. Justice offers the guidelines for using power in order to live well.

Politics cannot be understood without reference to both faces. On the one hand, without understanding a polity's conception of justice, or who should have power, one cannot understand clearly why certain people or groups get certain rewards, at certain times, in certain ways. On the other hand, one cannot focus properly on the pursuit of justice without also understanding the realities of the distribution of power. Both elements are present in all political questions, mutually influencing each other.

The Origins of the Polity

Since its beginnings, political science has identified three basic ways in which polities come into existence: conquest (force), organic development (accident), and covenant (choice). These questions of origins are not abstract; the mode of founding of a polity does much to determine the framework for its subsequent political life.

Conquest can be understood to include not only its most direct manifestation, a conqueror gaining control of a land or a people, but also such subsidiary ways as a revolutionary conquest of an existing state, a coup d'état, and groups of people—either a minority or a majority—conquering another or others in the land, or even an entrepreneur conquering a market and organizing his control through corporate means. Conquest tends to produce hierarchically organized regimes ruled in an authoritarian manner: power pyramids with the conqueror on top, his agents in the middle, and the conquered underneath the entire structure as portrayed in figure 5–1. The original expression of this kind of polity was the Pharaonic state of ancient Egypt. It was hardly an accident that those rulers who brought the Pharaonic state to its fullest development had the pyramids built as their tombs. Although the Pharaonic model has been

FIGURE 5–1
The Power Pyramid Model of Political Organization

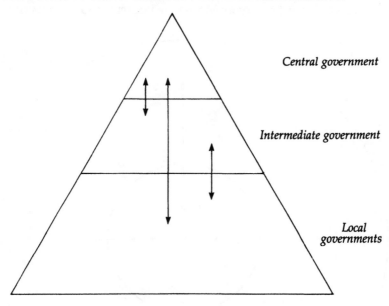

Central government

Intermediate government

Local
governments

SOURCE: Author.

judged illegitimate in Western society, modern totalitarian and racist theories, particularly fascism and Nazism, represent an attempt to give it a certain theoretical legitimacy.

Organic evolution involves the development of political life from families, tribes, and villages into large polities in such a way that institutions, constitutional relationships, and power alignments emerge in response to the interaction between past precedent and changing circumstances with the minimum of deliberate constitutional choice. The end result tends to be a polity with a single center of power, as portrayed in figure 5–2.

Classic Greek political thought emphasized the organic evolution of the polity and rejected any other means of polity building as deficient or improper. The organic model is closely related to the concept of natural law in the political order. Natural law informs the world and, when undisturbed, leads in every polity to the natural emergence of power relationships, necessarily and naturally unequal, which fit the character of its people.

The organic model has proved most attractive to many political philosophers precisely because at its best, it seems to reflect the

FIGURE 5-2
THE CENTER PERIPHERY MODEL OF POLITICAL ORGANIZATION

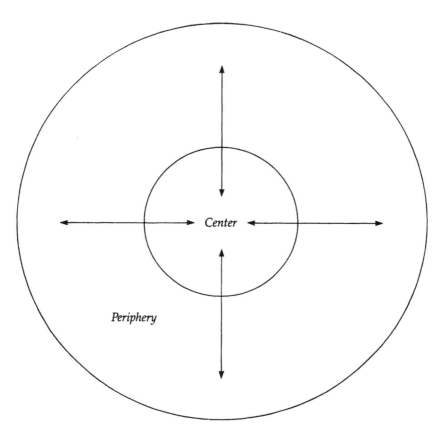

Center

Periphery

SOURCE: Author.

natural order of things. Thus it has received the most intellectual and academic attention. Just as conquest tends to produce hierarchically organized regimes ruled in an authoritarian manner, however, organic evolution tends to produce oligarchic regimes, which at their best have an aristocratic flavor and at their worst are simply the rule of the many by the few. In the first, the goal of politics is to control the top of the pyramid; in the second, the goal is to control the center of power.

Covenantal foundings emphasize the deliberate coming together of humans as equals to establish bodies politic in such a way that all reaffirm their fundamental equality and retain their basic rights. Even

FIGURE 5–3
The Matrix Model of Political Organization

Federal Government

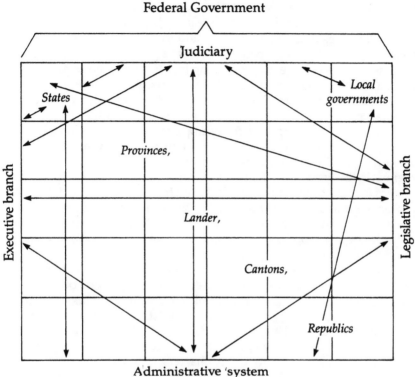

SOURCE: Author.

the Hobbesian covenant—and he specifically uses the term—which establishes a polity in which power is vested in a single sovereign, in principle maintains this fundamental equality. Polities whose origins are covenantal reflect the exercise of constitutional choice and broad-based participation in constitutional design. Polities founded by covenant are essentially federal in character, in the original meaning of the term (from *foedus*, Latin for *covenant*)—whether they are federal in structure or not. That is to say, each polity is a matrix (figure 5–3) compounded of equal confederates who freely bind themselves to one another so as to retain their respective integrities even as they are bound in a common whole. Such polities are republican by definition, and power within them must be diffused among many centers or the various cells within the matrix.

We find recurring expressions of the covenant model in ancient Israel, whose people started out as rebels against the Pharaonic model; in the medieval rebels against the Holy Roman Empire; in the Reformation-era rebels against the Catholic hierarchy; in the early modern republicans who were rebels against either hierarchical or organic theories of the state; and in modern federalists. Frontiersmen generally—that is to say, people who have gone out and settled new areas where there were no preexisting institutions of government and who, therefore, have had to enter a compact with one another to create such institutions—are to be found among the most active covenanters.

Each of these forms of founding has real implications for the character of the regime that emerges from it, in the structure of authority, in the mechanisms of governance, and in the forms the regime is likely to take. Thus, in regimes founded by conquest and force, we expect to find hierarchical structures of authority dominant, power pyramids in every sense of the word. In such regimes, administration, which is a matter of a top-down chain of command, takes precedence over politics and constitutionalism. Indeed, the major political arena in such regimes is that of the ruler at the top of the pyramid. In other words, it is court politics, with the kind of intrigue and jockeying for position associated with the politics of courts. If constitutionalism plays any role at all, the constitution takes the form of a charter granted by the ruler, whose status is at least formally controlled by him (although, as we know from feudal systems, under certain circumstances rulers who seem to be on the top of the pyramid can be forced to grant charters of liberties to subsidiary bodies, because there has been a redistribution of force as a result of external factors over which the top of the pyramid has no control).

The apotheosis of such a regime is an army. Indeed, one of the first modern models was Prussia, described by Voltaire as "an army transformed into a state." So, too, was Napoleonic France, where Napoleon's administrative reorganization of the country fixed its internal structure for the next 170 years regardless of wars, revolutions, coups, and regime changes. The worst manifestation of such regimes is the totalitarian dictatorship, whereby those at the top of the pyramid attempt, in the name of an ideology, to bring their pyramided powers to bear on every aspect of private as well as public life.

Organic polities that essentially develop by accident and are marked by their center-periphery configuration, organize their mechanisms of government differently. For them, politics takes precedence over administration, and both over the constitution. Since the most important political arena is in the center, the politics is the politics of the club or clubs where the elite gather and maintain relationships with one another, regardless of their stand on issues, simply because they belong to a common elite or network of elites. Administration is deemed much less important than politics and exists only to the degree that it is necessary, flowing from the center outward. At first, the same club members who dominate the regime's politics also undertake much of the necessary administration of functions, but as matters grow more specialized, a separate administrative elite is developed, drawn as much as possible from the same sources as the political elite and maintaining a common old-boy network.

The English system, where studies at Oxford and Cambridge are tickets of admission to either the political or the administrative elites, whose members speak the same language or at least in the same accents and belong to the same clubs, typifies this kind of regime. Constitutionalism is not unimportant in such regimes; however, it is not reflected in a single major document but in a set of constitutional traditions that may or may not have been set down in writing and transformed into law, again in the English model. The apotheosis of this model is parliamentary government along the Westminster system, while its excess is to be found in Jacobinism, where a revolutionary cadre seizes control of the center in the name of the masses and concentrates all power within it in the name of the revolution in order to reconstruct the regime. It never relinquishes control.

Covenantal regimes, founded on the basis of reflection and choice to establish a matrix of power centers, so that both its framing institutions and its constituent bodies share authority on a fundamentally equal basis, order the mechanisms of government quite differently. First and foremost come the constitution and the constitutional tradition it fosters. The constitution must, perforce, come first, because it is the basis on which institutions are organized and authority and power are shared and divided. Without the constitution, there can legitimately be neither politics nor administration. Pursuant to the constitution, there develops a politics of open bargaining in which access is guaranteed by the constitution and the constitutional tradition to all citizens who accept the rules of the game. The open competition of parties and factions is encouraged. Administration is subordinate to both constitutional and political standards and is further controlled by being divided between the framing institution and the cells of the matrix.

The apotheosis of this model is a federal democratic republic on the order of the United States or Switzerland. Its excess is anarchy, where the framing institutions and cells prove incapable of ordering the exercise of power within the structure.

While in real life many polities mix these models to establish their regimes, the classic examples of political organization tend to be relatively pure representations of one or the other. Both the purer cases and the mixtures teach us about important manifestations of political life (table 5–1).

South Africa and the United States—Some Comparisons

What do the American founders have to say that would be of use to the founders of the new South Africa? On the surface, the disparity in the two situations is great, especially since the American founders were faced with a situation like that in old South Africa, where, with some exceptions, nonwhites were excluded from citizenship in the polity. The genius of the American founders was that even if they were not as correct in their assessment of issues in the short run (for example, their belief that the central political issue of the new federal government would be small states versus large states), they knew what would be right in the long run. In other words, they founded a polity on correct fundamental principles, on a correct understanding of human nature.

Beyond that, the constitution that they wrote combines a proper degree of rigidity with a proper use of ambiguity. The times for elections were fixed, for example, unlike in parliamentary regimes. The president, vice president, representatives, and senators were to be elected for fixed terms with no possibility of changing those dates except by constitutional amendment. Where interpretation was necessary, however, a proper ambiguity of language was provided. This ensured that popular government would be maintained and that there could be no excuse for holding off popular elections, while at the same time allowing the kind of flexibility that a constitution needs.

Let me suggest a few comparisons between the United States and the Republic of South Africa. In both cases, we are speaking of one country. The United States was perceived or at least presented by its founders as homogeneous in population. In part, this was because of the exclusion of black slaves and Indians. This representation did not take into consideration the heterogeneity of the European population, which was already great by contemporary standards, or the country's religious heterogeneity, not only with so many Christian sects but also with Jews as full citizens.

The Republic of South Africa, in contrast, is recognized as highly

TABLE 5–1
MODELS OF FOUNDINGS AND TYPES OF REGIMES

Attributes	Conquest	Organic Development	Covenant
Founding	Force	Accident	Reflection and choice
Model	Pyramid	Concentric circles	Matrix
Structure of authority	Hierarchy	Center-periphery	Frame and cells
Mechanisms of governance (in rank order)	Administration: top-down bureaucracy	Politics: club-oligarchy	Constitution: written
	Politics: court	Administration: center outward	Politics: open with factions
	Constitution-charter	Constitution: tradition	Administration: divided
Apotheosis	Army	Westminster system	Federal system
Excess	Totalitarian dictatorship	Jacobin state	Anarchy
Most common form of revolution against	Coup d' état	Civil war among elites	Structural resort to arms

SOURCE: Author.

heterogeneous in several ways, not only in the division among black, white, Asian, and Coloured but also between those of English and those of Afrikaner background, plus European immigrants of many other groups and deep tribal divisions among the blacks.

The United States emphasized territorial democracy from the first. That is to say, citizenship, politics, and government were organized around territories, whether states, counties, townships, cities, or even less permanent electoral districts. In the Republic of South Africa, circumstances have modified its basic territorial democracy with a combination of other forms of democracy as well, principally resting upon the existence of primordial groups. The United States in 1787 did not have organized political parties; hence the Constitutional Convention was not divided along party lines. The Republic of South Africa in 1992 has well-organized political parties, in most cases reflecting the deepest cleavages in its civil society.

Further, it is well to remember certain points about the U.S. federal Constitution:

1. It was written by a committee. While there were outstanding figures at the Constitutional Convention and James Madison more than any other single person shaped the resulting constitution, still, the United States had no one founder. Rather, the Constitutional Convention functioned as a committee and made its decisions with all the differences of opinion that had to be covered within a committee.

2. The U.S. Constitution is incomplete without the state constitutions. Donald Lutz has made that point most effectively.[1] The U.S. Constitution was not meant to be other than an incomplete document, relying on the state constitutions for the fundaments of government and relating only to the constitution of the federal government and its basic relationships with the states.

3. The U.S. Constitution has silences that themselves have meaning. The Tenth Amendment, for example, was designed to clarify some of the silences with regard to the continuing status of the states in the new federal Constitution, though in fact it introduced ambiguities of its own. Similarly, there is no mention of local government in the U.S. Constitution, since that is constitutionally a matter for the states.

4. The U.S. Constitution has two dimensions. It reaffirms the rights of the states and their people to self-government and also guarantees them a share in the common government. One might refer to this as a combination of self-rule and shared rule, which is, by the way, an excellent definition of what federalism is all about.

5. The citizens of the United States are citizens as individuals; that is to say, they possess dual citizenship: they are citizens of their states and citizens of the United States. This was understood in the Constitution of 1787 but made explicit after the Civil War through the Fourteenth Amendment.

A central idea of the U.S. Constitution was to establish an extended republic, one in which there were no permanent majorities or minorities. This is the point of Madison's famous *Federalist* 10 extending the sphere of the republic. The founders perceived that the problem of previous small republics was that a permanent majority of the poor stood against a permanent minority of the rich and believed that with the extended republic, that problem would be solved. In it, there would be many interests, of which poor and rich could be only one, and those interests would constantly be forming coalitions with one another to form temporary majorities around specific issues. This would absorb and diffuse conflict by allowing all permanent interests fair expression.

It was assumed that this extended republic would be established by political compact. Its constitution would be established by a pact among its members. Indeed, the Constitution itself is such a pact. The reason it does not explicitly discuss the compact theory is that it follows in the path of the states, many of which did just that when they reestablished themselves during the Revolutionary War. Moreover, the Declaration of Independence can be read as the original covenant or compact establishing the United States of America. Elsewhere, I have demonstrated the covenantlike character of the Declaration.[2]

Some Questions

The United States was founded by uniting separate states that felt themselves to be akin to one another and that had conducted a revolution against the mother country together. The question before South Africa is, Can a unitary, highly centralized state be transformed into a federation? The record is not unambiguous. Spain, an example to which I will refer frequently and to which I suggest that South African constitution makers refer, is perhaps the most successful example of such a transformation in our times. After the death of Francisco Franco, and as part of its turn toward democracy, the Spanish political leadership made some critically important decisions to accommodate the country's ethnic minorities, at least two of which—the Basques and the Catalans—had become vociferous in their demands to the point of violence.

The Spanish political leadership brilliantly decided to avoid asymmetrical solutions, that is to say, limiting autonomy to those two or perhaps a few more minorities at the country's periphery, so that the issues would always be framed in the context of Spain versus its peripheral minorities. They determined to divide the entire country into autonomous regions while allowing those that wished to establish their own special constitutional relationships with Madrid to do so through bilateral negotiations. At the same time, the general law of regionalization required each region to establish a basic quasi-federal constitutional relationship in the intervening half-generation.

This was decided and embodied in the 1978 Spanish Constitution drafted in a convention that was highly partisan where the revived political parties of Spain covered the spectrum of political ideologies and attitudes, yet were able to negotiate a mutually satisfactory arrangement. In the intervening half-generation, the system has proved itself, as the major secessionist tensions have been eliminated or confined to a less-than-popular terrorist underground in the Basque country. The four unique regions—the Basque country, Catalonia, Galicia, and Andalusia—each negotiated its own constitutional status directly with Madrid, and the other regions adopted a common framework for regionalization, as they did not seek anything more than that. The plan, while avoiding the use of the word *federal* because of objections of the right-wing parties, has become essentially a federal one in all but name because the Spanish Constitution and the regional constitutions provide the kind of empowerment and protections that federal constitutions have.

Belgium is trying to do the same but has the problem of a dyadic division between Flemings and Walloons, which invariably leads to sharper confrontation. Nevertheless, because of its position in the European Community, it may be able to do so. The Federal Republic of Germany has had to undertake this task for its newly absorbed eastern part and, indeed, only accomplished unification by first reestablishing the five *Länder* in the east and then reuniting them with the eleven *Länder* of the west.

Austria, after it ceased to be the center of the Austro-Hungarian empire with its power-sharing features, then had to divide itself internally into a federation, which it did along the lines of its traditional provinces. This took place after World War I. Austria has tended to be a very centralized federation, but it is a federation and offers another example to be studied.

Brazil also transformed a unitary state that was quite centralized into a federation in the 1890s, shortly after it had ceased to be a monarchy. Brazilian federalism has had its ups and downs but has remained a powerful means of protecting liberties in that country, if often by unorthodox means themselves fostered by the existence of federalism.

Pakistan also formally transformed itself into a federal system upon achieving independence from the British and partition from India in 1947. Its federation is based on linguistic provinces and has been even more centralized than the others cited. Pakistan has had a military government for so much of its history that the extent of the existence of true federalism within its borders is questionable.

Even in these cases, it should be clear that the advantage of federalism is to allow a variety of ethnic accommodations. This would be true for South Africa as it has been for these other countries mentioned and still others. Moreover, as in the United States, federal protection of individual rights and the free flow of commerce will probably be essential for the achievement of the kind of liberal democracy that the peoples of South Africa seek.

The Critical Questions

Three critical questions for South Africa are: How will federalism affect economic growth; how will it deal with regional inequalities; and how will it affect redistributive policies?

As far as the United States is concerned, federalism certainly seems to have served the purposes of economic growth. While such growth always has a tendency to promote regional inequalities, in the long run it has kept those inequalities under control in the United States, in part because each region of the country had a strong political voice in national affairs, including national economic affairs. Certainly, federalism has had a redistributive role in the United States, since the existence of the states has ensured that federal government policies would take all states into consideration and thus serve redistributive functions.

The positive role of federalism in this regard may best be seen in the third world. In unitary states in the third world, economic development has generally meant the development of the capital city and the metropolis surrounding it, which have concentrated the wealth, new and old, in their hands. While the same inequities of concentration may have been present in third world federations, the existence of state capitals as well as the federal capital has ensured that at least these capital cities would become development nodes for their respective regions, offering a better distribution of wealth and addressing the problem of regional inequalities to a greater extent than in unitary states.

The economic dimension is a reflection of the difference between federalism and regionalism. In federalism, the subnational units have constitutionally entrenched powers, not easily subject to revocation by the federal government at the whim of those in power in the national capital. This is critically important for all concerned. In that sense, federalism is not functional devolution at the whim of the center but rather a constitutional division of powers designed to protect all citizens.

Federalism is also a way to overcome the disadvantages of metropolitanism in a country like South Africa, dividing the great metropolitan agglomerations, most specifically the great Pretoria Witwatersrand Verceniging (PVW) metropolitan agglomeration among several regional governments. Its governmental structures would serve a redistributive policy that will address major economic inequalities in the entire polity. Indeed, it may be the only way in which such redress can be brought about in fairness. If the PVW agglomeration is divided among several regional governments, either the regional governments will force the federal government to pursue a redistributive policy, or there will be a general metropolitan authority in which each region will be represented, with redistributive mechanisms and set-asides built in.

The question may be raised as to how important regional identities would be. Fortunately, South Africa has a basis for regionalization in the nine economic regions established several years ago that cut across the usual racial and ethnic lines sufficiently, where necessary, to establish a measure of fairness. These regions are already recognized. It may be necessary to establish one or two more by further dividing the nine, for example, another region in the PVW area or a new, predominantly Xhosa-speaking region based on Ciskei-Transkei and the South African territory in the middle. These regions will, once they are empowered, soon acquire an appropriate regional identity through their actions. As regional bodies of law and histories develop, sufficient regional integrity is established to give them identities but not identities that work against the common South African identity.

Designing a Federal Constitution for South Africa

The foregoing issues lead us to questions of constitutional design. Here I would like to try to emphasize those principles of constitutional design that are most appropriate for decision makers to consider. Several are conceptual, others theoretical, and still others very practical indeed. I will try to stress what I consider most important from the theoretical perspective of constitutional design. Constitutional design is a field in and of itself. Perhaps I can suggest some ways to use the knowledge accumulated in the field of constitutional design through experience in various parts of the world.

Political Will. The main problem to be faced in this regard is how much political will there is to federate, with all that entails—comity, power sharing, appropriate mutual trust, and respect. Based upon my experiences in South Africa, I believe that with appropriate leadership South Africans of all varieties will be able to find the necessary political will, although there are serious problems of trust among certain groups (not only between blacks and whites). If there is a will to have the political will, it will be possible.

An equally important question is, How much self-rule should be granted to the regions? It seems to me that it should be more rather than less, because the best way to encourage mutual trust is through the exercise of responsibility.

What needs to be ambiguous in the constitution, and what needs to be rigid? In my opinion, all those procedures that guarantee the preservation of democratic self-government need to be rigid—that is, dates of elections and basic issues of rights protection—whereas the exercise of powers or functions can be more ambiguous.

A major issue in the South African constitutional negotiations is the entrenchment of regional powers. The African National Congress wants no entrenchment, and the National party major entrenchment. Joe Slova's proposed compromise at Group Two of the Conference for a Democratic South Africa (CODESA) comes close to being a middle way and should be pursued. While there should be room for interpretation, basic regional powers should be constitutionally entrenched. Today, the trend in most federal states is away from centralization toward greater decentralization, because placing too great a burden on the federal government means that nothing gets done.

If South Africans need to find a word other than *federalism*, that should not be the problem. In Spain, for example, the federated states are called *autonomous communities*. Powers are the real issue.

We should not make ourselves slaves to questions of terminology—many mistakes have been made in both political science and philosophy by trying so hard to agree on terminology that we become slaves to the words. Still, unless we correctly understand not only each other but the things we are talking about as well, then it is difficult to try and communicate messages. In this respect, there are some issues of terminology that cannot be ignored.

Protecting Rights. The first question to be raised underpinning any polity is the question of rights. Is the local or the federal government the best one to protect the individual and private rights of citizens?

It depends on whom we want to protect. The American position, which is not wrong, is that if one wants to protect people who are different, who deviate from the local consensus, then indeed the federal government can do better. But today, there is some question in the United States as to whether needed local consensus is not at the mercy of every deviate who comes along and claims his or her constitutional rights. This is particularly important where national or group rights are involved because people obviously care passionately about their national rights, even if those national rights might be interpreted in another environment as going against their individual rights. Look today at what was Yugoslavia or the former Soviet Union.

People who care passionately about such things will have different ideas of protection. The problem that is faced in South Africa as in other parts of the world is, How do we find a balance in protecting both? Americans have been able to do that because we have had a clear conviction—a dominant consensus—that we are more interested in protecting the deviant individual than we are in protecting any kind of collective rights, a concept that we do not even formally recognize.

Avoiding the Reified State. The peoples of South Africa, especially those involved in the problems of constitutional design, must jettison the idea of "the state" as a reified entity, as something that exists in and of itself, regardless of its people, regardless of its regime. South African political language, influenced by European models, seems quite wedded to the idea of the state as a reified entity. In fact, the great revolution in modern democratic republicanism was to get rid of that idea of the state and to see the people as the source of political power.

Proper democratic theory holds that the people, in their various institutional combinations, delegate from their powers to governments—in federal systems, to local, state, federal, and special-purpose governments as necessary. Under democratic-republican theory, especially that animated by the principles of federal democracy, all governments are governments of delegated powers only. None possess powers in their own right, only such as their peoples delegate to them, and what can be delegated can be reassumed, transferred, reorganized, or shifted.

This is a conceptual matter but of immense importance, as it makes possible the distribution of powers and their separation and the constitutional protection of rights. If a reified state is "sovereign," then it decides if and how power should be distributed and divided—if it so chooses—but in fact it remains the final point of sovereignty where authority and power come together. Thus the state, which means for all intents and purposes those who run the state, determines who grants or guarantees rights and determines the final organization of powers. Whereas if the people are sovereign, then all rights, authority, and power inhere in them, and government is merely a vehicle for their exercise. Since rights are inherent, people are inherently protected, and rights do not come to them as a gift from some external state. Moreover, it is easier to understand government or governments as consisting of the governors, those who empower them, and the institutions and mechanisms for keeping those governors in their place, than when we are confronted by the ostensible majesty of the reified state. To restate matters, the three great elements of democratic republicanism—federalism, the separation of powers, and the bill of rights—are all made possible by the idea of popular sovereignty.

The idea of the reified state is a European invention. According to that theory, the only thing that democracy brings to the reified state is the possibility that peoples can change their regimes, sometimes democratically, but the idea that there is such a thing as a reified state makes it impossible to construct properly any kind of constitutional regime that will promise democratic republicanism and self-government, much less federalism.

In place of the state, Americans successfully developed a different approach to understanding how polities are organized. The people as a whole—and in a federal system, the people of their respective entities—are the source of political power or, if you will, political sovereignty. (I am not certain that we should not get rid of that term also simply because of the complications that it brings.) The people are politically sovereign. They are the source of the constituent power (in the words of Johannes Althusius, a great European political theorist of the late sixteenth century, who was ignored for three hundred years by all those who wanted to build reified states). The people delegate the constituent power to those governments to whom they choose to delegate it.

Under the doctrine of state sovereignty, as opposed to popular sovereignty, there is one state with its government. All the other jurisdictions are mere "authorities" subordinate to the sovereign state, not governments. The government is in the hands of the state.

Under the doctrine of popular sovereignty, the people can determine to delegate their powers to both general and constituent governments. The people can determine how they allocate the powers to govern themselves; to whom they entrust those powers; and to what institutions they entrust those powers. They do not grapple with abstract questions such as, Where is "the state"? Who is the state? What does the state do?

Individuals, people do things. Even "the bureaucracy" is an abstraction. There are people who are working in a bureaucratic framework with certain consequences because of the framework. But they are still people. Anybody who follows the infighting within and among bureaucracies knows how unhelpful it is to talk about a reified state bureaucracy. There are many state bureaucrats and departments and agencies who fight with each other for power as much as they fight with others, maybe more. So it is misleading to think that there is not real diversity even in the most centralized state, even if the words of reification camouflage it. The words of reification, by camouflaging the reality, hide the diversity from the people and allow bureaucrats to act irresponsibly.

Distribution of Powers. Look for the distribution of powers to build a political society that is democratic and republican. Whether federal or not, there needs to be a distribution of powers. In federal systems, the distribution of powers takes three forms. First of all, there is the form of federalism, the distribution of powers among territorial entities. A large, comprehensive entity that we call the federal government is constituted of smaller, comprehensive entities serving pieces of the territory, which we call states or localities. The total is a matrix of governments with the federal government as the framing institution (what earlier generations of Americans referred to as the general government), within which are constitutional regions or states and within those regions, others called local governments.

There is no "central" government, a term that implies that it is the center of all power and communication. As in a cybernetic system, power and communications flow in many directions, as needed. This is a vital distinction.

There also needs to be a separation of powers within each government: executive, legislative, and judicial. There have been efforts on the part of those inspired by certain forms of democracy to eliminate the separation of powers. They have not worked. Indeed, the trend has gone back to making the separation of powers more or less complete in order to preserve democracy in just about every case. The exceptions are in polities where the democratic tradition is so strong that it is able, to some extent, to substitute for a thorough separation of powers.

A Civil Society. Finally, there is the protection of the private rights of individuals through what we properly call *civil society*, a term from the age of democratic revolutions in the seventeenth and eighteenth centuries that has gained new currency in the former communist bloc, since its recent revolutions. *Civil society* is a term that teaches us that not all of society is political, that while framed by the polity, there is a large private sphere rightfully separate from government. Its revival in the East comes in time to remind us in the West that this is the term that properly describes our own liberties in which there is a separation of governmental and nongovernmental spheres and a distribution of powers between them.

I cannot overemphasize the importance of the idea of civil society, of limited government. The term itself is a great invention of seventeenth-century political philosophy that teaches us two good lessons: that no society exists without government, without some form for establishing order and security and allocation of powers, and at the same time, that government has to be limited so that there is a sufficient private sphere.

Indeed, in the most successful democracies, we have come to understand that civil society actually has three pillars: a governmental pillar, a private pillar, and a public nongovernmental pillar (a *civic sector* we call it in the United States), where people voluntarily come together (truly voluntarily, not coerced voluntarism) to do as much as possible on a cooperative basis, on a coproduction basis, before turning to government. Government does only what cannot be done privately or through the public nongovernmental civic sector. So look to the development of those three sectors.

Constituent Units with Real Powers. The constituent units of a federation need to have real power, including real powers of taxation. These may be implemented in the way that we do in the United States, where we have parallel federal and state officials in institutions working throughout the United States. Or it may be done the way it is done in Switzerland, where the federal government uses the institutions of the constituent units to implement federal legislation, and it has not tried to establish its own institutions throughout the country.

Each system is good in some places and poor in others. In the United States, for example, dual structures have worked rather well. The Latin American countries have allowed federal government, with its greater resources, to work locally, effectively preempting state and local efforts and defeating federalism because of the political culture. In Switzerland, the other system has worked rather well because of the ingrained federal political culture. It is somewhat more problematic in hierarchical Austria. What is necessary in either case is that real powers have to be constitutionally allocated and protected among governments.

Dualism and Cooperation. Federalism works through a combination of competition and cooperation. A dual structure is necessary in one or another of the forms I have described. But there will always be cooperative relationships within the structure because there are too many items that have to be done cooperatively by the governments involved. The United States learned that early. Cooperative federalism was the norm in this country within a few years after the adoption of the Constitution of 1787. But in our time, this thrust toward intergovernmental sharing has gotten out of hand somewhat, as it has been used by the federal government from time to time for coercive purposes.

A proper balance between cooperation and dualism is critically important, but both will always exist. What makes them work is what in American law is called *comity*; that is to say, a decent respect for the concerns of the other polity. Comity is protected through open bargaining and open government, in addition to formal constitutional provisions. This is critically important. There is no political system in the world that does not have bargaining. Even in the most closed and dictatorial system, at least those people who sit at the top bargain among themselves. The success of democratic systems is that their bargaining is sufficiently open and accessible to the vast majority of people who choose to make use of that access, and it is visible so that not too much can be done to strengthen the hands of the governors at the expense of the governed.

Slower but Firmer Results. Federalism, because it requires consent, is a slower way to get results, but its results are longer lasting. Sometimes a quick fix seems to be possible by the use of force or forceful intervention, but in the long run consensus has the ability of generating a wider and deeper desire to support the result. The history of the American confrontation with the problem of the rights of blacks and other nonwhite minorities is a case in point. The Americans used a combination of federal processes and the limited coercive power of the federal government, and the end result is that today there is sufficient change of heart among Americans in all parts of the country to make the reality of support for civil rights and rights protection much stronger.

I would like to conclude by mentioning three more points. One is that it is obviously easier to build democratic systems, federal systems, where the political culture lends itself to them. It is obviously more difficult where the political culture runs in contrary directions. Where it runs in contrary directions, the constitutional designers must find those elements that are most likely to be in favor of or supportive of democratic and federal institutions. In some cases, this is a matter of balancing oligarchies instead of securing broad-based participation. It is a matter of working with what is available.

This is especially difficult when it comes to ethnic federations. Some of the problems of unfavorable political culture can be overcome if there is sufficient political will. Such will is best when it can draw from the culture, but at times it is used even to modify and moderate the culture.

Fortunately or unfortunately, accidents of history have their role to play as well. Some have to do with the kind of leadership that appears. One wonders whether Yugoslavia would have been plunged into civil war if there had not been a certain kind of leader in Serbia at the time. But these are the accidents of history over which we have relatively little control. Proper leadership, however, is necessary for federalism to succeed.

Federalism and Democracy

Federalism is a rich and complex thing, a matter of formal constitutional divisions, appropriate institutions, patterns of political behavior, and, ultimately, political culture. Moreover, federal democracy offers a complete and comprehensive theory of democracy that stands in sharp contrast to the theories of democracy regnant in Europe until now—Jacobin democracy and parliamentary democracy on the Westminster model—not to speak of that monstrous development sometimes referred to as totalitarian democracy, where outside of the privileged elites, there is the "democracy" of the equality of repression.

Federal democracy addresses the great questions of political sovereignty and the distribution of powers (competences), the relationships between power and law or right, and the great issues of centralization and decentralization. It does so by vesting political sovereignty in the people who constitute the body politic rather than in states and requiring them to allocate competences or powers constitutionally among the governments of their creation. They must do so in a way that encourages multiple centers of power and in a manner that provides for both centralization and decentralization as needed, but always within a noncentralized framework whereby all exercise of powers is governed by law and related to the rights of the constituents.

What about Efficiency?

One question that is almost certainly to be raised is that, while federalism may be appropriate for accommodating pluralism and while it may even be helpful in initially promoting democracy, liberty will survive only if democracy can cope efficiently with the serious problems most of the newly liberated countries face. Is federalism not by definition inefficient? Even if justifiable for normative reasons, can it be at all justified when it comes to efficiency, namely, the minimum application of resources for the maximum results? Many claim that federalism, with its duplications, complexities, and redundancies, is a machine designed for waste.

This view is based on a widely accepted but erroneous understanding of what constitutes efficiency in government. That understanding is based on hierarchical thinking about governmental organization. We are now coming to realize that such thinking is not only outmoded but simply wrong. The hierarchies that appear to be so neat on paper do not work in practice. Sometimes the application of a great deal of coercion gets them to work for a while, but we have seen the results, neither fair nor efficient by any reasonable standard.

The development of cybernetics has given us a newer and truer understanding of how to achieve efficiency, one that has proved itself by revolutionizing the world. According to the cybernetic model, redundancies are vitally needed to achieve complex goals. At the least, in a world where people and machines are fallible and inevitably make mistakes or break down, fail-safe mechanisms and alternative channels are needed to keep things moving efficiently. Beyond that, such mechanisms are vital for the promotion of creativity and imagination.

As Martin Landau has pointed out, the American Federalists discovered this principle in patterns of government two hundred years ago.[3] Now their "new science of politics" (as they put it) has been confirmed by the new science of cybernetics. As a result, it is now beginning to be possible to talk about a federalist definition of efficiency.

The first step toward joining the issue is a clarification of normative positions. If one begins as a monist, assuming the desirability and feasibility of achieving one pattern of thought and behavior for everyone, then federalism is indeed inefficient and even wrong, because it enables the perpetuation and even the entrenchment of differences. If one begins as a pluralist, seeing the world as a heterogeneous place and properly so, then one must make a different evaluation of federalism as a means to protect and entrench liberty. Thus, monistic Jacobin and Marxian views have constantly rejected federalism as wrong in principle, even if they have had to compromise with reality and accept the temporary existence of pluralism. Federalist views, by contrast, embrace pluralism and seek means to protect it—one might say efficient means to do so—of which the constitutional division and sharing of power through a combination of self-rule and shared rule is primary.

Going beyond that, one can take as a starting point the human condition, both psychologically and sociologically, namely, that every individual and individual institution has its own goals, although to some extent each will share goals with other individuals and institutions. In recognition of that, the best way to move from A to B is to identify common goals and find a way for those same individuals and institutions to express those shared goals while allowing them to maintain and pursue their individual goals. That, indeed, is what federalism does.

A few years ago, as part of the effort to break through the paralysis of budgets rendered inflexible as a result of cumulative previous commitments, the idea of zero-based budgeting—of starting from scratch every year—was introduced. To implement this new form of budgeting, proponents of managerialism in public administration came up with the idea of Program Policy Budgeting System (PPBS). The premise of PPBS was that it was first necessary to identify agreed-on goals, then it would be possible to evaluate all budget items in light of their efficiency in the pursuit of those goals. PPBS failed precisely because, in any public framework, there is likely to be insufficient agreement on common goals to do that. People come together to pursue different goals, which at best can be harmonized so that they can be pursued through common effort and enterprise. That, indeed, is the federalist way. When forced to try to define a single comprehensive set of common goals, people could not do so, and PPBS could not be implemented except marginally.

Thus, in relatively complex public arenas, efforts to bulldoze directly, which would be termed efficient in other systems, might be the least efficient and might create great static and friction that would greatly waste resources, while the existence of multiple channels penetrating through multiple cracks might be a far more efficient way to achieve even the most common goals. The authors of *The Federalist* understood this.

Right now, all signs point to the fact that democracy and federalism have become closely intertwined and that together they represent the greatest opportunity that humans have yet had to achieve liberty and prosperity. But, as is always the case in human affairs, the problems are great, and the issue remains in doubt. One of the ways in which scholars of federalism can help resolve the issue in the right direction is by developing a federalist theory of efficiency that can be applied to assist the peoples and countries of the world in their application of the principles of federal democracy to secure life and pursue liberty and happiness.

No federation freely entered into that has lasted for at least fifteen years has ever failed of its own accord. The Soviet and Yugoslav federations were imposed by force. The results speak for themselves. What constitutes "freely entered into" may be a matter of discussion, but no such federation has failed of its own accord. Some have been eliminated by outside conquest, but where the people have chosen this course of political organization, they have generally stayed with it. As South Africa makes its new beginning, one can be hopeful that, whether internally or in their relations with one another, South Africans will be able to move from the government of force of the past to a useful and democratic federation of consent in the future.

6

Liberty, Commerce, and Prosperity—And a Bill of Rights

Dennis Davis

This is Radio South Africa, it's 6:00 P.M. on this the twenty-fourth day of November, 1995, and here is the news:

The chief justice today handed down the unanimous decision of the Constitutional Court in the case of *Die Blanke Boerevereeniging and the Government of the Republic of South Africa*. In its judgment, the Constitutional Court declared invalid the Reparation and Reinstatement of the Land Claims Act, which was passed by a narrow majority of Parliament last year. The act purports to authorize the government to expropriate land that had been acquired pursuant to the racist policy of apartheid removals during the 1960s. The Constitutional Court declared that this act was in contravention of Article 13 of the Bill of Rights, which provides for an entrenched right to private property save where the legislature, in the public interest, may authorize an expropriation against payment of reasonable compensation. The court considered that as the legislation authorized the executive to pay compensation in its sole discretion, there had been a contravention of the entrenched right of Article 13.

Reaction has been speedy and mixed. The chairman of the South African Agricultural Union, Mr. Barend du Plessis, and the leader of the opposition Democratic party, Mr. Tony Leon, welcomed the decision as being good for South Africa and even better for international investment. By contrast, the minister of justice announced that the court's decision

87

rendered it impossible for the government to redress the legacies of apartheid, which was the least that government supporters could expect from it. Consequently, the government was considering introducing legislation at the next session of Parliament which would curb the powers of the Constitutional Court. Eminent constitutional lawyer John Dugard warned that such a move would create a constitutional crisis the likes of which made the 1950 constitutional crisis appear "like a tea party."

This scenario might well be dismissed as poor political fiction. There is a point to the tale, however: unequivocal commitment to a free-enterprise–based bill of rights will condemn a constitutional enterprise in South Africa to instant failure.

All constitutions are a product of indigenous history. The American Constitution, with its quaintly drafted amendments, reflects a response to the legacy of English colonialism. The Third Amendment, for example, provides that no soldier shall, in time of peace or war, be quartered in any house without the consent of the owner, in a manner prescribed by law. Every word of this clause is saturated with the experience of the War of Independence and the impact of colonialism. The German Constitution reflects the attempt to reconstruct a *Rechtstaat* (constitutionalism) out of the ashes of Nazi Germany. The American Constitution emphasizes liberty, commerce, and prosperity, whereas the German Constitution creates a framework for a welfare state. Article 20(1) provides that the Federal Republic of Germany should be a democratic and social state, and Article 28(1) provides that the constitutional order in the *Länder* must conform to the principles of republican, democratic, and social government, based on the rule of this basic law. In short, there is no universal truth to which every constitution must conform.

In South Africa, no legal initiative that attempts to create a *Rechtstaat* can ignore the Land Acts of 1913, which reserved 87 percent of South African land for whites while forcing blacks to become laborers on white farms. Nor can it ignore trade union legislation that excluded blacks from the definition of "employee." Nor can it ignore job reservation laws that excluded blacks from most of the better paid occupations, or discriminatory social security payments and discriminatory wages in the civil service that biased economic progress in favor of whites. Neither can it omit the pass laws, which broke down family life and kept a large proportion of the black population in rural areas; or Bantu education, which was designed to educate black South Africans to remain slaves in the land of their birth. Doubtless it will be argued that this legislation has now been repealed, but its effect remains.

Inequality in income distribution in South Africa is among the highest in the world. Between 20 and 25 percent of children under the age of six are malnourished; only 20 percent of black families earn incomes above the minimum effective level; whites, who constitute but 15 percent of the population, receive more than one-half of the national income and own more than 90 percent of the wealth of the country. More than 20 percent of all black South Africans between the ages of fifteen and sixty are unemployed, and in some areas unemployment exceeds this percentage. No constitutional enterprise can ignore these facts.

Notwithstanding this reality, the debate in South Africa is not between a centrally planned state buttressed by a constitution that provides for the absence of civil society on the one hand and laissez-faire capitalism on the other. Even enthusiastic advocates of capitalism would argue for some measure of state intervention. Robert Dahl warns against the limitations of competitive markets. He suggests there is a conflict between democratic processes and competitive markets, because persons who believe themselves injured by the market will cooperate to achieve economically efficient outcomes only if they act from a commitment to the general good rather than from rational self-interest. A belief in the general good is unlikely to come in any form of rational self-interest. Second, arguments in favor of nonintervention are often too abstract and obscure to be persuasive to the general public. Furthermore, people who believe themselves to be injured by free markets and who cannot be persuaded by rational argument to accept the system might be compelled to do so. Often, therefore, democracy and a competitive market involve a trade-off, which has been advantageous in the so-called miracle economies of the Pacific Basin.[1]

These persuasive arguments have not dispelled the enthusiasm of free-market advocates. A bill of rights that promotes the free-market system will, they argue, achieve growth for society and hence prosperity for all. The crudity of this argument ignores the criticisms raised by Dahl as well as the history of South Africa. More subtle proponents of free-enterprise constitutionalism ignore that market outcomes are often morally arbitrary, such as unequally distributed opportunities and existing unequal distribution of skills. As Sunstein notes, "The goal of a legal system is not merely to ensure autonomy by allowing satisfaction of preferences but also more fundamentally to promote autonomy in the process of preference formation."[2]

Doubtless, free-enterprise advocates will argue that a democratic society affords an opportunity to each citizen to choose from a variety of alternatives and that the principle of choice is its fundamentally characteristic value. But is there choice when many citizens face constraints imposed on the free development of their preferences and beliefs?

In the context of the purpose of this chapter, only economic constraints on the free development of the preferences and beliefs of millions of South Africans will be noted. About 17.5 million people—that is, 47 percent of the South African population—live in households with incomes below the minimum living level. Of these, more than half are to be found in the homeland rural areas. It is true that the distribution of income between South Africans has not been stable for many years, as the proportion of personal income accruing to white people has dropped and that accruing to Coloured and Asian people has risen. But these increases have generally been between rich and poor black households. Upward mobility and increased entrepreneurial activity, along with increased unemployment, have had an impact on the distribution of wealth.[3]

Similar racist patterns exist in almost every area of social and economic life in South Africa. In 1985, two-thirds of the white population had achieved full secondary or tertiary level education, and Asians and so-called Coloured populations had an intermediate attainment, yet more than half of the economically active African population had not completed primary level schooling.[4] The imbalance in wealth and education alone is grounds for concluding that equality of autonomy does not exist in South African society. A democratic enterprise would surely view such a failure of autonomy as a reason for a collective response to promote a democratic society. More than half the South African population suffer from an absence of information and a lack of opportunity to participate meaningfully within the political process. To ignore this material reality is to confirm what critics of the market have argued for a long time—namely, that

> incorrect acclaim of something called the market in respect of private arrangements embodies governmental neutrality. Private preferences are partly a product of available opportunities, which are a function of legal rules. Those rules allocate rights and entitlements; that function is simply unavoidable short of anarchy. The allocation will in turn have a profound effect and will indeed help to constitute the distribution of wealth and the content of private preferences.[5]

Such inequality not only threatens the social equilibrium of South African society but negates the principle of equality so inextricably linked with the concept of democracy. As Arblaster notes,

Inequality and welfare and economic power . . . is a form of political inequality which contradicts the principle of political equality expressed in the slogan "One person—one vote". To those that possess the kind of power to influence events or determine political outcomes, the possession of the single individual vote would seem by comparison as a trivial and irrelevant form of participation. Other forms of inequality, social, racial and sexual also run counter to the political equality. No one with experience of political meetings or grassroots political organisations can fail to have noted how easily and naturally such groups and gatherings are dominated by white, bourgeois, educated males. The advantages and privileges attaching to class, race and gender make it seem quite "natural" that this should be so.[6]

In short, the democratic enterprise in South Africa could well be stillborn if adequate consideration is not given to the linkage between economic and political inequality. First, ignorance of history in the formulation of the constitution endangers the legitimacy of such a document. Second, the integrity of a constitution's proclamation of equality is placed in question when it operates within the context of profound economic inequality. On this point, the Law Commission's *Interim Report on Human Rights 1991* fails.[7] Notwithstanding its otherwise imaginative, bold, and timely proposals, the Law Commission's approach to the economy illustrates the danger of the self-proclaimed neutrality of free-enterprise constitutionalism. It is to this we now turn our attention.

The Law Commission and the Economy

Article 15 recommends that everyone has the right individually or jointly to become the owner of private property and that legislation may authorize the expropriation of such property against payment of just compensation that shall be determined by a court of law in the event of a dispute. This recommendation contrasts with that of the African National Congress in its draft bill, which provides that compensation shall be just, taking into account the need to establish an equitable balance between the interests of the public and of those affected. The ANC's draft also provides that the provisions dealing with land should not be interpreted as impeding the right of the state to adopt the measures deemed necessary in any democratic society for the control, use, and acquisition of property. This is to be done in accordance with the general interest, with preservation of the environment, with the regulation or curtailing of monopolies, or with securing the payment of taxes, other contributions, or penalties.

Behind these provisions, the Law Commission saw "naked and arbitrary nationalisation of private property of whatever nature without the courts being able to protect those prejudiced in any way whatsoever."[8] There is little discussion in the Law Commission's report, with even less appreciation of the problem of historically legitimate claims of those who were removed from their land as a result of apartheid. For these people, there must be something ironic in the sudden conversion of many lawyers to the idea of the sanctity of private property, a principle that was hardly mentioned during the dark days of apartheid, when the removal policy formed a key principle of the policy of social separation.

But the Law Commission goes further. It not only entrenches private property, but it rejects any possible provision for economic and social rights in a bill of rights. The ANC's draft bill provides that all men and women have the right to enjoy basic social, educational, economic, and welfare rights. In an attempt to reconcile the legitimate demands of South Africans for basic standards of living with the limitations of the public purse, the ANC draft bill proposes that resources be diverted from richer to poorer areas and timetables be established for the phased extension of legislation and minimum standards from area to area. These measures would help to achieve a common floor of rights for the whole country. The draft further provides that the state should ensure the introduction of minimum standards of nutrition throughout the country and, in collaboration with private bodies where appropriate, should dismantle compounds, single-sex hostels, and other forms of accommodation associated with the migrant labor system. Instead it could embark on and encourage an extensive program of house building.

In many countries' constitutions, these particular clauses are well known. Indeed, since World War II, much jurisprudence has concentrated on attacking the artificial divisions among the first, second, and third generations of rights. This suggests that a constitution that simply provides first-generation rights produces a distorted concept that must be concerned with minimum standards of welfare for all citizens in the country. Hence the European Social Charter of February 1985 provides for the right to work, the right to fair remuneration, the right to bargain collectively, the right to health protection, and the right to social and medical assistance. The International Covenant of Economic, Social, and Cultural Rights, which came into effect in 1976, recognized the right of everyone to just and favorable conditions of work, including a decent living and healthy working environment, the right to enjoy the highest attainable standard of physical and mental health, and the right to receive free compulsory primary education.

In the context of South Africa's history, the case for providing the minimum floor of economic and social rights becomes all the more compelling. As David Dyzenhaus writes, a constitution that protects rights to private property and would prevent redistribution of resources "would create a constitution at war with itself by proclaiming in the same document commitments to democracy together with a commitment to an economic status quo premised on the inequality of the majority of its political community."[9] But this is precisely what the Law Commission's draft achieves. Having entrenched private property, it rejects any provision for economic and social rights in a bill of rights. Its rejection of a full program of such rights—a program far greater than that provided for in the ANC's draft bill of rights—appears to be predicated on two fundamental grounds. The first is a traditional argument that rights that impose an economic cost on the state cannot be enforced by a court. The second is the absence of a consensus regarding such rights for inclusion in the constitution.

Both these arguments are spurious. In the first case, a number of so-called first-generation rights impose economic costs on the state, the most significant of which perhaps is the right to a fair trial. Indeed, the commission's draft Article 25, which provides that every accused has the right not to be sentenced or punished without a fair and public trial, must of necessity include the cost of a judge, prosecutor, police, and court system. The commission's Article 25 provides the right to be represented by a legal practitioner. These provisions impose economic costs on the state, yet this is not regarded as an obstacle to the inclusion of such an article in the bill of rights. Economic affordability and the problem of competing claims for scarce resources cannot be considered adequate justifications for the exclusion of social and economic rights. Each right must be separately evaluated in terms of the broad justification for the constitutional enterprise in general and the inclusion in a bill of rights in particular. If a bill of rights is committed to democracy and hence to the right of each citizen to participate in the political process, economic affordability cannot be regarded as a major justification for the inclusion or exclusion of a right from a constitutional document.

But if the first justification offered by the Law Commission for its exclusion of social and economic rights is troubling, the second is pregnant in irony. The commission suggests that

> for practical purposes consensus regarding such rights for inclusion in the constitution or a bill of rights is unattainable,

particularly in this country where widely differing economic views are held by the main political parties. There is a potential for deadlock regarding the creation of a new constitution for this country, with unthinkable consequences—and that on a matter where there will be no conflict because consensus on it is not necessary, as has been shown. Once a new constitution has been written and an election held, it can be left to the winning party or parties to translate their socioeconomic policy into statutes.[10]

It seems extraordinary that the commission is not able to grasp the inconsistency between its advocacy of the entrenchment of private property and its recommended exclusion of social and economic rights from a bill of rights. Its exclusive reliance on first-generation rights represents a commitment to a particular economic viewpoint, and thus one laden in theoretical choice. It is unsatisfactory for the commission to suggest that its free-enterprise–orientated bill of rights is neutral and represents consensus, whereas the ANC social democratic recommendations reflect a particular viewpoint about which there is no consensus. This point is used once more by the commission to reject the inclusion in the constitution of directives of state policy, as was the case in Namibia following the Indian and Irish precedents. The commission states,

> It is rather unlikely that consensus is going to be reached on socio-economic ideals and principles between even the main negotiating political parties and organisations. This could wreck the whole process of negotiation and plunge the country into chaos were the matter not being the subject of dispute in the first place. Therefore much as one would like to see a compromise the compromise of directive principles is no compromise because it poses a great danger for this country.[11]

While the commission advocates a range of labor rights that would represent considerable progress, its failure to provide for socioeconomic rights reflects its free-enterprise bias. Indeed, its only concessions are the suggestions that everyone has the right lawfully

- to make provision for any costs that may arise from one's own mental or physical illness and that of dependents
- to make provision for the maintenance of a reasonable standard of living
- to provide for one's own proper education and training and that of dependents
- to claim available state assistance to provide for necessary subsis-

tence where a person is unable to provide for such needs, by reason of physical or mental illness or disability, and where no one else may by virtue of support be compelled to provide for such needs

The right to insurance, which is included in this bill, must surely be a unique South African contribution to constitutional jurisprudence. Together with the other rights described above, it reflects an economic choice on the part of the Law Commission that will doubtless run counter to the wishes of millions of South Africans and illustrates a disappointing rejection of the historical realities on which any legitimate constitution must be grounded.

Property and Democracy

We may reject the contention that the ordering of institutions is always defective because the distribution of natural talents and the contingencies of social circumstances are unjust, and this injustice must inevitably carry over to human arrangements. Occasionally this reflection is offered as an excuse for ignoring injustice, as if the refusal to acquiesce in injustice is on a par with being unable to accept death. The natural distribution is neither just nor unjust; nor is it unjust that persons are born into a society at some particular position. These are simply natural facts. What is just and unjust is the way institutions deal with these facts. Aristocratic and caste societies are unjust because they make these contingencies the ascriptive basis for belonging to more or less closed and privileged social classes. The basic structure of these societies incorporates the arbitrariness found in nature. But there is no necessity for men to resign themselves to these contingencies. The social system is not an unchangeable order beyond human control but a pattern of human action.[12]

South Africa adopted a racial class system during the vicissitudes of its history. To ignore this is to imprison future generations of South Africans in the past. Not only is this unjust and undemocratic, but it is unwise if the country is to emerge from authoritarian violence into democratic equilibrium. The folly of the free enterprise–cum–Law Commission approach to constitutionalism in the area of economics is best illustrated in the area of property. The government and the Law Commission are committed to the idea that the constitution is negotiated in a political vacuum. As Geoff Budlender has noted

The constitution that is now being negotiated is not to be written for England in the time of John Stuart Mill. It is being written for South Africa in the latter stages of the

95

twentieth century, and the twenty-first century. We should note the deep irony of the situation. The present pattern of property relations is the result of generations of laws and practices that would not have survived for a minute in a bill of rights society. The beneficiaries of systematic human rights abuses now seek to create and rely on a bill of rights to protect what they have acquired. In the present historical context, property rights for the property-less are likely to be overwhelmed by a competing constitutional right for the property holders.[13]

A right to property as proposed by the Law Commission would run two risks, either of which would thwart attempts to transform South African society away from its racist past. First, the entrenchment of property in a bill of rights could have an impact on a range of other legislative initiatives. In one period of its history, the U.S. Supreme Court interpreted the due process clause as more than simply procedural limits on the deprivation of life, liberty, and property. By employing a concept of substantive due process, the Court struck down state laws that provided for minimum wages, for maximum hours of work, and for protection of employees against antiunion activities.[14]

Opponents of a property clause in the Canadian Bill of Rights have argued that such a clause would place at risk possible rent control legislation; minimum wage and pay equity plans; occupation, health, and safety regulation; matrimonial property regimes that provide for the division of property and separational divorce; environmental controls; and natural resource management schemes.[15] The effect of this approach was well illustrated in the American case of *Pennsylvania Cola Company v. Mahon*, where the court held in favor of a mining company whose underground operations in relation to a particular parcel had been prohibited by state law. The owner of the adjoining land obtained an injunction preventing the company from mining in a way that contravened the statute and damaged his property. An agreement between the claimant's predecessor and the mining company had permitted such activity. The Supreme Court ruled that the legislative denial of the mining company's underground rights amounted to an uncompensated loss. Protective and environmental legislation was characterized as essentially redistributive and hence unconstitutional. As Laurence Tribe has observed:

> In broad outline the underlying philosophy held that the only legitimate goal of government in general and of the police power in particular, was to protect individual rights and otherwise enhance the total public good; if they were to

be upheld, governmental regulations had to promote "the general welfare" and not be "purely for the promotion of private interests." As a corollary it follows that any statute which was imposed upon individuals and corporations in order to redistribute resources and thus benefit some persons at the expense of others . . . would extend beyond the explicit boundaries of legislative authority. Such law would thus violate natural rights of property and contract, rights lying at the very core of the private domain.[16]

The second major implication of the absolute protection of property rights is to prevent any future government from addressing the skewed pattern of land tenure created by apartheid in general and the removals policy in particular. To protect private property and make expropriations subject to compensation at market value regardless of the legal cause of existing ownership of the land would render expropriation financially impossible and legitimize the ill-gotten gains of apartheid. Even libertarian philosophers like Robert Nozick would not seek to legitimize ownership derived from theft. It would be beyond the ability of the treasury department to initiate expropriation plans after paying market value to each landowner, regardless of the basis on which such land was acquired. Hence apartheid tenure patterns would continue.

The Law Commission opposes the placement of such limitations on the democratic enterprise. Indeed, in its earlier report it concluded

To the vast majority of all South Africans a bill of rights without a property clause would be totally unacceptable. Our impression is that, so far as the right to property and means of production are concerned, the aspirations of all in our country will be satisfied if i) the right to property is guaranteed, ii) all discriminatory impediments to the acquisition, retention and ownership of property and means of production of any kind are abolished, iii) the possibilities created that the state, where necessary, will be able to expropriate property and means of production against fair compensation to be determined by the Supreme Court if it is not possible to reach an agreement on the matter, iv) the objects of affirmative action are taken into account with regard to the powers of expropriation, v) it is left to the normal political process in a democratic state to meet fluctuating economic needs on a continuous basis.[17]

The commission's claim that the vast majority of South Africans would regard a bill of rights as unacceptable without a property clause is debatable. Doubtless the vast majority of South Africans would want their property protected, but many would want to make a claim against the moral expropriation and state-induced loss of property during apartheid.

The lack of attention to historical detail by the commission would doubtless bring the constitution, if implemented, into immediate conflict with a democratically elected legislature. The experience of India's courts and their relationship with the Indian Parliament concerning the state's power and property is particularly illuminating. The approach of the Indian legislature was that the power to determine compensation for expropriation lay exclusively with Parliament. But the courts, through a series of cases, appropriated to themselves the power of establishing the quantum of compensation. They furthermore imposed substantive and procedural tests of reasonableness with regard to the exercise of police powers and the power of eminent domain.[18] The legislature decided simply to circumvent the courts. It introduced a series of amendments to the constitution. In 1967, the Indian Supreme Court, in *Golak Nath v. Punjab*,[19] held that the legislature had no power to amend the fundamental rights contained within the constitution and hence could not eliminate market value as a test for compensation. This case raised fundamental questions about the capacity of the Indian legislature to implement any socioeconomic reforms. Eventually the courts backed down in *Kesavananda v. Kerala*[20] and held that Parliament had the power to amend the fundamental rights contained within the constitution, provided such amendments did not abrogate the basic structure of the constitution. Finally, after twenty-five years of dispute, Parliament obtained an ascendancy.

If a constitutional enterprise is to retain its integrity, the issue of property cannot be swept under the free-enterprise carpet. The myopia of the Law Commission's approach can be contrasted with that of the agreement reached between East and West Germany before their unification.[21] The question arose as to the legality of property takings by the East German government. Some lawyers argued that when a sovereign government expropriates property from its citizens for economic or political purposes, as had East Germany, other sovereign governments must recognize the expropriation as long as that state acted within the bounds of its own authority. This view was rejected for three major reasons. In terms of the August 22, 1978, Vienna Convention on Succession of States in respect of Treaties, an attempt was made to strike a balance between stability and continuity on the one hand and beneficial change on the other. By honoring legitimate claims to property, the new German government accomplished both these objectives. It promoted continuity in the international system as well as the interests of justice and fairness. Second, it would have been extremely difficult for the West German government to enforce the expropriation policy of the East German government when the former had never formally accepted the legitimacy of the latter. Furthermore, given the volatile political climate in united Germany, politicians negotiating the unification agreement felt significant pressure from those citizens who demanded that the German government return their dispossessed properties.

All three justifications have resonance for the South African experience. A new South African government would assume the obligations of the former South African state. As with the new German government, a future South African government would not have to be obligated to its predecessor's policy of expropriation as the valid acts of another sovereign, but rather should exercise its own control of land to rectify past injustices. Furthermore, apartheid was declared a crime against humanity in terms of international law, and millions of South Africans never considered the Pretoria government to be legitimate. The problem of political pressure and legitimacy that was applicable to the German experience is equally applicable to that of South Africa.

There can be no moral justification for entrenching a tenure pattern fashioned by apartheid. Even Robert Nozick, who holds that economic goods arise already encumbered with rightful claims to their ownership, refuses to extend his theory to property that was stolen. Nozick's theory would support the contention that no morality justifies ownership of property that was acquired through the removal policies of South African governments.[22]

The critique of the Law Commission's proposals illustrates the lack of neutrality inherent in a proposal designed to protect existing property relations in particular and the free-market system in general. Were a bill of rights to be drafted that takes account of competing interests, it would need to balance the protection of property with the need to address the apartheid legacy. In this connection, there is useful international precedent. Article 13(1) of the Malaysian Constitution provides that no person shall be deprived of property save in accordance with law. Article 13(2) provides that no law shall provide for the compulsory acquisition or use of property without adequate compensation. This clause could be further extended to quantify "adequate": such compensation being determined after a consideration by a court of the interests of society, of the affected party, and of whether the property was acquired in circumstances that would have been in contravention of this article, had it been enforced at the time of such acquisition.

By means of such a formulation, the provision could achieve a far greater measure of reliability than is the case with the Law Commission's formulation, and it would enable a court to examine the basis on which such property was acquired by the affected persons and the interests of other claimants. The amount of compensation should be different, for example, in the case of an owner who acquired property at market value, from the case of a speculator who acquired a piece of land from which the state removed a tribe for a negligible consideration, and who acquired the same knowing the reasons for such a windfall.

Conclusion

Any constitutional formulation that treats current ownership in absolute terms will create a constitution "at war with itself." If Jennifer Nedelsky's superb analysis of the American Constitution is any guide, absolutizing property along the lines of the Law Commission will have an even more profound effect on our constitutional enterprise. Nedelsky suggests that by adopting property as the paradigmatic right, the Madisonian Constitution created a system of government that reinforced the political power of the rich and limited the potential for popular participation. The framers' preoccupation with property generated a shallow conception of democracy and a system of institutions that allocated political power unequally and failed to foster political participation.[23]

A South African constitution that purports to entrench present property relations reinforces present patterns of inequality and constitutes a major obstacle to popular political participation. Like Madison, advocates of the absolute position are perhaps not interested in the possibility of popular political participation. Such a lack of interest could possibly be discounted in eighteenth-century America, but to exclude its possibility by constitutional provision in twenty-first century South Africa is to invite constitutional disaster.

But a constitution must do more than refuse the offer to entrench existing property rights. A constitution born of the economic inequality of present-day South Africa cannot ignore the post–World War II effort to incorporate the social dimension of law and justice into constitutional instruments. Whether economic and environmental rights should be incorporated into a bill of rights as first-generation rights or should be formulated as directives of state policy is debatable. But a constitution that excludes such rights, as is the case with the Law Commission's proposals, will inevitably distort the meaning of human rights within the modern context. As Cappelletti has noted:

To exclude social rights from a modern Bill of Rights, is to stop history at the time of laissez-faire; it is to forget that the modern state has greatly enlarged its reach and responsibilities into the economy and the welfare of the people.[24]

South African constitutional lawyers might well adopt the format of directives of state policy because social rights require different enforcement machinery for their implementation. The enforcement of the right to housing and education involves a protracted economic commitment to such constitutional rights. Furthermore, judges are less proficient in dealing with the allocation of resources than in defending against state action. Hence the enforcement of second- and third-generation rights is far more complex than the enforcement of those of the first generation, which are essentially negative and are designed to prevent excessive governmental interference and liberties of the ordinary citizen.

To exclude social and economic rights on the basis of jurisprudential complexity, however, is to promote a distorted view of equality that even in the Law Commission's formulation enjoys centrality of place.[25] By introducing state policy directives into a bill of rights to provide the flesh on the skeleton of judicial review, it would be possible for the courts to review a broad range of governmental expenditure designed merely to promote the interests of bureaucrats and party officials, not to fulfill a commitment to social and economic upliftment as enshrined in the bill of rights. If the president were to acquire an expensive jet aircraft, for example, in circumstances of fiscal discipline that otherwise prevented the government from building houses or providing schools, then the court might well examine such a decision. An extended process of judicial review along these lines would also prevent the endemic corruption that has characterized the National party government since its accession to power and has recently been personified by the corruption in Lebowa, Kwa Ndebele, and the Department of Development Aid. The importance of judicial review, which holds the government to the promises made in the bill of rights, cannot be underestimated, particularly in the context of the governmental immorality the National party has bequeathed to South Africa.

The transition from authoritarian rule to democracy is extremely fraught at present. Many issues divide the major parties, but on one point there appears to be agreement: a bill of rights is essential for a democratic enterprise in South Africa. A bill of rights would create space for individual autonomy, free political activity, and conditions in which all citizens have an equal opportunity to participate in the formulation of decisions that shape their lives and the lives of their society. In launching this democratic enterprise, cognizance must be taken of the inegalitarian status quo in South Africa that was born of racism and sustained by an apartheid legal system. To ignore this reality and still suggest that a constitution should be committed to democracy is to stultify the aspirations of millions of South Africans and run the risk that a government, albeit elected by overwhelming majority, will not be able to satisfy the legitimate claims and aspirations of its own supporters. The justification for a bill of rights is the promotion of equality among the citizens of South Africa and hence the principle of meaningful individual autonomy. This can be achieved neither by ignoring the past nor by failing to address a status quo that is the antithesis of these principles.

7

American Democracy and the Acquisitive Spirit

Marc F. Plattner

The essay that follows—originally written for How Capitalistic Is the Constitution? *(AEI 1982)—took as its starting point a debate that raged during the late 1970s among American intellectuals and policy experts over the desirability and propriety of large-scale income redistribution. It sought to put this controversy in a broader context by exploring the views of the founders of the American republic concerning the linkages among political democracy, a capitalist economy, and the rights of private property. Although that policy debate was soon superseded by the march of events and the rise of new issues and concerns, the broader exploration retains its relevance not only for those seeking to understand the thought of the American founders, but more generally for all who are interested in the relationship between economic systems and political liberty.*

Obviously, the new democracy that one hopes will be born in South Africa will come into being under circumstances very different from those that attended the founding of American democracy two centuries ago. The brutal legacy of apartheid cannot simply be wished away or ignored. Yet no matter how special the situation of South Africa may be, there are certain general principles governing the relationship between the political and economic spheres that cannot be overlooked without putting democracy in grave peril. My contention is that the American founders discerned such principles, and that these apply not merely to the American case but to modern democratic politics as such. Thus it is my hope that this essay may be of some value to South African readers engaged in the effort to construct a stable and prosperous democratic order in their own country.

More and more critics nowadays contend that there is a fundamental tension—or even contradiction—between America's capitalist economic order and its democratic political order. The late Arthur Okun opened his influential *Equality and Efficiency* with a discussion of the "double standard of capitalist democracy, professing and pursuing an egalitarian political and social system and simultaneously generating gaping disparities in economic well-being."[1] In a similar vein, Kenneth Keniston, in his foreword to Richard de Lone's *Small Futures*, writes of "the inherent conflict between the inegalitarian consequences of a liberal economy and the egalitarian ideal of a liberal political democracy." De Lone spells out this view at greater length in the book:

> There is . . . a deep tension in liberal thought between the political and economic traditions. The political tradition emphasizes the equal *rights* of all individuals, rights conferred by the natural law from which human reason draws its strength. The economic tradition emphasizes not so much the rights as the *prerogatives* of individuals in the pursuit of self-interest, e.g., the accumulation of property and wealth. Rights and prerogatives often clash. The political tradition of rights embraces equality while the economic tradition of prerogatives leads to inequality.[2]

These critics are quite willing to affirm the democratic character of America's liberal political tradition and its commitment to guaranteeing equal political rights and liberties to all. They do not dispute the fact that the liberal tradition has historically been associated with support for a capitalist economy. What they do seem to deny is that there is any intrinsic connection between the political system whose protection of equal rights and liberties they applaud and the economic system whose inegalitarian outcomes they deplore. Accordingly, their prescription for the reform of American society consists chiefly of a call for a redistribution of incomes aimed at undoing the inequalities generated by a capitalist economy. They see no danger that such a policy might threaten the liberal political fabric that guarantees our liberties.

I believe that this view derives from a shallow and incorrect understanding of the bases of the American regime, one that overlooks certain critical connections between liberal democracy and capitalism. It is my contention that where the contemporary critics see only an adventitious and ill-matched association, the founders both of liberal political theory and of the government of the United States saw an intimate and indispensable link. In short, I believe that the regime instituted by the Constitution was understood by the framers to be essentially capitalistic. By the equivocal term "capitalistic" I do not mean, in this context, a "free market" economy devoid of any government interference or regulation. Rather, I refer more broadly to an economic system that allows all citizens freely to acquire, possess, and dispose of private property and encourages them to devote themselves to the pursuit and enjoyment of wealth.

The Federalist and the Constitution

For anyone seeking to understand the political and economic thought of the framers of the Constitution there can be no more authoritative source than *The Federalist*. Even Thomas Jefferson, some of whose own views might seem to be in conflict with *The Federalist*, referred to it as a work "to which appeal is habitually made by all, and rarely declined or denied by any as evidence of the general opinion of those who framed and of those who accepted the Constitution of the United States, on questions as to its genuine meaning."[3] Of the eighty-five essays that compose *The Federalist*, number 10, in which Publius elaborates his theory of the large republic as the remedy for the diseases of popular government, is widely and justly regarded as the most fundamental.[4] At the heart of his argument appears the following passage:

> The diversity in the faculties of men, from which the rights of property originate, is not less an insuperable obstacle to a uniformity of interests. The protection of these faculties is the first object of government. From the protection of different and unequal faculties of acquiring property, the possession of different degrees and kinds of property immediately results.[5]

This statement—and the critical position it occupies in the all-important argument for the large republic—reveals that the framers of the Constitution recognized that an economic system that permitted material inequalities was not merely compatible with but was an essential aspect of the political structure they sought to establish. It also indicates two other key features of the economic theory that informs *The Federalist*. First, contrary to Richard de Lone's suggestion that the liberal tradition primarily emphasizes economic "prerogatives," Publius speaks here and in several other places of the *rights* of property. Government has the same kind of obligation to protect the

105

rights of property as it does to protect citizens' rights to life and liberty. Second, Publius emphasizes that government is obliged not simply to concern itself with the preservation of property but also to protect people's ability to acquire more of it. The economic theory of *The Federalist* holds that men should be encouraged to exercise to the full extent their "different and unequal faculties of acquiring property," despite the inequality this inevitably produces. A more detailed analysis of *The Federalist's* argument can appropriately begin with the latter point, the encouragement of acquisitiveness and its role in the theory of the large republic that underlies the Constitution.

The Issue of Faction

Federalist 10 is devoted to an analysis of the problem of faction, the "dangerous vice" that has everywhere led to the destruction of popular government. Publius states that there are two ways of remedying "the mischief of faction": "by removing its causes" or "by controlling its effects." And there are, in turn, two ways of removing the causes of faction. The first is the obviously unacceptable expedient of eliminating the liberty that allows factions to grow. The second, which Publius rejects as "impracticable," is to give "to every citizen the same opinions, the same passions, and the same interests."[6]

Stated in this fashion, this alternative sounds utterly unrealizable. Yet the notion that a republic will be happier and freer of faction to the extent that its citizens share a set of common opinions, passions, and interests is not at all implausible. In fact, roughly speaking, this may be taken as the viewpoint of classical political philosophy. Even more to the point in this context, however, is that this is the well-known view presented by Montesquieu in his *Spirit of the Laws*, which is far and away the most frequently cited and discussed work of political theory in *The Federalist*.[7]

According to Montesquieu, the animating principle of republics is virtue. He defines this virtue as "the love of the laws and of our country," and states that it "requires a constant preference of public to private interest." As such, it demands a rigorous restraint of the private passions for pleasure, for wealth, and for personal superiority. Consequently, a well-ordered republic must be characterized by great austerity or purity of morals. Moreover, not only must there be an equality of property, carefully regulated by the laws, but the level of wealth enjoyed by each person should be small: "Since every individual ought here to enjoy the same happiness and the same advantages, they should consequently taste the same pleasures and form the same hopes, which cannot be expected but from a general frugality." Finally, Montesquieu asserts that a republic built on the principle of virtue can subsist only in a small territory, for "in an extensive republic the public good is sacrificed to a thousand private views."[8]

This Montesquieuan version of republicanism—a small democratic polity characterized by public-spirited virtue, austerity of morals, simplicity and homogeneity of manners, and equally distributed and strictly limited property—is explicitly and emphatically rejected in *The Federalist*. In *Federalist* 9, Publius points out that a strict adherence to Montesquieu's ideas in this regard would require splitting up most of the American states into several smaller polities, which would create "an infinity of little, jealous, clashing, tumultuous commonwealths, the wretched nurseries of unceasing discord and the miserable objects of universal pity or contempt." In *Federalist* 6 he disparages the two most famous historical examples of the virtuous republic: "Sparta was little better than a well-regulated camp; and Rome was never sated of carnage and conquest." In *Federalist* 10 he argues that such small democratic regimes "have ever been spectacles of turbulence and contention; have ever been found incompatible with personal security or the rights of property; and have in general been as short in their lives as they have been violent in their deaths."[9]

In thus rejecting the Montesquieuan model of the small, virtuous, poor republic, however, Publius is in considerable measure following the lead of Montesquieu himself. For after generally praising the ancient republics in the first part of *The Spirit of the Laws*, Montesquieu turns in Book 9 to the issue of political liberty, where he concludes that the general opinion that democracies are the freest form of government is an error, which arises from the fact that "the power of the people has been confounded with their liberty." Political liberty does not consist in the self-rule enjoyed by the citizens of a virtuous republic; indeed, the power such a government exercises over the private lives of citizens places strict limits on their freedom. Montesquieu defines political liberty instead as "a tranquility of mind arising from the opinion each person has of his safety. In order to have this liberty, it is requisite the government be so constituted as one man need not be afraid of another."[10]

Montesquieu takes as the model of such a government modern England, the "one nation . . . that has for the direct end of its constitution political liberty." England does not readily fit into the category of either republics (the principle of which is virtue) or monarchies (the principle of which is honor) established in the first part of *The Spirit of the Laws*. Although its political institutions have some republican and some monarchical aspects, it is animated neither by virtue nor by honor. In England, "all the passions [are] unrestrained"; the English are "a trading people," who "have ever made their political interests give way to those of commerce." England emerges in Montesquieu's description as having political institutions plainly superior to those of other nations, and especially to the ancient republics. The chief source of this superiority, and the guarantor of its liberties, is the separation it maintains among the legislative, executive, and judicial branches of its government, so that "power [is] a check to power."[11] This separation of powers is, of course, a key element in the new science of politics espoused by Publius, who defends the Constitution's faithfulness to this concept by invoking the authority and the reasoning of "the celebrated Montesquieu."[12]

Having dismissed the possibility of forestalling factions by giving the citizens a common set of opinions, passions, and interests, Publius turns next in *Federalist* 10 to an examination of how the effects of faction can be controlled. In a republic, he notes, regular elections limit the power of minority factions, but they can do nothing to check the potential excesses of a majority faction, that great danger to all popular government. How can a republic be protected from such a faction? The first and most important part of Publius's answer is that "the existence of the same passion or interest in a majority at the same time must be prevented."[13] In other words, far from seeking the greatest possible unity among the citizens, as the legislators of the small, virtuous republic did, the framers of the American Constitution chose precisely the opposite course, of encouraging multiplicity and disunity. Or, as Madison sums it up in a letter to Jefferson that mirrors much of the argument of *Federalist* 10, "*Divide et impera*, the reprobated axiom of tyranny, is, under certain qualifications, the only policy by which a republic can be administered on just principles."[14]

Diversity and Capitalism

The way to achieve the internal divisions required to prevent the formation of a majority faction, Publius contends, is to "extend the sphere" and thus "take in a greater variety of parties and interests." The large republic founded on the Constitution will embrace "so many separate descriptions of citizens as will render an unjust combination of the whole very improbable, if not impracticable." Simply enlarging the nation's territory, however, will not by itself achieve the requisite diversity unless the different citizens thereby included have genuinely distinct interests. Moreover, since Publius is committed to finding a wholly "republican remedy" to the problem of faction, he cannot rely on that part of Montesquieu's scheme which involves checking the popular interest with those of the nobility and of the monarchy. It is critical to *The Federalist*'s concept of the large republic, therefore, that the population be divided into a considerable diversity of *economic* interests. This, in turn, requires a relatively advanced and complex economy. "At present," Publius notes in *Federalist* 56, "some of the States are little more than a society of husbandmen. Few of them have made much progress in those branches of industry which give a variety and complexity to the affairs of a nation."[15] An overwhelmingly agricultural society would not provide the multiplicity of interests essential to the large republic.

Unlike Jefferson, then, who asserts in his *Notes on the State of Virginia* that "the proportion which the aggregate of the other classes of citizens bears in any state to that of its husbandmen, is the proportion of its unsound to its healthy parts."[16] Publius favors the growth of commerce and manufacturing. This preference is visible in many parts of *The Federalist*, but it receives its fullest statement at the beginning of *Federalist* 12:

> The prosperity of commerce is now perceived and acknowledged by all enlightened statesmen to be the most useful as well as the most productive source of national wealth, and has accordingly become a primary object of their political cares. By multiplying the means of gratification, by promoting the introduction and circulation of the precious metals, those darling objects of human avarice and enterprise, it serves to vivify all the channels of industry and to make them flow with greater activity and copiousness. The assiduous merchant, the laborious husbandman, the active mechanic, and the industrious manufacturer—all orders of men look forward with eager expectation and growing alacrity to the pleasing reward of their toils.[17]

In praising the political utility of commerce, Publius acknowledges that it prompts men more actively to pursue their private gratification. Far from encouraging public-spirited virtue, it promotes what traditionally has been considered a vice—namely, avarice. Indeed, the concern with private gain, Publius later acknowledges, will make the citizens unwilling to contribute their time to manning the garrisons necessary to defend their republic's frontiers:

> The militia would not long, if at all, submit to be dragged from their occupations and families to perform that most disagreeable duty in times of peace. And if they could be prevailed upon or compelled to do it, the increased expense

of a frequent rotation of service, and the loss of labor and
disconcertion of the industrious pursuits of individuals,
would form conclusive objections to the scheme. It would be
as burdensome and injurious to the public as ruinous to
private citizens.[18]

How, then, can the promotion of commerce and the "pursuits of
gain," which clearly weaken public-spiritedness, redound to the
public good? The first answer, as has been suggested, is that a great
diversity of competing economic interests can supply the foundation
of a free and stable government, provided that those interests are
channeled by properly constructed political institutions. "Neither
moral nor religious motives," Publius argues in *Federalist* 10, "can be
relied on as an adequate control" for the oppressive tendencies of
faction. What virtue cannot be trusted to accomplish, however, the
division of society into a multiplicity of interests can. Such a division
impedes the formation of oppressive majority factions, so that "a
coalition of a majority of the whole society could seldom take place
on any other principles than those of justice and the general good."[19]

In his discussion of the separation of powers, which is also based
on the principle not of restraining the passions but of counteracting
them with the passions of other men, Publius states, "This policy of
supplying, by opposite and rival interests, the defect of better motives, might be traced through the whole system of human affairs,
private as well as public."[20] He does not specify how this policy
operates in private affairs, but he may well have been thinking of the
benefits of economic competition, which received their classic exposition from Adam Smith:

> Every individual is continually exerting himself to find out
> the most advantageous employment for whatever capital he
> can command. It is his own advantage, indeed, and not that
> of the society which he has in view. But the study of his
> own advantage naturally, or rather necessarily leads him to
> prefer that employment which is most advantageous to the
> society.[21]

In any event, if increasing national wealth—that is, economic
growth—is taken as a desirable political goal, as it clearly is by the
authors of *The Federalist*, encouraging individuals to pursue their own
private gain becomes a means toward promoting the public good.

Finally, the avarice stimulated by commerce, though undeniably
a selfish passion, is nonetheless conducive to habits of industry,
prudence, and sobriety—in short, to regularity of morals.[22] Men
under the sway of this passion tend to go about their business quietly,

seeking gratification in the pleasing reward of their private activities, with little to be gained and much to be lost by disturbing the public tranquility. This self-regulating mechanism makes it possible for government to be relatively unconcerned with the private lives and opinions of its citizens, and to allow them a great measure of personal liberty. At the same time, what Tocqueville called "self-interest rightly understood" leads the citizens freely to support "a government which will allow them to acquire the things they covet and which will not debar them from the peaceful enjoyment of those possessions which they have already acquired."[23]

Advantages of the Large Republic

The authors of *The Federalist*, then, fully understood that opting for the large republic characterized by representative government, separation of powers, religious toleration, and personal liberty required unleashing the acquisitive or commercial spirit. At this point, it is worth inquiring briefly into the theoretical grounds for their preferring this "modern" alternative to the older ideal of a small republic characterized by direct democracy, religious unity, public-spiritedness, frugality, and economic equality.

In the first place, Publius rejects the classical small republic as "impracticable." Despite their attempts to foster public-spiritedness, unity, and equality among their citizens, regimes supposedly based on virtue have always been afflicted by civil discord: "Theoretic politicians who have patronized this species of government, have erroneously supposed that by reducing mankind to a perfect equality in their political rights, they would at the same time be perfectly equalized and assimilated in their possessions, their opinions, and their passions."[24] In fact, however, men's self-love generally leads them to prefer their private advantage to the public good, and the diversity in their faculties causes them to resist efforts to reduce them to an equality of condition. In particular, men are always inclined to pursue their economic self-interest; hence, despite all efforts to suppress it, a distinction inevitably emerges between rich and poor. Religion and morality are simply too weak to counter—at least over the long run—the human tendency toward self-seeking. The small, poor, virtuous republic is ultimately doomed to failure because it goes against the grain of human nature.

Publius's rejection of the ancient republican model does not seem to derive from considerations of practicability alone, however. The classical political philosophers also were aware of the practical problems posed by men's selfish passions, yet they persisted in their

preference for the small, virtuous, poor republic because they regarded virtue not merely as a means toward maintaining republican
government but as the end or goal of political life. From such a
perspective, it would hardly have made sense to favor a kind of
regime that encouraged citizens to pursue their selfish passions.
There is almost no evidence of this classical viewpoint in *The Federalist*, however. Publius nowhere suggests that the large republic
founded on the Constitution would have as its aim the inculcation of
virtue or piety.[25] Instead, emphasizing the inability of morality and
religion to control men's passions, he advocates a set of political
arrangements that depends on allowing self-interest considerable
liberty. In apparently discarding virtue as a political goal, Publius
removes the need for the onerous self-sacrifice and restraint on
individual liberty demanded by the classical republic. The ancient
republican model thus is rejected for being intrinsically undesirable
as well as impracticable.

The Federalist does not offer a systematic discussion of the goals
of political life, but where its authors do touch on this great question,
they tend to emphasize such ends as security (or safety), liberty, and
property.[26] In particular, they echo the thought of John Locke in
speaking of the "great principle of self-preservation," the "original
right of self-defense," and the violence and uncertainty of men's
condition in the "state of nature" which prompts them to "submit to
a government."[27] Now, John Locke does of course address this
question directly, most conspicuously in the chapter "Of the Ends of
Political Society and Government" in his *Second Treatise*. Here he
states, "The great and *chief end* therefore, of Men uniting into Commonwealths, and putting themselves under Government, *is the Preservation of their Property*."[28] But Locke also considers the question in a
less well known but most revealing passage of his *Letter Concerning
Toleration*. This passage, which I shall take the liberty of quoting at
length, is preceded by a paragraph in which Locke, after asserting
that "every man has an immortal soul, capable of eternal happiness
or misery," nonetheless concludes that "the care of each man's
salvation belongs only to himself" (that is, it is no business of
government):[29]

> But besides their souls, which are immortal, men have also
> their temporal lives here upon earth; the state whereof being
> frail and fleeting, and the duration uncertain, they have
> need of several outward conveniences to the support
> thereof, which are to be procured or preserved by pains and
> industry. For those things that are necessary to the comfort-
> able support of our lives are not the spontaneous products

of nature, nor do offer themselves fit and prepared for our use. This part therefore draws on another care, and necessarily gives another employment. But the pravity of mankind being such that they had rather injuriously prey upon the fruits of other men's labors than take pains to provide for themselves, the necessity of preserving men in the possession of what honest industry has already acquired, and also of preserving their liberty and strength, whereby they may acquire what they further want, obliges men to enter into society with one another, that by mutual assistance and joint force they may secure unto each other their properties, in the things that contribute to the comfort and happiness of this life, leaving in the meanwhile to every man the care of his own eternal happiness, the attainment whereof can neither be facilitated by another man's industry, nor can the loss of it turn to another man's prejudice, nor the hope of it be forced from him by an external violence. But, forasmuch as men thus entering into societies, grounded upon their mutual compacts of assistance for the defense of their temporal goods, may, nevertheless, be deprived of them, either by the rapine and fraud of their fellow citizens or by the hostile violence of foreigners, the remedy of this evil consists in arms, riches, and multitude of citizens; the remedy of the other in laws; and the care of all things relating both to one and the other is committed by the society to the civil magistrate. This is the original, this is the use, and these are the bounds of the legislative (which is the supreme) power in every commonwealth. I mean that provision may be made for the security of each man's private possessions, for the peace, riches, and public commodities of the whole people, and, as much as possible, for the increase of their inward strength against foreign invasions.

These things thus explained, it is easy to understand to what end the legislative power ought to be directed, and by what measures regulated; and that is the temporal good and outward prosperity of the society, which is the sole reason of men's entering into society, and the only thing they seek and aim at in it.[30]

In short, it is Locke's contention that the care and improvement of men's souls—the cultivation of virtue and piety—is not the province of government. Political society is properly concerned only with men's "temporal lives"—that is, their bodily or material existence. What men above all require for their temporal lives are those "outward conveniences" that provide them with "comfortable support." These things are not supplied ready-made by nature, however; they can be acquired only through "pains and industry." The acquisition of "the things that contribute to comfort and happiness in this life," therefore, is naturally men's chief task. But because in the state of nature some men seek to take away the fruits of others' labor, men must unite into political society to achieve the security of their present possessions and future acquisitions on which their well-being depends.

It is easy to see why, in this view of the origin and purpose of political society, "the protection of [men's] different and unequal faculties of acquiring property" might be regarded as "the first object of government." According to Locke, acquiring and enjoying private wealth are the legitimate and reasonable aims of the individual citizen, and hence ensuring the security of these pursuits is the proper task of political society. In this light, the attempt of the small, virtuous republic to impose strict limits on private wealth in the name of the public good is unreasonable, for it contradicts the very purpose of men's entering society—the preservation and enlargement of their possessions.

Although Locke's view of human nature and political society devalues virtue understood as devotion to the common good or as self-sacrifice for the benefit of others, it brings to the fore a particular notion of justice: in essence, that "justice gives every man a title to the product of his honest industry."[31] A man may justly pursue his own self-interested desire for gain to the full, provided he confines the means of that pursuit to "honest industry" and does not seek to deprive others by fraud or rapine of what their own honest industry has procured. Justice consists in respecting the private rights—and particularly the property rights—of others.

But would not this standard of justice allow industrious men to amass such great riches that their less industrious fellows would be left with none of the "outward conveniences" of life? Locke in effect answers this question in the chapter "Of Property" in his *Second Treatise*. Because "the far greatest part of the value of things, we enjoy in this world" is created by human labor rather than bestowed in fixed proportions by nature, the man of superior industry "does not lessen but increase the stock of mankind." Hence even its poorer members benefit from living in a society that protects and encourages industry; the worst-off Englishman "feeds, lodges, and is clad" better than a "king of a large and fruitful territory" among the Indians of America.[32] Utility as well as justice requires that the rights of property be secure.

The Rights of Property

Providing security for the rights of property is an absolutely central concern of the authors of *The Federalist*. Indeed, Madison, in the letter to Jefferson already cited, suggests that the encroachments of unjust state laws on citizens' rights of private property were the principal factor that led both to the Constitutional Convention and to public readiness to accept "a general reform."[33] *The Federalist* itself is filled with condemnatory references to these problems, specifically attacking state laws that violated private contracts and paper-money measures and more generally deploring the mutability of state laws.[34] It is in these contexts, moreover, that Publius most frequently and emphatically invokes the language of justice and morality: "such atrocious breaches of moral obligation and social justice"; "an accumulation of guilt, which can be expiated no otherwise than by a voluntary sacrifice on the altar of justice of the power which has been the instrument of it"; "practices . . . which have . . . occasioned an almost universal prostration of morals"; "a rage for paper money, for an abolition of debts, for an equal division of property, or for any other improper or wicked project."[35]

The introductory paragraph of *Federalist* 10 alludes to the instability and injustice of state governments, which Publius holds responsible for "that prevailing and increasing distrust of public engagements and alarm for private rights which are echoed from one end of the continent to the other." In the systematic analysis of the problem of faction that follows, he leaves no doubt that it is the violence and injustice prompted by economic motives that are his chief source of concern:

> The most common and durable source of factions has been the various and unequal distribution of property. Those who hold and those who are without property have ever formed distinct interests in society. Those who are creditors, and those who are debtors, fall under a like discrimination. A landed interest, a manufacturing interest, a mercantile interest, a moneyed interest, with many lesser interests, grow up of necessity in civilized nations, and divide them into different classes, actuated by different sentiments and views. The regulation of these various and interfering interests forms the principal task of modern legislation and involves the spirit of party and faction in the necessary and ordinary operations of government.[36]

Because in a republican government political power naturally comes to reside in majority factions, and because the rich are always in a minority, holds Publius, the greatest danger to property rights is that the poorer members of society may unite to defraud or despoil the wealthy. As we have seen, Publius's principal solution to the problem of faction is to enlarge the territory of a republic to encompass "a greater variety of parties and interests" (by which he appears primarily to mean economic interests). The purpose of this solution is to make the "various" distribution of property more politically salient than its "unequal" distribution. If both the poor and the rich earn their livelihood in a great variety of ways, there will be divergent and competing interests within each group, as well as certain common interests cutting across economic strata. Thus, Publius suggests, poor mechanics will be inclined to vote for the rich merchant as "their natural patron and friend," and a unity of political interest will exist between the "wealthiest landlord" and "the poorest tenant." Furthermore, the extended republic, with its large election districts, would be more likely to choose for its representatives men of "the most diffusive and established characters"—that is, presumably, men of greater wealth.[37] In sum, the large republic is meant to be structured so as to minimize the likelihood that a poor majority will coalesce to violate the property rights of the more prosperous.

The inviolability of the rights of property appears to have been accepted by the full range of American political thinkers of the constitutional era—anti-Federalists as well as supporters of the Constitution, agrarians as well as proponents of commerce and manufacturing.[38] Even Jefferson, despite the notably egalitarian character of some of his views, remained firmly committed to a concept of property rights which promoted and justified unequal material rewards. In his second inaugural address as president of the United States, he affirmed his wish that "equality of rights [be] maintained, and that state of property, equal or unequal, which results to every man from his own industry, or that of his fathers."[39] In a letter to Joseph Milligan, he stated:

> To take from one, because it is thought his own industry and that of his fathers has acquired too much, in order to spare to others, who, or whose fathers have not exercised equal industry and skill, is to violate arbitrarily the first principle of association, "the guarantee to everyone of a free exercise of his industry and the fruits acquired by it."[40]

This is not to deny that Jefferson, along with others of the founding generation, believed that a wide distribution of property, without vastly disproportionate wealth or acute poverty, best comported with republican government.[41] In a letter to the Reverend

James Madison (a cousin of his more famous namesake), Jefferson suggests as one "means of silently lessening the inequality of property" the use of progressive taxation, a policy that had been approved by both Montesquieu and Adam Smith.[42] But the principal instrument advocated by Jefferson (and others) for preventing inequality of fortune sufficient to threaten republicanism was laws encouraging the equal partition of inheritances. Shortly after the Declaration of Independence was adopted, Jefferson returned to the Virginia Legislature, where he led a successful fight to abolish the laws of primogeniture and entail (which required that landed estates be passed intact to the eldest son). In his autobiography he explains the purpose behind these reforms as follows:

> To annul this privilege, and instead of an aristocracy of wealth, of more harm and danger, than benefit, to society, to make an opening for the aristocracy of virtue and talent, which nature has wisely provided for the direction of the interests of society, and scattered with equal hand through all its conditions, was deemed essential to a well-ordered republic. To effect it, no violence was necessary, no deprivation of natural right, but rather an enlargement of it by repeal of the law [of entail]. For this would authorize the present holder to divide the property among his children equally, as his affections were divided; and would place them, by natural generation, on the level of their fellow citizens.[43]

If Tocqueville's account can be believed, the reformed law of inheritance fully achieved the democratizing effect Jefferson had intended. During the Revolutionary War, almost all the states had abolished the old aristocratic English laws of inheritance; sixty years later, "the law of partition [had] reduced all to one level." By this assertion Tocqueville means that the permanent concentration of vast wealth in certain great families had been eliminated:

> I do not mean that there is any lack of wealthy individuals in the United States; I know of no country, indeed, where the love of money has taken stronger hold on the affections of men and where a profounder contempt is expressed for the theory of the permanent equality of property. But wealth circulates with incredible rapidity, and experience shows that it is rare to find two succeeding generations in the full enjoyment of it.[44]

Results of the Framers' Work

The economic aspects of the framers' political theory may be summarized, then, in the following four points: (1) Industry and the pursuit of gain should be encouraged. (2) Superior industry and skill justly merit the greater material rewards they naturally tend to reap. (3) The rights of private property must be secured, both on grounds of justice and as a necessary condition for promoting industry. (4) The laws should favor the free and rapid circulation of property. so that all may have a chance to become rich and so that distinct and permanent classes of either the very rich or the very poor are unlikely to form.

The political ends these economic principles were meant to serve are the now traditional liberal goals of liberty and prosperity. National prosperity is the product of individual industry, supported by the security afforded to private property. Liberty is made possible because, given the proper political institutions (representative government, separation of powers, and a large territory), men devoted to industrious pursuits can largely be left to go their own way. The extended republic based on economic self-interest protects the private sphere and gives it unprecedented room to expand. In comparison with the classical republican ideal, the Madisonian version can be said to foster a far-reaching depoliticization of human society. Government no longer need closely supervise the morals, religion, and opinions of the people, for extraordinary public-spiritedness is neither demanded nor needed. The calculating pursuit of economic advantage and the habits of industry provide a check on people's most dangerous and politically destructive passions, and citizens readily give their allegiance to a government that guarantees their liberty and supplies the political conditions they need for prosperity.

I believe it is safe to say that Publius's vision of the large republic animated by economic self-interest has been remarkably successful in bringing the United States almost two hundred years of freedom and material well-being. I believe it is also fair to say that the economic views of the framers, at least as embodied in the principles summarized here, continue to prevail in this country today. To be sure, there have been enormous changes over the past two centuries in technology, in economic organization, and above all in the role played by the federal government in the economy. The modern welfare state certainly goes well beyond anything the framers of the Constitution might have envisioned. And it cannot be denied that the expanded scope of government activity has created difficulties for our political system that have not yet been fully resolved. But whatever the practical problems caused by the proliferation of government programs in the areas of regulation, social insurance, equal opportunity, and aid to the needy, I believe that on the level of principle, the welfare state remains compatible with the liberal capitalist society established by the Constitution—a society that guarantees the security of private property and generally allows material rewards to be allocated according to the "industry and skill" of individuals.

I would argue, however, that proposals for making it an explicit aim of government policy to combat economic inequality directly are a very different matter. In the first place, by focusing on the political competition among income classes (as opposed to that among interest groups formed along other lines), frankly redistributionist policies would intensify the very conflict between the rich and poor that the framers sought to minimize. Moreover, a direct governmental assault on economic inequality would seem to me even more fundamentally incompatible with the basic economic theory underlying the Constitution. It is no accident that the more sophisticated arguments for income redistribution are accompanied by an explicit denial that superior skill or industry conveys a just title to the greater material rewards it normally brings. (This denial is found in Okun's *Equality and Efficiency*, and it is a crucial premise of the most influential work in political theory of the 1970s—John Rawls's *A Theory of Justice*.)[45] Having government determine the level of people's income by redistribution can be morally justified only if those who originally earn income have no legitimate right to it.

By making the political process rather than the "honest industry" of private individuals the arbiter of each person's income, redistribution undermines the notion of genuinely private property. For the implicit assumption of such a policy is not that a society's wealth is the sum of the wealth of its individual citizens, but that individuals' wealth is merely the share of the society's wealth that government decides to allot them. By making everyone's income directly dependent on governmental largesse, a policy of explicit redistribution must necessarily politicize society. In effect, each citizen would become the equivalent of a government grantee or a welfare recipient, and it is hard to see how anyone could hope to avoid the government's solicitude about how he or she was spending the public's money. In addition, with everyone entitled to a goodly share of the society's total output, there would be inevitable pressure to regulate the contributions people make to the production of that output. Decisions about whether, where, and when individuals ought to work would tend to become subject to political determination. It seems unlikely, therefore, that a redistributionist society could maintain the protection of the private sphere necessary for personal liberty to flourish.[46]

One way of describing the error into which I believe the advocates of redistribution have fallen is that they seek to impose on the large republic an economic egalitarianism more appropriate to the small republic. Indeed, I think a very large portion of contemporary hostility to capitalism comes down to a longing for certain attractive features of the small republic—not only economic equality, but intense political participation, a strong sense of community, and selfless devotion to the public good. Few of the contemporary critics of capitalism, however, are willing to sacrifice the blessings of the large, modern, capitalistic republic—unprecedented wealth and personal liberty. Thus they often seem to wind up calling for a utopian combination of contradictory elements—diversity and unity, individualism and community, a high standard of living without resort to the pursuit of private gain. The danger, of course, is that trying to achieve this hybrid in practice will cause us to lose the advantages of the large republic without gaining the advantages of the small republic. In fact, modern totalitarianism can be viewed in some respects as the unfortunate result of just such a misguided attempt.

Lest I be misunderstood, let me hasten to make clear some things I do *not* mean to imply: that the large republic demands an unqualified reliance on self-interest and unbounded libertarianism, that it can or should *totally* dispense with every characteristic of the small republic, or that a capitalist economy is a sufficient condition for political liberty. Indeed, I think the gravest weakness of *The Federalist's* case for the large republic is its taking for granted the moral and customary props that are essential to the maintenance of self-government in any society. In this respect, an excellent supplement (or corrective) to *The Federalist* is provided by Tocqueville, with his emphasis on the importance of such factors as religion, local government, civil association, and domestic morals to the health of American democracy. Tocqueville constantly stresses, however, the need to adapt these supports to the worldly and commercial spirit of a liberal capitalist society. For he perceived that self-interest—"rightly understood"—was the only reliable basis for political freedom in the modern world.

Certainly the historical record does not reveal any noncapitalist society that has given its citizens a high degree of personal liberty, or any large noncapitalist society that has long maintained a republican government. One hesitates, however, to rely too heavily on the evidence of the past in matters like these, remembering Publius's plea in behalf of "the experiment of an extended republic": "Hearken not to the voice which petulantly tells you that the form of government recommended for your adoption is a novelty in the political world; that it has never yet had a place in the theories of the wildest projectors; that it rashly attempts what it is impossible to accomplish."[47] Perhaps a country as large and diverse as the United States could continue to enjoy republican government and personal liberty even if it ceased to have a capitalist economy. This possibility will have to be taken seriously when it comes to be defended with the theoretical insight and persuasive power displayed in *The Federalist*.

8

Human Rights and the Rule of Law in Postapartheid South Africa

John Dugard

The constitutional experience of the United States has had a profound effect on the present constitutional debate in South Africa.[1] The failure of the British Westminster system to provide an adequate constitutional mechanism for the protection of individual rights has compelled South African jurists and political scientists to turn to other models for guidance. Inevitably, the Constitution of the United States and its Bill of Rights have provided the main inspiration for the constitutional protection of human rights. In some quarters, in both South Africa and the United States, the success of the U.S. documents has led to the simplistic belief that the U.S. Bill of Rights could be transplanted in the barren soil of South African constitutionalism with few changes. Such a view is both naive and dangerous, as it fails to take account of different historical developments, jurisprudential traditions, and changed attitudes toward rights. At the outset, it is essential to focus attention on these differences to explain why South Africa's founding fathers-to-be face a more daunting task than did those who drafted the American Bill of Rights and why the U.S. model does not provide a complete answer to South Africa's constitutional problems in the field of rights and liberties.

America was colonized at a time when the natural-law tradition of Edward Coke and John Locke was the prevalent jurisprudential influence.[2] Legal positivism was unheard of. In these circumstances, it is not surprising that the Declaration of Independence of 1776, the

Constitution, and the amendments to the Constitution that have come to be known as the Bill of Rights should be premised on the notions of a higher law and of the inalienable rights of the individual. That the inalienable rights were civil and political rights—first-generation rights in modern parlance—is also not surprising. These were the rights denied to the American colonists by Britain. It was the denial of these rights that had sparked a revolution.[3] Moreover, social and economic rights were not part of the natural-law philosophy of the eighteenth century. This was fortunate for the Founding Fathers, as the group of distinguished constitution builders who gathered together in Philadelphia in 1787 were unlikely to be enthusiastic about such rights: they were men of substance—landowners and in some cases slaveholders.

South Africa's founding fathers face a more complex task. They are expected to draft a bill of rights that guarantees the rights denied by forty-two years of apartheid and that takes account of contemporary national bills of rights and international human rights conventions that extend beyond the limited first-generation rights of the U.S. Bill of Rights to protect social and economic rights, women's rights, children's rights, workers' rights, and environmental rights. To aggravate matters, they have no shared legal philosophy of the kind that guided their American counterparts.

Natural law—the obvious guiding jurisprudence for a bill of rights—has had a bad time in South Africa. Unlike the United States, South Africa was colonized when legal positivism and parliamentary supremacy dominated legal thought.[4] Natural law, the jurisprudential creed of Hugo Grotius (1583–1645) and the Roman-Dutch jurists,[5] had been rejected as a ridiculous "abstraction,"[6] and the notions of a higher law and inalienable rights, the necessary concomitants of natural-law philosophy, were repeatedly dismissed by those in authority. In 1896, South African President Paul Kruger condemned judicial review of legislative and executive acts as "a principle of the devil"—one that had been introduced into paradise to test God's word.[7] Apartheid's prime ministers and presidents have vilified human rights: none more clearly than John Vorster, who rejected the rule of law and human rights as being the instruments of international communism.[8] Pleas for a rigid constitution (that is, a higher law) and a bill of rights were rejected on the enactment of South Africa's constitutions of 1910,[9] 1961,[10] and 1983.[11] National party opposition to the legal protection of rights has been premised on three different jurisprudential creeds.[12] First, positivism, whose strict insistence on the separation of law as it *is* from law as it *ought* to be, has been invoked as a justification for the rejection of legal idealism.

123

Second, the historicism of Friedrich von Savigny (1779–1861), which sees law as the expression of the spirit of the people (*Volksgeist*), in the South African context has been interpreted to mean that law is the expression of the spirit of the Afrikaner people represented by the National party. Third, Calvinism, according to some, rejects human rights and the rule of law as manifestations of an unacceptable humanist philosophy that challenges the authority of the state.[13]

The attitude of the liberation forces toward natural law has vacillated. In its early years, the African National Congress, under the leadership of Albert Luthuli and Z. K. Mathews, was essentially a civil rights movement not unlike that in the United States under Martin Luther King. In 1955, it endorsed a rights philosophy in the Freedom Charter. At the same time, it engaged in a passive resistance campaign inspired by the philosophy of Mahatma Gandhi. After it committed itself to the armed struggle in the 1960s, however, its concern for rights was substantially replaced by demands for power. Its Marxist associations confirmed this approach. To the Marxists of this time, the concern for human rights was simply a bourgeois preoccupation with the cosmetic improvement of the superstructure of white domination.

Throughout the apartheid period, liberals protested against the invasion of human rights and advocated a bill of rights and judicial review. Although their influence was considerable, their number was few. Their voices will still be heard in the negotiations for a new constitution, but it is the opinion of those who wield political power that will prevail.

The purpose of this examination of jurisprudential attitudes in South Africa is not to suggest that natural law is the only "true" theory of law. Positivism, historical and sociological jurisprudence, and economic theories of law all contribute to an understanding of the nature of law. What is suggested, however, is that natural law, despite its many weaknesses, has provided the inspiration for both national and international instruments aimed at the protection of human rights. Undoubtedly, it assisted the Founding Fathers of the American Constitution and Bill of Rights. Unfortunately, those responsible for the drafting of a bill of rights in South Africa do not share a common jurisprudential outlook; more particularly, they do not share a jurisprudential outlook that recognizes the inalienability of the rights of the individual. Instead, our "founding fathers" bring to the negotiating table jurisprudential baggage that is likely to hinder rather than to promote the advancement of rights.

The Current Debate

Attitudes toward a bill of rights have changed radically and rapidly in South Africa.[14] Less than a decade ago, the ruling National party summarily dismissed proposals for a bill of rights in the 1983 constitution.[15] Liberation, not rights, was the main goal of the ANC. Only since the late 1980s have both principal players in the drama of South Africa shown an interest in the legal protection of human rights.

The first sign of change on the part of the National party came in 1985, when it enacted a declaration of rights for Namibia as part of its evolution to independence.[16] The following year, the minister of justice, Kobie Coetsee, announced in Parliament[17] that he had requested the South African Law Commission, a statutory body whose members are appointed by the government,[18] to investigate the role of the courts in protecting group and individual rights and to consider the desirability of instituting a bill of rights. As this announcement coincided with the declaration of a state of emergency that resulted in a large-scale violation of basic rights, few took it seriously. Cynics construed it either as an attempt to legitimize the notion of group rights at the expense of individual rights or as a last-ditch attempt to forestall sanctions by the U.S. Congress by sending a belated message that South Africa was prepared to model its constitutional order on that of the United States.

Shortly before the law commission completed its report, the then-outlawed African National Congress published *Constitutional Guidelines for a Democratic South Africa,*[19] which advocates the inclusion of a bill of rights based on the Freedom Charter in a new constitution. Since then, a bill of rights has featured prominently in ANC constitutional pronouncements.[20]

The year 1989 saw the publication of the South African Law Commission's report, which proposed the adoption of a bill of rights to protect individual civil and political rights.[21] By asserting "the right of all citizens over the age of eighteen years to exercise the vote on a basis of equality"[22] and by dismissing the idea that a bill of rights was the appropriate instrument for the protection of *group* rights,[23] the law commission won credibility for itself and provided a major impetus to the cause of a bill of rights.

Although the National party was unhappy because the law commission refused to extend its recommendation for the protection of rights to group rights,[24] the party has nevertheless unequivocally supported the inclusion of a bill of rights in any future constitution.[25] Its allies in the negotiating process—mainly the national states—have followed suit. Today, every political party or movement committed to the negotiation of a new constitution for South Africa accepts that a bill of rights will form part of the constitution.

The 1991 discussions of the Convention for a Democratic South Africa devoted little attention to a bill of rights, as the ANC, the National party, and the nonaligned Democratic party are in agreement that such a mechanism should be included in the constitution. The debate has been taken a step further, however, by the publication of two working papers—A *Bill of Rights for a New South Africa*[26] and *Constitutional Principles for a Democratic South Africa*[27]—by the ANC Constitutional Committee and of a follow-up report—termed an interim report—by the South African Law Commission.[28] Unfortunately, the National party, unlike the ANC, has failed to publish its own blueprint for a bill of rights.

Politicians in search of consensus have refused to be drawn into the debate over a bill of rights. Instead, they have focused on more obviously divisive issues such as federalism and the powers and composition of the upper house. This is understandable, as those issues on which there is a semblance of consensus should not be too readily abandoned when the course of negotiations is uncertain. Conversely, the fact must be faced that the agreement over a bill of rights is more apparent than real. Serious disagreements already exist over both the purpose and the content of a bill of rights. At some stage, these areas of disagreement will have to be acknowledged. This chapter addresses some of the potentially most controversial issues.

Purpose of a Bill of Rights

For the National party, a bill of rights is probably intended to serve a limited and straightforward purpose, namely, the direct protection of individual rights and the indirect protection of group rights. This was spelled out by the state president in his address to the Federal Congress of the National party on September 4, 1991: "A Charter of Fundamental Rights must be constitutionally protected and legally enforceable. This will equip the citizen to protect himself against unlawful action by government. Effective protection of the fundamental rights of the individual will at the same time offer important protection of the interests of groups and communities."[29]

For the ANC, a bill of rights is intended to serve goals beyond the protection of rights. For it, the bill of rights must signal an end to apartheid and to the denial of rights inherent in that policy. This view is made clear by the introductory note to the ANC Constitutional Committee's working document *A Bill of Rights for a New South Africa*: "In South African conditions, a Bill of Rights becomes the fundamental anti-apartheid document. It guarantees equal rights of all citizens, and defends each and every one of us against the kinds of tyranny and abuse which have flowed daily from the apartheid state."[30] A bill of rights is therefore to constitute a visible sign of the victory of the liberation forces over apartheid. In this way, it will give legitimacy to the constitution.[31]

As a logical implication of this, the ANC will insist on the denunciation of apartheid in the bill of rights. The form this denunciation will take is as yet unclear. The most low-key and least divisive method would be a condemnation of apartheid along the lines of article 3 of the International Convention on the Elimination of All Forms of Racial Discrimination.[32] The ANC may, however, insist that, like the International Convention on the Suppression and Punishment of the Crime of Apartheid of 1973, the bill of rights should declare that "apartheid is a crime against humanity" and that "inhuman acts resulting from the policies and practices of apartheid" are crimes according to the general principles of law recognized by the community of nations.[33] Such a provision accompanied by a clause of the kind found in both the European Convention on Human Rights[34] and the International Covenant on Civil and Political Rights,[35] exempting such crimes from the prohibition on retrospective penal laws, would open the way for the retrospective punishment of "apartheid's criminals" like a statute modeled on the International Convention on the Suppression and Punishment of the Crime of Apartheid. Such a course would be totally unacceptable to the National party, and it would probably find itself compelled to accept a compromise of the kind contained in the International Convention on the Elimination of All Forms of Racial Discrimination. The failure of the National party to tolerate even a denunciation of apartheid at this stage[36] suggests that it has failed to consider this piece of jurisprudence rooted in international human rights conventions.

Another issue that deserves more attention is whether the purpose of a bill of rights is to create or to declare rights. The South African Law Commission, which approves a natural-law approach to rights,[37] sees the bill of rights as declaratory of certain basic rights that inhere in the individual qua person without the need for state intervention.[38] A similar philosophy is espoused by the ANC Constitutional Committee.[39] The National party's position here is undeclared, but given its long hostility to natural law and its ideological commitment to the state as the repository of all rights and powers, it may insist that the compact on the bill of rights should be exclusive.

If this happens, those who favor a natural-law approach may insist on a clause along the lines of the Ninth Amendment to the U.S. Constitution, which states that "the enumeration in the Constitution, of certain rights, shall not be construed to deny or disparage others retained by the people." Alternatively, they may be satisfied with a preambular paragraph recognizing that the rights contained in the bill of rights "derive from the inherent dignity of the human person."[40]

Controversial Areas in a Bill of Rights

The consensus over a bill of rights relates principally to first-generation rights, that is, basic civil and political rights such as the liberty of the person; freedom of speech, assembly, and association; the right to a fair trial; freedom from torture; and the right to vote. The most important areas of potential disagreement follow.

Individual or Group Rights. As mentioned, the National party's original interest in a bill of rights stemmed from the belief that such an instrument could be used to protect group rights,[41] which in political terms is a euphemism for white, and particularly Afrikaner, rights. The idea that a bill of rights could serve such a purpose has, however, been rejected by both the law commission and the ANC.

The law commission is not unsympathetic to the protection of group or minority rights. It does, however, make it clear that the political protection of group rights is a matter to be determined by the constitution itself. A bill of rights can protect the group only by means of the individual,[42] although it can guarantee the right of every person, individually or together with others, to practice freely his culture or religion and to use his language.[43]

The government reluctantly[44] accepted the advice of the law commission and has turned instead to the constitution to protect minority group rights. Federalism, an upper house whose composition is disproportionately weighted in favor of minorities, a clear constitutional separation of powers, and an independent judiciary are now part of the government's strategy to create a multiparty democracy in which minorities are able to play a meaningful role.

Some of these constitutional mechanisms—particularly federalism—are opposed by the ANC. If the government is dissatisfied with the protection accorded to minorities in the constitution, the government may turn again to the bill of rights for this purpose. This would seriously disturb consensus over a bill of rights, as the ANC is implacably opposed to such a course.

Freedom of Speech. In the United States, the First Amendment's recognition of freedom of speech is seen as the pivotal feature of democracy.[45] The notion that any particular ideology or viewpoint may be proscribed is greeted with horror by American civil libertarians. For them, the correct approach to this freedom was enunciated by Justice Douglas in his dissent in *Dennis v. United States*:

> When ideas compete in the market for acceptance, full and free discussion exposes the false and they gain few adherents. Full and free discussion even of ideas we hate encourages the testing of our own prejudices and preconceptions. Full and free discussion keeps a society from becoming stagnant and unprepared for the stresses and strains that work to tear all civilizations apart.[46]

In South Africa, there are those who support Justice Douglas's philosophy.[47] But many argue that South Africa's legacy of racism warrants a prohibition of the advocacy of apartheid and racism.[48] Thus the ANC Constitutional Committee envisages that the bill of rights will not permit the distribution of material that insults "any racial, ethnic, religious, gender or linguistic group."[49] Although such a qualification on free speech has a precedent in international convention[50] and in the Namibian Constitution of 1990,[51] it opens the door to abuse. Serious consideration should be given to Denise Meyerson's criticism of the "Left's" support for such a restriction:

> Those on the left should not be quick to betray the values of the tradition from which their views derive. It is conservatives, not progressives, who appeal to revealed truth and the infallibility of authority, and who want the state to save us from false beliefs. Those on the left have always put their faith in a very different route from the truth, namely that of democracy, debate, reason and autonomy. They have always and rightly asked for truth by demonstration, not revelation, and they have always celebrated, not distrusted thought. It can only be a backward step to switch allegiances now, enlarging the powers of the state in what is essentially a reactionary way.[52]

Private Discrimination. The equal protection clause of the U.S. Fourteenth Amendment seeks to curb the action of states, not of individuals within the states. Thus it did not outlaw the discriminatory practices of private citizens in the case of privately owned facilities open to the public. This led to a substantial case law in which the courts sought to define what constituted state action for the purposes of the Fourteenth Amendment.[53] Ultimately, Congress was obliged to intervene and adopt the 1964 Civil Rights Act prohibiting racial discrimination in all facilities open to the public.[54] The question of discrimination by private clubs and associations remains a vexed question.

There are fears that the history of the United States will be repeated in South Africa, as the process of privatizing apartheid has already begun. Whether it will receive the approval of the bill of rights is an open question. The ANC Constitutional Committee clearly envisages that racially exclusive private bodies will be prohibited.[55] The law commission, however, recognizes the right of groups to exclusive association—provided no public money is spent on racially exclusive associations.[56] This right, which would seem to recognize the right of one racial group to exclude members of other racial groups from private schools, hospitals, clubs, and suburbs, is bound to be divisive in negotiations and a cause for friction if adopted.

Economic Policy. It is not the function of a bill of rights to entrench a particular economic theory, whether it be capitalism or communism. The contrived constitutions of failed socialist states bear testimony to this, as does the history of the U.S. Supreme Court's failure to enact Herbert Spencer's *Social Statics* into the Fourteenth Amendment. As Justice Oliver Wendell Holmes declared in *Lochner v. New York*, "A constitution is not intended to embody a particular economic theory."[57]

The South African Law Commission, emboldened by the collapse of socialism in Eastern Europe, discards the advice of Justice Holmes and, after stating that it "knows of no economic system which has functioned successfully this century and was not based on free market principles,"[58] proposes that the bill of rights include the following clause: "Everyone has the right freely and on equal footing to engage in economic enterprise, which right includes the capacity to establish, manage and maintain commercial undertakings, to acquire property and to procure means of production and to offer or accept employment against remuneration."[59]

Although the ANC appears to be gradually abandoning its socialist principles, it will likely find this clause too hard to swallow. In its 1988 *Guidelines for a Democratic South Africa*,[60] the ANC declares that "the state shall ensure that the entire economy serves the interests and well-being of all sections of the population," that "the state shall have the right to determine the general context in which economic life takes place and define and limit the rights and obligations attaching to the ownership and use of productive capacity," and that "the private sector of the economy shall be obliged to co-operate with the state in realising the objectives of the Freedom Charter in promoting social well-being."

Clearly, there is no room for agreement on economic policy at this stage in South Africa's history. In these circumstances, it would seem wise to heed the advice of Justice Holmes and to omit any clause on economic policy from the bill of rights. It will then be left to a democratically elected government to determine the economic policy of the country without the restraining hand of the bill of rights.

Property Rights. The formulation of a right to property that satisfies all the major negotiators will be difficult to achieve. In these circumstances, it is tempting to suggest that a South African bill of rights, like the international human rights covenants, should refuse to include such a right.[61] Politically, such a course is impossible, as whites look to a bill of rights for protection against nationalization and the redistributive policies and programs threatened by the ANC. After all, even the moderate ANC constitutional lawyer, Albie Sachs, has warned that

> any entrenchment of property rights has to take account of the fact that a reality has been constructed in terms of which 85 per cent of the land and probably 95 per cent of productive capacity is in the hands of the white minority. What is required is a constitutional duty to rectify these percentages, not one to preserve them.[62]

The ANC Constitutional Committee adopts a conciliatory stance on this subject.[63] It accepts that "all are entitled to the peaceful enjoyment of their possessions, including the right to acquire, own, or dispose of property" but recognizes the right of the state to "take steps to overcome the effects of past statutory discrimination in relation to enjoyment of property rights." No person may be deprived of his possessions "except on grounds of public interest or public utility," in which case "just" compensation is to be paid, "taking into account the need to establish an equitable balance between the public interest and the interest of those affected." A dispute over compensation is to be settled by "a special independent tribunal, with an appeal to the courts."[64]

The vehement rejection of these proposals by the normally restrained and moderate law commission forewarns of the likely response of the National party to any clause that fails to provide an absolute guarantee of property rights. It categorizes the ANC's provisions on property as "chicanery" and as permitting "naked and arbitrary nationalization of private property." It accordingly "feels obliged to sound a serious warning against the introduction of such provisions in any proposed bill of rights."[65]

Affirmative Action. There is general agreement that the historical injustices to which blacks have been subjected in South Africa warrants affirmative action to provide for true equality or, in the parlance of a nation saturated with sport and sporting idioms, to level the playing field. Inevitably, recourse is made to the experience of the United States.[66]

The law commission is particularly influenced by the experience of the United States[67] and gives its support to affirmative action, where it seeks to provide equal opportunities to all by means of "education and training, financing programmes and employment."[68]

For the ANC, affirmative action is to play a different role.[69] It is to redress historical injustices meted out not to minorities but to the overwhelming majority of South Africans. It is, therefore, to be used to redistribute wealth, to restore land to the dispossessed, and to Africanize the civil service. No equality before the law clause or a right to property clause in a bill of rights will be permitted to obstruct these goals. The ANC's Constitutional Committee proposes that the affirmative action clause be formulated in the following terms:

> Nothing in the Constitution shall prevent the enactment of legislation, or the adoption by any public or private body of special measures of a positive kind designed to procure the advancement and the opening up of opportunities, including access to education, skills, employment *and land*, and the general advancement in social, economic and cultural spheres, of men and women who in the past have been disadvantaged by discrimination.[70]

As the ANC's affirmative action clause is seen as a device aimed at the redistribution of wealth,[71] like the property clause it will inevitably be an obstacle in the path of agreement on a bill of rights.

Social and Economic Rights. The U.S. Bill of Rights is a product of eighteenth-century natural law. This is reflected in its exclusive concern for "first-generation" rights. While Americans, for whom the Bill of Rights has become a symbol of liberty, see no need for the recognition of social and economic rights in a constitution, to many foreign observers it seems that the failure of the Bill of Rights to concern itself with such rights seriously limits its effectiveness in a society in which poverty, homelessness, and environmental decay present major problems.

South Africa, as it seeks to draft a bill of rights in the 1990s, has little choice in this matter. Social and economic rights must find their place in the constitutional compact, if it is to have any legitimacy. Radical claims that the purpose of a bill of rights is to entrench white privilege are directed at the idea of a bill of rights that seeks to protect only civil and political rights and fails to concern itself with poverty, housing, unemployment, poor working conditions, and the breakdown of family life—the legacy of forty years of apartheid.[72] Such issues must be addressed in a bill of rights. Another compelling factor is that modern human rights instruments—notably the International Covenant on Economic, Social and Cultural Rights[73]—have changed attitudes toward rights: social and economic rights are seen, in the international perspective, as an essential component of human rights. If South Africa is to regain its place among the community of nations, it must accept the norms and expectations of this community.

While there is consensus over the need to provide for economic and social rights in a bill of rights, there is an awareness of the difficulty in enforcing these rights in the same way as civil and political rights.[74] First-generation rights are negative in nature and prohibit the state from doing something to the individual, such as detaining him without trial or denying his freedom of speech. Courts may enforce these rights by ordering the state to release the detainee or to recognize his right to free speech. Second-generation rights, conversely, are positive in nature and require the state to improve the quality of life of the individual by making resources available for this purpose. It is not the normal function of the judge to order the state to make funds available for health care, nutrition, education, or employment. Consequently, it is said that these rights are nonjusticiable or unenforceable.[75]

This distinction has led to the suggestion that economic and social rights should be included not in a bill of rights but in a separate constitutional chapter on directives of state policy, as in the Indian[76] and Namibian[77] constitutions. An emerging consensus, however, is now developing that these rights—or at least some of them—should be included in the bill of rights itself. The ANC Constitutional Committee has categorized the rights to nutrition, education, health, shelter, employment, and a minimum income as "basic human rights" and would require the state "to devote maximum available resources to their progressive materialization."[78] The South African Law Commission, more concerned with the problem of enforcement than the ANC Constitutional Committee is, proposes that the bill of rights should include only those second-generation rights that can be protected in the same "negative way" as first-generation rights, that is, against state infringement. In support of this proposal, it cites the right to work. "Why should it not be possible," it asks,

> to recognize this right as a fundamental right of every individual in the sense that everyone is entitled, and regard being had to the demand for his or her labour, to obtain work? Then there would be not duty on the state to provide work for a particular individual, but the state may not make any law which unreasonably makes it impossible or difficult for the individual to obtain employment.[79]

Although there is still a wide gap between the ANC and the South African Law Commission on this issue, it seems to be premised more on attitudes toward justiciability and enforcement than toward ideology. In this context, the views of Etienne Mureinik are important: he shows that courts may have a wider review power over social and economic rights than is normally accepted.[80] Courts can, he maintains, review governmental action that is lacking in sincerity and rationality. This would enable the courts to set aside governmental action that addressed social and economic issues in a dishonest or irrational manner. He argues:

> The court . . . would be reviewing policy choices, not making them. That would of course limit its powers, but they would be far from meaningless. Under a constitutional right to health care, for instance, a court might well have been able to quash the legislation which created fourteen departments of health. The court would have asked whether any plausible argument could be advanced to show that to be a sensible way of delivering medical assistance. If it found multiple bureaucracies to be a senseless squandering of precious resources, the court would have been bound to intervene. Likewise if the annual Budget appropriated funds to build a replica of St. Peter's, or perhaps a nuclear submarine, before the rights of education promised by the Constitution had been delivered. The question in each case would be: given the constitutional commitment to these economic rights—to eradicating starvation, to supplying primary education, to delivering basic health care, can this government pro-gramme be justified? The prospect of having to answer that question would be sufficient incentive to most public ser-vants to consider their programmes carefully enough to guarantee their capacity to survive judicial scrutiny. But some programmes would fall, and rightly so.

While this argument may not completely overcome the distinc-tion between first- and second-generation rights in respect to justiciability, it does narrow the gap between the two. Certainly, a responsible court could do more to advance social and economic rights in a rational manner than a government committed to free-market economic ideas. Whether this would meet the expectations of those determined to restructure South African economic life is another matter. This suggestion may be interpreted to imply that, like economic policy, social and economic rights are best left to the political sphere and have no place in a bill of rights. While there is some basis for this argument, it fails to take account of the legacy of the past, the distrust that many South Africans have for legislative, social, and economic engineering, and the need to provide legitimacy for the bill of rights. Clearly, some social and economic rights must be included in a bill of rights. It would, therefore, be wise to include a provision for judicial review of such rights along the lines suggested by Mureinik.

The Right of Self-Determination. Many international human rights conventions recognize the right of self-determination.[81] This right has featured prominently in the practice of the United Nations, particularly in the process of decolonization.[82] It is a right frequently invoked by the ANC; indeed, the ANC struggle for liberation has been portrayed as a struggle for self-determination. The ANC, however, has consistently claimed that this is a right to be exercised by all South Africans within the 1910 borders of South Africa. In this, the ANC has been supported by the United Nations and by the Organization of African Unity, which have both insisted on the preservation of the territorial integrity of South Africa within its 1910 borders. One of the reasons advanced for the nonrecognition of Transkei, Bophuthatswana, Venda, and Ciskei (TBVC states) is that their creation and continued existence violate the principle of territorial integrity.[83]

Although the right of self-determination is an accepted third-generation right, it finds no mention in the draft bill of rights of either the ANC or the law commission. One suspects that this is a deliberate omission, based on the awareness that the recognition of the right of self-determination will encourage secessionist moves by some factions within the South African body politic.

The law commission addressed this question in its interim report in response to the argument that "the Afrikaners are a nation; that a nation has a right to self-determination; that in the case of the Afrikaners in South Africa the need for self-determination can be satisfied only by partition and self-government."[84] Relying on the strong tendency to limit the right of self-determination to peoples with a distinct territorial claim,[85] the law commission dismissed claims to secession principally on the ground that "no national group occupies a distinct territory only."[86] This is certainly not the end of the matter. The dissolution of Yugoslavia has given new hope to secessionist groups. It is highly likely that the white Right, Bophutha-tswana, Ciskei, and possibly Kwa Zulu (or the Inkatha Freedom party), which seem to be torn between a loose federation of states and outright secession, will insist at least on the inclusion of the right of self-determination in a bill of rights to lay the foundation for a later secession from a unitary or federal South Africa.

Formulating a Bill of Rights

Americans, proud of their own Bill of Rights, argue that any bill of rights should be short, couched in general terms, and phrased negatively. Much debate over a bill of rights has focused on the question of negative versus positive rights. Many Americans oppose the inclusion of positive social and economic rights in a bill of rights; many South Africans are sensitive to the need for the inclusion of such rights. Little attention has been paid to the form that such an instrument should take.

During the apartheid years, when the South African judiciary justified its abstentionist, hands-off approach to laws violating the most basic rights by invoking a formalist-positivist judicial philoso-phy,[87] many South African lawyers[88] turned to the jurisprudence of the Warren Court for support. Why could the South African courts, it was argued, not destroy or ameliorate the laws of apartheid by activist interpretation in favor of racial equality and human rights? Many South African lawyers are still captives of this time. They believe that a short, broadly phrased bill of rights would provide the judiciary with the best instrument for judicial activism, which, it is apparently assumed, will characterize judicial conduct in a new South Africa.

The South African Law Commission and the ANC Constitutional Committee are in agreement on this subject. In advocating a bill of rights couched in "broad general terms," the law commission main-tains that it is this characteristic that has enabled the American Bill of Rights to retain "exceptional viability in spite of radically changed circumstances."[89] The ANC Constitutional Committee is even more open in its acknowledgment of the influence of the American model:

> We have aimed at open and accessible language. This is in the tradition of the first great modern Bill of Rights, namely, that contained in the Amendments to the American Consti-tution. . . . In our view, a Bill of Rights should set out

general principles and not attempt to deal with each and every eventuality in advance.[90]

It is necessary to raise a word of caution on this issue in the context of the judicial history of the United States. It is true that the Supreme Court has expanded liberty by means of the Bill of Rights. It has outlawed racial segregation,[91] promoted political toleration[92] and the free exchange of ideas, and extended the rights of the criminal suspect.[93] But there is another side of the coin. The Supreme Court has also condoned slavery,[94] authorized racial segregation,[95] obstructed social and economic reform,[96] permitted the internment of Japanese Americans,[97] and participated in the hysteria of the McCarthy period.[98] On occasion, like its South African counterpart it has preferred abstention to activism: even the Warren Court refused to become embroiled in the controversy surrounding the legality of the Vietnam War.[99] More recently, it has condoned the execution of juveniles,[100] the harassment of gays,[101] and the flouting of the most basic norms of international law.[102]

To a large extent, this fluctuation in judicial philosophy is the product of the broad language of the Bill of Rights. Does a future South Africa really wish to run the risk of such vacillations in judicial lawmaking? Surely it would be wiser to draft the bill of rights more precisely and more legalistically. Ideally, the drafters of a bill of rights should chart a middle course between the Scylla of generalization and the Charybdis of precision, so that the judiciary may make law in such a manner that "they are confined from molar to molecular motions."[103] Judicial lawmaking cannot and should not be discouraged. But the judiciary should not be given the license that the judiciary of the United States enjoys under the Bill of Rights.

The more carefully worded and less generously phrased international human rights conventions offer a better model for a South African bill of rights. These instruments recognize and protect the most fundamental rights but, all the same, acknowledge the need for the qualification of certain rights. There is a further advantage in such a course. In all probability, a future South Africa, sensitive to human rights, will seek to accede to international human rights conventions, such as the International Covenant on Civil and Political Rights. By fashioning its bill of rights on this covenant, it would be easier for South Africa to ensure that its domestic law coincided with its international commitments. At the same time, it would provide South Africa with a rich source of jurisprudence on which to draw, as the decisions of the European Court and Commission of Human Rights[104] are more helpful and instructive than the conservative judgments of the present Supreme Court of the United States. The Canadian experience in this respect is worth following: the 1982 Charter of Rights and Freedoms is modeled on international conventions, and, in consequence, the Canadian courts have been able to invoke the jurisprudence of international human rights tribunals for their interpretation of the charter.[105]

The Judiciary

Guided by conservative public opinion, today's U.S. Supreme Court is unwilling to exercise an enlightened leadership on the moral issues of the day. This has not always been so. The Warren Court (and other federal courts) desegregated American society at a time when Congress, sensitive to racist public opinion, was unprepared to act.[106] Its decisions on criminal justice, which created a new code of conduct for the treatment of criminal suspects, were also in advance of public opinion.

There is strong support for judicial leadership in modern South Africa. Inherent in the present support for constitutionalism is a rejection of majoritarianism on key issues. The adoption of a bill of rights would place certain issues—such as equality before the law, standards of criminal justice, the right to privacy, and the basic political, economic, and social freedoms—beyond the reach of the political majority as special, more demanding amendment procedures will be made applicable to the bill of rights. Both the National party and the ANC appear to accept this. More important, this philosophy has the backing of the black majority, which throughout South Africa's racist history has directed its appeals against the injustices of successive Parliaments to the courts. The courts have not always, or even generally, responded positively to such appeals, but they have done so sufficiently to make the courts appear more sympathetic to black needs than the legislature has been. This history provides a sound basis for the exercise of judicial leadership.

Ironically, the South African judiciary will be called on to exercise wider powers than it has ever enjoyed when it still faces a serious crisis of legitimacy. For a bill of rights will give it review powers that it did not have under successive Westminster-type constitutions,[107] and this at a time when it has yet to redeem its reputation from years of close association with apartheid.

The reputation of the South African judiciary has been tarnished by apartheid. After a period of resistance during the first decade of National party rule,[108] the courts succumbed to apartheid for thirty years. Much has been written about the performance of the judiciary during this period.[109] At the one extreme, it is argued that judges had no alternative but to abstain from involvement. The task of the judge is to declare the law as he finds it and not to attempt to soften its impact where this is not clearly directed by Parliament. Judges are to be congratulated for having maintained their integrity and independence by failing to "take sides" in the debate over apartheid.[110] At the other end of the spectrum,[111] it is argued that the South African judiciary collaborated with the National party government by upholding the laws of apartheid, refusing to confront it, and, on occasions, expanding its severity.[112]

The truth is probably somewhere in the middle. South African judges, with a few notable exceptions, did not confront the laws of apartheid, nor did they use the interpretative powers available to them to reduce the harsh injustice of the system. They chose a policy of abstention, because they believed that detachment and aloofness from political disputations were the hallmarks of judicial independence. Some, particularly Chief Justices L. C. Steyn and F. L. H. Rumpff, "collaborated" in the sense that they allowed their judicial office to be used to promote the interests of the National party. But most aspired to "neutrality," forgetting that in the apartheid state neutrality was itself a position. In this way, judges gave legitimacy to the apartheid legal order. As a result, the reputation of the judiciary is today suspect and its legitimacy questioned.

Since 1989, when M. M. Corbett became chief justice, the image of the South African judiciary has undoubtedly improved. Gradually, in response to changed circumstances, the judiciary is beginning to retrieve its lost reputation. New judges of relatively liberal persuasion have been appointed to the bench. This does not, however, address the real problem. South African judges (again, with a few notable exceptions) are a product of a narrow, positivist training at the South African bar, which has equipped them to administer the law under the Westminster system, in which Acts of Parliament may not be reviewed. Professionally and intellectually, most lack the ability to exercise the power of review, which requires a judge to balance competing social and political interests in the context of the values of the legal system in the course of construing a constitution or bill of rights. Under apartheid, they have come to believe that deference to the will of the executive and legislature is a judicial virtue and that activism, courage, and creativity are not the attributes of a judge. Apart from one black man and one white woman, all are upper- and middle-class white males. Finally, the overwhelming majority were appointed in the apartheid era and have no enthusiasm for a new legal order.

There are three solutions to this problem. One is to entrust the new legal order to the old judiciary. How conservative judges of the *ancien régime* obstructed the reforms of the Weimar Republic is sufficient reminder of the perils of such a course. A second is to retire those judges considered unsuitable for office in a postapartheid society and to replace them with new judges appointed from the bar. The objection to this solution is that, given the fact that there are only three senior counsels of color and two women, the composition of the court is unlikely to change in representativeness or professional outlook. The third course is to encourage judges out of sympathy with the new order to retire, to appoint new judges from the bar to fill their places, and to create a special constitutional court, representative of the people of South Africa and intellectually qualified to exercise the power of review. This course has the support of the law commission, the ANC,[113] and, in all probability, the National party.[114]

The South African Law Commission considers the desirability of a constitutional court in its *Report on Constitutional Models of 1991*.[115] It concludes that a constitutional court should form part of the appellate division and that this division "should consist of two Chambers, namely a General Chamber and a Constitutional Chamber. The latter would deal with all issues arising from the bill of rights, the constitution and the field of administrative law."[116] In essence, the law commission favors the decentralized American model, which empowers all courts to entertain challenges to the constitutionality of a law, rather than the continental centralized system, which establishes a single court of judicial review to which all questions relating to the constitutionality of a law are referred. Consequently, the law commission proposes that the constitutional chamber would not have original jurisdiction but that each application would have to follow the normal course through the existing structure of the courts. The law commission also accepts that the present system of judicial appointments by the executive is inappropriate and recommends that judges should be appointed by a judicial service commission, comprising judges, lawyers, legislators, and the minister of justice. Judicial appointments will no longer be confined to practicing advocates: attorneys and academics will also be eligible for appointment.

The debate over a constitutional court is aimed as much at the restoration of judicial legitimacy as at the establishment of an appropriate review court. The major premise of this debate—often inarticulate—is the failure of the judiciary to promote racial equality and human rights during the bleak years of apartheid. This is a healthy and hopeful sign, as it evidences an awareness that the far-reaching powers of judicial review cannot simply be handed over to the existing judiciary. Whether a representative court with members not drawn exclusively from the bar can restore the reputation of the judiciary is a question that time alone can answer.

Rights, the Rule of Law, and the Legacy of Apartheid

There have been momentous changes in declared attitudes toward human rights in South Africa in recent years. No longer is the protection of human rights seen as a manifestation of sickly humanism, as an instrument of international communism, or as a bourgeois ideology. Instead, respect for human rights is seen as a necessary component of democratic society, which must be institutionalized in a bill of rights. Whether human rights are more secure in South Africa today than before February 1990 is another question. Discriminatory and repressive laws have been repealed, but political violence, unemployment, and increased crime and poverty have spawned new forms of human rights violations.

The harsh reality is that South Africa still has far to go before it can claim to be a society in which the rule of law prevails and human rights are respected. A bill of rights and a constitutional court exercising powers of judicial review are a significant start. But such institutions have failed in other countries. Why should it be different in South Africa? To this question, the optimist replies that there is a determination among leaders of all factions to build a new South Africa out of the ashes of apartheid and that this consensus provides a sound foundation on which to build. This may be so. But there is also a less hopeful reply. The necessary foundations for a society committed to human rights and the rule of law are absent. Until a rights culture is created and apartheid erased from our consciousness, there is no hope for such a society.

A handful of human rights lawyers, judges, and clergy is not enough to constitute a culture. Respect for human rights is not part of the popular consciousness of public life. Few political actors have committed themselves fully to this ideal. The ANC is still principally a liberation movement in which the struggle for power takes priority over its Constitutional Committee's commitment to constitutionalism. The rights policy of the Inkatha Freedom party is based primarily on the Second Amendment of the U.S. Constitution—which recognizes "the right of the people to keep and bear arms." Worse still, there is no evidence that the leopard has changed its spots—that the National party has really changed its attitude toward human rights. Its attempt in the closing days of the 1992 parliamentary session to introduce legislation on detention without trial[117] in the worst tradition of the apartheid era speaks for itself. Above all, there is little evidence that any of the three major political actors is prepared to abandon violence as a means to achieving or maintaining political power. Until violence is repudiated, there can be no real development of a rights culture.

Finally, the problem of apartheid remains. Most of its laws have been repealed. Government spokesmen describe it as a policy that failed, hence the preparedness to explore a new policy. There is no remorse, no acknowledgment (with the exception of a statement by Minister Leon Wessels) that apartheid was an offense to mankind, which, like slavery and Nazism, caused immeasurable suffering to millions in the name of "law." The National party is still unprepared to admit that apartheid was not merely a failed policy but an abomination, that its decrees were not law but an abuse of law. Many still feel no guilt over the wrong that has been perpetrated against South Africa and its people.

The ANC has announced that it is opposed to Nuremberg-type trials for the main exponents of apartheid. This does not mean that it condones apartheid. If the government itself does not denounce apartheid while it is yet in power, there are those who will surely do so when it is no longer in power. Whether this denunciation will take the form of Nuremberg trials or of a commission of inquiry into the crimes of apartheid along the lines of commissions established in Argentina, Uruguay, and Chile after military rule[118] remains to be seen. Until something of this kind is done, the legacy of apartheid will remain. South Africa cannot build a rights culture on this legacy, and without such a culture, a bill of rights, however skillfully fashioned, will not succeed.

9

What Is a Bill of Rights, And What Is It Good For?

Robert A. Goldwin

"What use then it may be asked can a bill of rights serve in popular governments?"[1] James Madison posed that question to himself and to Thomas Jefferson at the moment, in the year 1788, that both were contemplating the addition of a bill of rights to the new Constitution of the United States. Now, at this decisive moment in their history, when South Africans are being urged to write and adopt a new constitution and bill of rights, it is critically important to focus serious attention not only on the many answers being provided to Madison's question but also, and especially, on the question itself. Is it not remarkable that a man renowned for his devotion to the cause of the rights of the people, the architect of the Constitution of the United States of America and the chief author of its Bill of Rights, should have asked such a question, as if a staunch devotee of the rights of the people could have doubts about the beneficent nature of a bill of rights?

As good democrats, today we assume that a bill of rights is necessarily benign, and powerfully so. Madison made no such assumption. He saw a bill of rights as problematic, especially in a constitutional republic, and complained that the bills of rights of his time, for instance in his home state of Virginia, were least effective when they were most needed.[2] He never doubted that securing the rights of the people was the primary purpose of government, but he expressed doubt that a bill of rights was an efficacious instrument for

143

doing so. In this chapter, I propose to take seriously Madison's question and others suggested by it, to explore what a bill of rights is and what it is good for, what it can and cannot do, and what must be accomplished by other means to secure the fundamental rights of the people.[3]

Character and the Security of Rights

Statesmen and others concerned with good government have long been attentive to doctrines and institutions that improve the character of the people, striving to make citizens public-spirited and considerate of their fellow citizens. Ancient teachers of politics devoted themselves to the question of what virtue is and how to develop it in the political community. With the advent of modern political thought, however, political attention moved away from a fundamental concern with virtue toward an emphasis on liberty and the primacy of individual rights.

Even in a modern nation that devotes full attention to individual rights, though, virtue and the character of the people cannot be ignored. The connection of character with security of rights is obvious and direct: vicious people will not respect the rights of others unless they are strictly controlled by the superior force of authority. And if the authorities have enough power to restrain multitudes bent on using force to abuse the rights of others, the government is likely to become so powerful that the rights of the innocent may also be in jeopardy from the probable misuse of that power. Thus, rights are most secure among a people of good character, who defend their own rights and respect the rights of others, with little or no governmental compulsion.

If the government is to be limited in its power over the behavior of the people and restrained in its control over their thought, speech, writing, education, and religion—those things that have always been considered essential to the inculcation of citizen virtue—then control of behavior must be sought in some new way. This is one description of the turning point and essential difference between ancient and modern political thought and practice—the search for new ways to make individual liberty and public order compatible. It is also one way to describe the advent of modern constitutionalism.

Liberty and Restraint

The principal task of ancient political thought was to make good men, to make us better than we are. One would search classical political philosophy in vain for discussions of the protection of individual rights, although there was in those writings abundant condemnation of tyranny, cruelty, oppression, and all other forms of injustice. Justice was the central concern of ancient political thought, not liberty or rights. But once the political task was looked at in a new and different way, once the objective became to build a society fit for men as they really live, not as they should live,[4] politics was transformed. If, in addition, human beings are themselves seen as the natural source of all political power who can be governed by others only with their own freely given consent,[5] then the objectives of politics become something else entirely. It ceases to be a proper function of government to exercise control over our personal development to make us as good as we ought to be. The private realm thus comes into existence, and it becomes possible and true to say that some things, including some of the most important things, are none of the government's business.

The classical rule was, "Where the law is silent, there you are forbidden." We say to a child or to a soldier, "Who said you could do that?" implying that if one has not been given prior permission, that action is forbidden. But such a challenge is not acceptable to an adult civilian of a modern constitutional democracy. We need no permission; we are free to do whatever is not prohibited. The rule of modern liberal politics is, "Where the law is silent, there you are free."

One of the problems thus created by modern political thought is that individuals and groups within the political society are more at the mercy of other individuals and groups than they would be under a government that could and would intervene in what we now consider private affairs. The right to do whatever is not forbidden gives us more freedom to benefit ourselves as we see fit, but it also leaves others more free to harm us as they see fit, unless they are restrained. And to the extent that the government is called on to restrain them, the intrusive power of government increases, and our realm of privacy potentially diminishes.

Are there ways to secure our rights, both private and civil, that do not strengthen the government's power to tyrannize over us, that do not extend its reach into things that are not its business and thereby endanger what we seek to protect? That is the question the framers of the U.S. Constitution posed for themselves; their affirmative answer to the question is what they called "the new science of politics."[6]

That answer was a setting forth of effective ways of ordering political society and its institutions and constituting it in accord with certain fundamental principles. They contended that new ways had been developed to shape a society whose uncoerced citizens, taken as they are, not as they ought to be, would see that it was in their self-interest to conduct themselves in a civil manner, as self-restrained, civic-minded, public-spirited citizens behaved as of old, and all this consistent with effective, even energetic government. In short, they thought that sound popular government and individual liberty could coexist if the behavior of the citizenry was characterized by moderation. They proposed novel ways to achieve that moderation, without governmental efforts to influence behavior by indoctrination or regimentation. The connection between moderation and the security of rights is vital.

American voters were once encouraged by a presidential candidate to believe that "extremism in the defense of liberty is no vice, and moderation in the pursuit of justice is no virtue."[7] Nothing could be further from the thinking of the framers of the Constitution. If they were asked whether there are ever circumstances when extremism is not vice and moderation not virtue, they would have answered yes, but they would have described such circumstances along these lines: a revolutionary situation, a struggle against the tyranny of a dictatorial despot ruling without law, when *political* resolution of controversies is not possible and when physical safety can be defended only by force. The right to resist tyranny is a natural right acknowledged by Locke and enshrined as a basic American principle in the Declaration of Independence.[8] For citizens living under a constitution of limited government, however, whose offices are to be filled by candidates standing in a freely contested election, whose election results are determined by universal adult suffrage and immediately accepted as valid by the entire electorate, including especially the defeated candidates and their supporters, it is wildly untrue to argue that extremism is "no vice" and moderation "no virtue." In such a setting of civil institutions and practices for determining political leadership and national direction of policy, moderation in pursuit of justice—moderation in pursuit of anything—is virtue and no vice.

Some leaders of populist thought and action seek the euphoria of revolutionary principles, glorying in the blare of trumpets and the glare of fireworks, unwilling to accept fully the inglorious drudgery of establishing civil restraint and constitutional peace. While committed to the abstract principles of liberty and justice, unsullied by practice, they lack the same fervor for the constitutional institutions that embody those principles because, by necessity, they embody them imperfectly. This is moral greed, about which I have more to say.

Once the step was taken beyond the success of revolution to the more difficult task of embodying the principles of revolution into the structure and constitution of political society, new characteristics and new activities came to the fore. The fundamental principle, set down in the Declaration of Independence, was that no one can be governed justly without his own consent. The common aim of both the American Revolution and the Constitution of the United States was to secure the blessings of liberty, to protect the rights of individuals. The Constitution set out to do this by means of popular government, which necessarily led to political competition. Liberty and politics are inseparable, because when people are left free, they develop different interests and opposed opinions. But political competition means that there will be winners and losers, and where there are losers, there is danger to their rights. For just as powerful as the natural human inclination to assert and defend our rights is that opposed natural inclination to abuse the rights of others to advance our own interests, unless we are held back either by government or by inner restraints. What will the restraints be, and how will they be made strong enough to cope successfully with this powerful natural inclination?

Small-Group Loyalty and Divisiveness

With few exceptions throughout the world, modern democratic societies are heterogeneous, comprising peoples of different languages, religions, nationalities, and races. In this respect, South Africa is much like most other nations—typical, not atypical. Although the dominant community in international political life is the nation-state, experience almost everywhere in the world reveals that the most powerful human loyalties are to communities other than, and usually smaller than, the nation-state. Thus, we see in most nations not the "domestic tranquility" that the Preamble to the Constitution of the United States pledges to ensure but instead, almost everywhere, an intense domestic hostility—of Protestant and Catholic Irish, of Muslim and Christian Lebanese, of Jews and Palestinians in Israel, of white and black Americans, of Dutch-speaking and French-speaking Belgians, of Russians and non-Russians in the former Soviet Union, of English-speaking and French-speaking Canadians, of Hindu and Muslim Indians, of Castilian-speaking and Catalan-speaking Spaniards, of Sinhalese and Tamil Sri Lankans, of Malayan and Chinese Malaysians, and, of course, among the numerous tribal, racial, and language communities in South Africa.

This brief list of nations suffering internal discord and strife is incomplete, as every knowledgeable observer knows. This hostility *within* national boundaries is sometimes restrained and even civil, as for instance in Switzerland; sometimes violent, even lethal, as in Bosnia; but even when restrained, it is strongly felt and persistent. The primary fact is a powerful, natural, fraternal bond among persons of the same sect or tribe or nationality or language group; the secondary fact is that this bond has an opposing tendency, to exclude others—hence the hostility.

This small-group loyalty is one of the great facts of modern political life. It underlies much of the constitutional politics in every country, whether it is a government based on rights or some other form of rule.[9] Different nations seek to cope with the problem in different ways, but none can escape dealing with it, except that small number of nations whose populations are homogeneous. To think straight and usefully about how a nation's constitution deals with the relations of different groups in society, we must start with a clear recognition of the power and universality of this human sentiment of attachment to persons of one's own kind.

Only by keeping in mind the tremendous power of this human force can we truly appreciate the daring of the American constitutional attempt to combat it almost entirely by silence, by denying to it any constitutional legitimacy. Other constitutions acknowledge the existence of these groups, naming them, whether by language or religion or race, and granting to them certain assurances, benefits, guarantees, or preferences. These provisions sometimes assure one group or another that they will have a certain proportion of seats in the national legislature or that if the president is a member of one group, the prime minister will be a member of another group. Some provisions name certain groups and assure them that their language or their religious practices will be protected. By doing so, they seek to reassure the citizens who belong to these groups that they will be safe or that they will have a fair share in the political and economic life of the country. Unavoidably, however, such provisions set these groups apart from the rest of the citizenry, raise their separateness to a constitutional level, and emphasize, strengthen, and perpetuate the divisions within society.

Unlike the others, the Constitution of the United States lays the foundation for establishing one body politic in which no one is separated out, by making no mention of any group within the body of the people—no race, no language group, no religious sect, no nationality. (The only exception is American Indians, who are mentioned by name explicitly to exclude them from being counted for purposes of representation.)[10] There were, at the time of the founding, scores of religious sects in America, profoundly concerned for the safe perpetuation of their church. Some were concerned, rightly, for their physical safety; all were concerned for the protection of the religious practices most dear to them. None of these sects is named in the Constitution, nor are they, or *any* group, singled out for protection as a group.

Protections under the Constitution of the United States are for individual persons, and all persons are considered equally, no more nor less than any other. (I am speaking here about the text of the Constitution, not the American society, which practiced not only racial discrimination but also centuries of human slavery based on race and sanctioned by state constitutions and state laws. The American society has been powerfully influenced for the better by the nonracial character of the Constitution of the United States, especially in the past half-century, and yet is still not as good as the document that governs it.)

Contrary to frequent complaints that women were left out of the Constitution, a careful reading of the text reveals that it makes no distinction between men and women; there are no nouns or adjectives that refer to sex.[11] No distinction is made among different sects of Christians, nor among Christians, Jews, and Muslims. There is no mention of race or color; the words *black* or *white* do not occur. Although slavery existed for the Constitution's first seventy-five years, the word *slave* does not occur in the original Constitution, and where it is clear that slaves are being referred to by circumlocution, they are called, without exception, "persons."

The purpose seems to have been to combat the power of small-group loyalties and animosities by refusing to give them constitutional standing. The result sought was assimilation, a society in which no person is excluded, in which all persons are included indiscriminately on a basis of equality. One example is striking. Jews had not been full citizens of *any* nation *anywhere* in the world since the destruction of the Second Temple in 70 A.D. Full U.S. citizenship for Jews was accomplished in two ways. First is a simple negative: "No religious test shall ever be required as a qualification to any office or public trust under the United States."[12] Second, but much more sweeping in its scope and effect, Jews were simply not mentioned. Since there were several thousand Jews in North America at that time, many of them born there, when the Constitution was ratified in 1789, Jews became full citizens of a nation for the first time in more than 1,700 years. And it was accomplished by the method of meaningful silence.

This means of using silence to combat the divisive tendencies of human nature, the natural inclination of some groups not only to distinguish themselves from others, but to use the distinctions as grounds for abusing others and depriving them of their natural rights, is distinctive in the Constitution of the United States, a method too little noted probably because silence does not draw our attention. This silence is little appreciated even in the United States, where today it is under relentless attack by advocates of group rights and group preferences in education, in employment, and in society generally, with the predictable divisive effects that such policies of group preferences have had wherever they are practiced throughout the world.

Multiplicity of Interest

How are rights best protected? The answer today's American is most likely to give is, "By the Bill of Rights and an independent judiciary." I will examine this answer, but first it is important to observe that the question, What truly serves to protect our rights? is rarely asked today. For some reason it is not considered to require serious thought. In contrast, to James Madison it was a question of paramount importance, and some of his best writing, especially in *The Federalist*, was devoted to seeking answers to it. Much of the superficiality of human rights doctrine today and much of the futility of human rights activism are related to the failure to ask and to ponder this question seriously.

The Federalist was first published as a series of newspaper articles in 1787–1788 as part of the effort to win ratification of the new Constitution in the state of New York. It is a detailed commentary on the Constitution with one persistent theme: that the chief purpose of the government to be established under the Constitution is to secure the rights of the people. Jefferson wrote to Madison from Paris, where he was serving as the American minister, that in his opinion it was "the best commentary on the principles of government which ever was written."[13] And to this day, *The Federalist* is considered by many to be still, by far, the finest exposition of the Constitution of the United States. But as we read it, we must remind ourselves that at the time these papers were being written the Constitution did not contain the Bill of Rights; it was added in 1791, as the first ten "articles in addition to, and amendment of," the Constitution. Alexander Hamilton and Madison, therefore, in writing on this subject in *The Federalist*, could not have given the answer an American citizen is now likely to give. How was the argument made that the Constitution, without the Bill of Rights, secures the rights of the people?

In fact, in the body of the original Constitution the word *right* occurs only once, in the provision known as the copyright and patent clause. There it is clear that "the exclusive right" of authors and inventors to benefit from "their writings and discoveries" is not a natural or fundamental right; Congress is granted the power to secure the right, but it is secured only to the extent that Congress legislates to secure it.[14] In other words, the document that Madison and the other framers designed to protect the rights of the citizens did not even mention such rights, let alone guarantee their free exercise; instead they relied on a quite different approach.[15]

Madison's answer to the question of what truly protects rights follows from the principles of a properly constituted free society: that rights are primary and that the public good is best served by the habits developed by citizens exercising their rights in opposition to other citizens doing the same thing. "In a free government," Madison said,

> the security for civil rights must be the same as that for religious rights. It consists in the one case in the multiplicity of interests, and in the other in the multiplicity of sects. The degree of security in both cases will depend on the number of interests and sects.[16]

Madison later became the chief author of the First Amendment[17] and would today no doubt agree with us that it is a powerful force in protecting civil and religious rights. Yet I doubt that he would modify his argument that the more interest groups we have and the more religious sects we have, the more security there is for civil and religious liberty. A follower of Madisonian reasoning would contend that the First Amendment continues to be effective in protecting rights (though identical constitutional provisions have proved ineffective in other countries) in large part because of the multiplicity of American interest groups and religious sects. He would argue, for example, that one of the most important consequences of the First Amendment (especially the injunction against an established church combined with the protection of the free exercise of religion) has been its encouragement of the increase in the number of religious sects. And Madison would add that, even with the First Amendment as a valid addition to the Constitution, religious freedom would be in jeopardy in the United States, as in many other countries, if at some time *any* one religious sect became dominant.

Institutions established under the Constitution were designed to multiply the number of interests and allow them to assert themselves. The scheme of representation, for example, gives voice to a tremendous diversity of interests, giving them every chance to compete, as well as strong incentives to cooperate, and making it difficult, if not impossible, for one of them to dominate as a persisting majority. The federal structure, moreover, makes it possible to have republican government over an extended territory with greatly varied regional characteristics, which also adds to the multiplicity of economic interests.

There is little that is morally demanding in this formulation of how best to secure the rights of the people. Madison had no illusions, for instance, about disinterested congressmen with nothing in their minds and hearts but a patriotic concern for the common interest. We all know that it is wrong for any man to be the judge in his own cause, but, Madison asked, "What are the different classes of legislators but advocates and parties to the causes which they determine?"[18] From time to time, statesmen of moral excellence and religious conviction may appear on the scene, seeking to protect our rights rather than to promote their own advantage. When that happens, it is a benefit for which the community can be truly grateful, but we cannot rely on such appearances.

There is, in fact, the opposite assumption: that Americans, like human beings everywhere, are not angels and, when given the chance, they are likely to abuse others and violate their rights. The constitutional design, therefore, seeks to minimize the opportunities to tyrannize over others. Madison bluntly expressed his view of unrestrained human behavior: "Wherever there is an interest and power to do wrong, wrong will generally be done."[19] The *interest* to do wrong is ever-present in human nature and difficult, if not impossible, to eradicate, especially in a free society. The more sensible and effective constitutional task is to seek to make the interest ineffective by concentrating instead on eradicating, or at least minimizing, the power to do wrong. The Constitution addresses the problem of power by dispersing it in many hands at many levels, preventing that concentration of power necessary "to do wrong," no matter how intense and persistent the interest may be.

But even with the American devotion to the primacy of rights, the Constitution, the Bill of Rights, the separation of powers and federalism, and the multiplicity of interests and sects, the whole history of American legislation and litigation—federal, state, and local—has nevertheless been one long procession of groups and individuals struggling to deprive other groups and individuals of their rights. The best Americans can say for themselves, and it is indeed a lot to say, is that the principles, laws, and institutions are almost all arrayed on the side of securing rights and against the efforts to violate them. In that struggle, what Americans have been habituated to rely on is not a disinterested self-restraint but the energetic pursuit of self-interest by others, if they are equally free, and the clash of interests and ambitions where there are enough competitors and none with an overwhelming and persisting concentration of power. In this way, to use Madison's phrases, ambition counteracts ambition and "the private interest of every individual may be a sentinel over the public rights."[20]

The expectation is that the clash of interests and ambitions will be guided, constrained, and ultimately transformed by the regular procedural channels established by the Constitution for passing, executing, and interpreting the laws of the land. Those procedural pathways force some sort of mutual accommodation among the crudest forms of interest and ambition, and, as I have argued, over time such accommodation, compromise, and mutual consideration become habitual. The result is behavior perhaps distinguishable from, but nevertheless very similar to, that of restrained, considerate, public-spirited citizens. Thus moderate behavior is achieved without regimentation or indoctrination.

No American who loves liberty would be willing to repeal the First Amendment, but we should be clear that by itself it cannot protect our rights of religion, speech, press, assembly, and petition. The Soviet Constitution of 1977, to give only one example from scores of such constitutions, had a list of rights that included all those in the Bill of Rights and many more and in addition guaranteed those rights in a way that the American Constitution does not attempt. Yet we know that the exercise of the rights of religion, speech, press, petition, and assembly in the Soviet Union was insecure, if not nonexistent.

Words on paper cannot secure rights unless they are buttressed by a certain ordering of the institutions, the society, and the economy of the nation. The written constitution must correspond to the way the nation is truly constituted. If it does not, its protections of rights are a mere "parchment barrier,"[21] easily shredded by malevolent forces. In any nation with a concentration of economic and political power and little or no diversity of interests and religious sects, the most that can be hoped for in securing rights is the occasional concession in individual cases when, for one reason or another of policy, it suits the advantage of those in power to make those concessions. But there can be no internal basis for security of rights— and exhortation or moral fervor will be ineffective. Madison put the point this way: "We well know that neither moral nor religious motives can be relied on as an adequate control." He urged instead a "policy of supplying by opposite and rival interests, the defect of better motives."[22]

Making Rights Secure

The astonishing political developments of recent years in Eastern Europe and the former Soviet Union, as well as the different kind of changes in South Africa, demonstrate dramatically how strong the longing is for political freedom and how well human beings know, in their hearts, the old self-evident truth that we are all equal in our fundamental rights. But these same developments have also shown once again what history has taught repeatedly: it is one thing to overthrow despotic rule in the name of the rights of the people and quite another to succeed in replacing it with a constitutional government capable of making those rights secure. That constitutional effort has been successful in only a few nations, and usually only after long and painful struggles.

It is not an easy matter to answer the question, What truly secures rights? By way of answer, I cite one of the most successful efforts at securing rights, that is, the addition of the Bill of Rights to the Constitution of the United States. The true story of the writing of the American Bill of Rights is not inspiring, romantic, or morally elevating, but it is instructive for anyone faced with the task of constitution building.

As is well known, the Constitution of the United States was written and ratified without a bill of rights. This was not an oversight; that there should be a bill of rights was proposed, debated, and voted on in the Constitutional Convention; it was voted down, after deliberation, by an overwhelming majority of the delegates, in fact, by unanimous vote of the participating states. But as soon as the convention was over, agitation for a bill of rights began and support for amendments grew stronger, so that as the ratification process moved from state to state, the voting became closer and closer, putting ratification by the required number of states in danger.

The opponents of the proposed Constitution, the Anti-Federalists, sought to prevent ratification and to convene a new convention to write a quite different constitution. Short of that goal, the Anti-Federalists' fallback position was to demand numerous amendments as a prior condition of ratification. They did not prevail in any state in winning these prior amendments, but in several state conventions they did win the concession that their recommended amendments would be considered after ratification, by the First Congress, by subsequent amendment rather than prior amendment. In the Virginia convention, ratification was won by Madison and his fellow Federalists only by pledging to support such amendments, and Madison was later elected to Congress, again only after making that pledge as part of his election campaign.

More than a hundred amendments had been proposed in the several state ratifying conventions, but they broke down into two categories: structural amendments and protections of individual rights. The Anti-Federalist leaders were much more interested in the structural articles—to take away from Congress several essential powers and assign them to the states: the power to levy direct taxes, to control elections, and to establish a standing army. They also sought to eliminate all the federal judiciary except the Supreme Court and the courts of admiralty. In short, their chief concern was the allocation of powers in the federal system because of their suspicion that a powerful general government would be a threat to the liberty and rights of the people.

Madison, without the benefit of modern public opinion surveys but with an abundance of the skills of an expert and experienced politician, sensed that the widespread popular support the Anti-Federalists enjoyed, not a majority but a significant minority, was linked to the proposed articles to protect rights, not to the articles that would alter the structure of the government. And so he devised a strategy that protected the new Constitution from structural amendments while at the same stealing away the Anti-Federalists' popular following.

When the First Congress gathered, Madison proposed in the House of Representatives, against almost universal opposition, a set of amendments that were substantively very close to the Bill of Rights as we now know it in its final form. He was opposed by the Anti-Federalists because, they said, he left out all of what they considered the most important amendments. He was also opposed by the Federalists, his own colleagues, supporters of the Constitution, because they saw no point in making concessions to the Anti-Federalist minority when they had an overwhelming majority in Congress. But Madison had his reasons, on at least two levels. The first level was masterful democratic politics. By moving his amendments, he won over most of the remaining dissidents, those honest citizens who were uneasy about this powerful new constitutional government with so many strange innovations. As soon as his speech proposing the amendments was published in the newspapers, doubts and fears were eradicated, and all the popular support for a second convention to write a different constitution melted away. In this way, Madison thwarted the Anti-Federalist movement and kept out of the Constitution amendments that would have weakened the powers of the Union. When Madison was finished with them, the Anti-Federalist leaders were left at the head of a movement without followers.

More interesting today for anyone involved in constituting or

155

reconstituting a nation that will provide security for the rights of all the people is the second level of Madison's reasoning. Madison was a dedicated advocate of popular government, of rule by the majority, who also saw clear dangers in majority rule that had to be acknowledged, faced up to, and coped with.

The greatest potential danger to the rights of the people in any political society, he argued, always stems from the most powerful force in that society. In a monarchy, the most powerful force, and therefore the most dangerous, is the king; in a representative republic, the most powerful force is the majority of the people, and therefore a bad majority, inclined to oppress the minority, poses the greatest threat to the safety of the rights of the people.

In a republic, what can stop the majority? That is, where the majority rules, how can a malevolent majority, determined to oppress the minority and deprive them of their rights, be restrained? All the "auxiliary precautions" for which Madison is so well known—separation of powers, extended territory, multiplicity of interests, a federal structure, a bicameral legislature, even ambition counteracting ambition—are designed to prevent the formation of such an oppressive majority or to restrain it should it develop.

Madison's own response, which he characterized as the true principle of republican government, was that in a properly constituted republic, governed ultimately by public opinion, something must be more powerful than the majority of the moment, something persistent, pervasive, and transcendent. That something, he insisted, must be an almost universal allegiance to the constitution. When he realized, therefore, that the opposition of a significant minority of honest citizens could be converted to allegiance to the Constitution simply by reassuring them that their rights would be secure, Madison became the chief advocate of a bill of rights that he himself would compose. For he saw that winning over the popular opposition to the side of the Constitution was an extraordinarily powerful means of restraining an otherwise unstoppable oppressive majority. That is, he saw that a constitution, unlike ordinary legislation, must have the support of more than a majority; it must have the support, in his words, of "the great mass of the people." Only with the support of just about everyone can a bill of rights be effective in restraining an oppressive majority.

Consider, for example, the first words of the Bill of Rights, that "Congress shall make no law" to do certain things, such as "abridging the freedom of speech, or of the press." What can it mean, in the constitution of a republic, ruled in all things, ultimately, by the voice of the majority, to have a negative command such as this, that there are some things the majority shall not do? Who or what is to stop them? Madison saw that the answer has to be everybody, the great mass of the people.

For if the First Amendment means anything, it means that even if a clear majority of the citizens (acting through their representatives in Congress) vote to silence the objectionable speech of some lowly, impotent, obnoxious person, they *all* say (through their allegiance to the Constitution and their acceptance of Supreme Court decisions) that such a law is constitutionally invalid and shall not be enforced. A democratic constitution that hopes to protect the rights of the people, in short, needs more than majority support; it will be effective in securing rights against an oppressive majority only if it has universal support. And so when Madison presented his proposed amendments to the House of Representatives, the chief reasons he gave were that they would do no harm (since he had blocked all the structural amendments that the Anti-Federalists had proposed) and that they would win the allegiance to the Constitution of the great mass of the people.

Madison did not think that his amendments, explicitly addressed to such fundamental rights as freedom of religion, speech, press, and peaceable assembly, could, in themselves, secure rights. The real basis of security for the rights of the people is a sound constitution built on sturdy principles that include separation of powers, federalism, checks and balances, an extended territory, a diverse society and economy with a multiplicity of interests, and energy in all parts of the government; but to be effective and sustainable over a long time, a constitution must be universally respected.

Alexander Hamilton had argued that the original Constitution was itself a bill of rights and therefore it was superfluous, at the least, to add a bill of rights to it.[23] In none of Madison's set speeches and arguments in the debates in the First Congress that resulted in the addition of the Bill of Rights did he express disagreement with Hamilton's formulation. But Madison saw that a bill of rights was the best means of winning the allegiance of all the people and was therefore a powerful instrument for curbing an ill-intentioned majority.

All this, in my opinion, is consistent with the contention that only because the original Constitution provided the real basis for securing rights has the Bill of Rights appended to it been at all effective.

Denials of Power

Given the many incidents of domestic violence the world has experienced in recent decades, no one needs to be reminded that the cause

157

of civil rights has enemies in this world, bloody-minded and bloody-handed enemies who persecute, kidnap, torture, maim, and slaughter their victims, most of whom have committed no offense greater than trying to exercise the natural rights of all men and women to live a productive, private, decent life.

When we look at the human rights situation throughout the world, we must admit it presents a dismal picture. Few bright spots or signs of improvement are evident, despite worldwide efforts by governments, the private sector, research institutes, international organizations, innumerable conferences, and a flood of publications. In many places, now including South Africa, great emphasis is placed on enacting into law a sweeping and extensive bill of rights to provide what is thought will be effective protection of a long and even comprehensive list of the rights of the people. And yet the efforts prove mostly ineffectual. We must conclude that the policy approach is wrong or our understanding of the task is faulty—or both. Why is it so difficult to protect the rights of the people? What are the advocates of rights doing wrong? What could be done to be more effective?

Thinking about securing rights must always start with the most basic aspects of human life. We must all breathe, eat, drink, and work in order to live, and we must do these in a certain way in order to live well. Advocates of the so-called second- and third-generation rights consider it important to label these necessities as rights. Such a bill of rights goes beyond the standard civil and legal rights and proceeds to enumerate not only the right to a job at a living wage for everyone but also the rights to, for example, clean air, an adequate diet, and unpolluted water. These rights have been included in many national and international documents as the newest generations of rights and are not included in the old American documents such as the Declaration of Independence, state constitutions, and the Constitution of the United States. Those who have great faith in the efficacy of declarations or bills of rights, and rely on them more than on constitutional arrangements for the security of rights, strongly advocate enumeration of these new rights and many more.

The starting point of all natural-rights teaching, beginning more than three hundred years ago in the writings of Thomas Hobbes and John Locke, is that all human beings, either because of the fear of violent death or because of the strong desire for self-preservation, know that they have the right to life and to the means necessary to sustain it. That right, asserted in the Declaration of Independence, is enshrined as fundamental law in the Constitution's Fifth Amendment ("No person shall . . . be deprived of life, liberty, or property without due process of law") and is extended in the Fourteenth Amendment ("nor shall any State deprive any person of life, liberty, or property, without due process of law"). We weaken the protection of fundamental rights by adding to legal documents a long list of second- and third-generation rights. I see two dangers immediately apparent in the codification of such a list: first, it can give a false sense that asserting the rights in some way addresses such problems as obtaining adequate food, potable water, clean air, and gainful work; second, it can have the effect of increasing the power of government agencies in new and unwelcome ways.

Declaring the right to an adequate diet does not increase the supply of food or improve its distribution. If we think of the plight of desperate peoples in many parts of Africa, with hundreds of thousands dying of malnutrition as the result of the combination of drought, corruption, and intertribal civil warfare, how does it help to insist that these people have the right to an adequate diet? The problem is not whether they have the right but how to get food to them, how to correct the problems that led to the lack of food, and how to restore some semblance of domestic order and reestablish government capable of putting their agricultural production and distribution on a sounder footing. Can we take seriously the contention that the way to deal with the violence, hatred, corruption, and incompetence that are causing the mass starvation is to declare in a bill of rights that every person has the right to an adequate diet?

There is, second, a threat to the security of rights resulting from adding to the powers of government. It is common for Americans to speak of their constitutional guarantees of rights, but, as a matter of fact, none are guaranteed. The First Amendment rights, for example, are spoken of as preexisting; the security they have is that "Congress shall make no law" to abridge or prohibit their exercise. The formulation is negative, a restraint on the government, a *denial* of power. The positive formulation found in many other present-day constitutions, in which the government guarantees a long list of rights, *adds* to the power of government, authorizing it to act in an area forbidden by the American Bill of Rights. Where the state guarantees freedom of the press, the first action, typically, is to establish a government agency to ensure that the press remains "free," by putting it under government supervision and regulating its daily operations.

The strategy of the Constitution of the United States is to rely on denials of governmental power and to avoid additions of governmental power over rights. The word *guarantee* does not occur anywhere in the Constitution in regard to rights, but only in the aptly

159

named "guarantee clause": "The United States shall guarantee to every State in this Union a Republican form of government."[24]

There is a real danger in enumerating a long list of affirmative rights, and the danger is intensified if the rights are guaranteed. If the guarantees to the rights to education, housing, and jobs, for instance, are taken seriously, the state will almost inevitably end up supervising and controlling most, if not all, of the system of education, construction and allocation of housing, and the employment market. In many countries, one effect of a long and detailed bill of rights has been that the government became the sole schoolmaster, landlord, and employer. These state monopolies are a harsh reality for the citizenry; they represent a frightening concentration of power. If, in addition, the list is extended to guarantee everyone's right to health care, paid vacations in government-owned resorts, summer camps for children, retirement pensions, funeral benefits, and such, as was done under many Communist constitutions, the government can come to control almost every aspect, the totality, of life—which is what we mean when we speak of a regime as totalitarian. For this reason, the accretion of power rather than the denial of power, rights are more secure where the constitutional list is short, negative, and free of guarantees.

The cause of protecting the rights of the people would be greatly strengthened if we understood better that a bill of rights is an integral part of a constitution, not something that stands well alone. The American Bill of Rights is a set of ten articles appended to the Constitution; the human rights provisions in the United Nations Charter are in the preamble and three articles of a document of well over one hundred articles. Each is part of a document that establishes institutions and assigns and limits responsibilities and powers. The extent to which they work well is a direct consequence of the soundness and efficacy of the constituting document to which they are appended.

The Bill of Rights added to but did not alter the original Constitution. In the First Congress, both those who voted for the amendments and those who voted against them agreed that these amendments changed nothing, which was why one side voted for them and the other voted against them. The majority, the supporters of the Constitution, held that the Constitution did not need to be changed because it already constituted the nation in such a way that the rights of the people were secured. But they were willing to vote for additional articles that did no harm to the structure of the Constitution and at the same time blocked the passage of other amendments that would alter the structure. In short, the authors of the Bill of Rights understood the body of the Constitution to be the real instrument for securing the rights of the people.

Now many Americans take the body of the Constitution too much for granted and speak about the Bill of Rights as if it were the Constitution.[25] Harm is done thereby, but not as much as would be the case if the institutional arrangements established by the Constitution were not in place, functioning and jealously guarded.

It is otherwise where constitutions are weak or badly drawn and where enumerations of rights are lengthy, affirmative, and guaranteed. There great harm is done by talking about declarations of rights as if they were self-sufficient and self-activating, which they are not. It is but another example of a curious faith in the magical power of words, a false reliance that distracts our attention from the real dangers and the real remedies and can add only frustration, disappointment, and bitterness to the suffering that we seek to diminish.

The Dark Side of Human Rights

This leads me to my final difficulty with the arguments of those who assume that any bill of rights is benign, especially one setting forth a long list abounding in affirmative guarantees of many generations of rights. They seem to ignore what might be called the dark side of human rights. It is not true that human rights teachings come from our religious heritage; if I am not mistaken, no passage in the Bible speaks of rights. The reader of the Bible is instructed in duties, not rights. Jefferson knew that it was not necessary to connect religion and rights; he was able to speak of the self-evident truth of the equality of men in their rights without referring to a divine source. All the prayerful phrases in the Declaration of Independence—"endowed by their Creator," "appealing to the Supreme Judge of the world," and "with a firm reliance on the Protection of Divine Providence"—were absent in Jefferson's original draft but were added by committee, after the argument of the Declaration was complete.[26] Rights and religion can be made compatible, but one is not the source of the other.

There is also reason to doubt the connection of rights and morality. The authors of the great works of ancient classical political philosophy, especially Plato and Aristotle, wrote lengthy and profound works on the subjects of ethics and politics but never wrote about natural rights. John Locke, in contrast, writing near the end of the seventeenth century, based his teachings about the origin, extent, and end of civil government on the primacy of rights. His other works—on philosophy, psychology, economics, theology, and education—abound in discussions of morality. But in his principal work on politics, the word *morality*, or anything like it, does not occur. Locke's *Two Treatises of Government*, one of the chief sources of the doctrines of political liberty for the American founders, is the first significant writing to set forth a comprehensive account of political society that does not include a discussion of justice. Natural rights displaced and replaced the word *justice*.

In Locke's writings, the most influential of the teachings of the political primacy of individual rights, rights derive naturally from the powerful human desire for self-preservation. It is self-evident that we have a right to do what we can to preserve ourselves; we *know* we have a right to life. We have a right, therefore, to actions that defend our life—a right to liberty. We also have a right to those things necessary to sustain and nourish ourselves—a right to property. Our awareness of these rights to life, liberty, and property—their self-evidence—is strong, natural, and innate and requires no instruction.

The exercise of these rights in society with other human beings, however, leads to difficulties, because we come into conflict and competition as we exercise our rights. It becomes clear, to some at least, that the ability to enjoy my rights depends to a great extent on protecting your rights and the rights of all others. That consequence of natural rights is obviously not clear to all of us, however, and does require instruction, and much more than instruction: it requires rules, commands, judgment, and enforcement. What comes naturally does not suffice; we need to be taught, as Locke put it, that "where there is no law, there is no freedom"—and that has not been an easy or natural lesson for mankind.

To make it easier to accept this unnatural outcome of natural-rights teaching, we acknowledge powers exerted over us as legitimate, as political rather than dictatorial, but only if those powers derive from our own consent. There are some things it is assumed we will not consent to. That is the meaning of the opening words of the American Bill of Rights; even if a majority of Congress, truly representing a majority of the people, wants to abridge the freedom of speech or prohibit the free exercise of religion, nevertheless "Congress shall make no law" of that sort. If the government should use its power to prohibit the free exercise of religion, that would not be a constitutional use of political power but an exercise of dictatorial power, not legitimized by the Constitution, not "just powers" because not derived "from the consent of the governed."

In extolling the importance of individual rights, we must realize that they stem from a political teaching based on strife and harsh competition, with pain, suffering, deprivation, and misery often resulting. A nation whose political scheme is based on the primacy of individual rights is one of confusion, turmoil, and ferment—and, unavoidably, more than a little injustice. It is not a design for calm and harmony in national life. It is a design for a stormy, tumultuous, and chaotic peace, but one we can nevertheless readily consent to.

Most human beings throughout the world and throughout history have never had the chance to live under a government they would or could consent to. Their choice has been limited to resistance or submission. In despotic societies, human rights have no standing, no matter what deceptive rhetoric is used. In such a society, if one is fortunate enough to be given a public trial or is interrogated without torture or is allowed to emigrate, such generous treatment is not a matter of right but only of policy, a gift or privilege bestowed by the state. For that reason, the protests by human rights activists of abuses of the rights of individuals in despotic societies have no general or lasting effect.

Some think it sullies the ideals of political liberty and human rights to acknowledge their dark and lowly origins, but this is a shallow view. It is one of the greatest ironies of the human condition that, on the one hand, despicable tyrannies—the fundamentalist Ayatollah Khomeini's Iran being only one of the most recent examples—are often born of lofty ideals, like the love of God, which become corrupted, distorted, and unrecognizably disfigured and that, on the other hand, the greatest modern political achievement, a government of sustained, ordered liberty, an inspiration to humankind for centuries, is born of the basic human desire for self-preservation and the fierce determination—natural in us all—to be independent and look out for ourselves.

Independence and individualism can be nurtured as well as governed in a skillfully constituted society and, at the same time, can be shaped and expanded to inculcate in the citizenry a reasoned concern for the well-being and freedom of others. We can be prouder of the system of liberty, and better able to expand and continue it, if we understand its lowly origin. It is not unknown in nature, after all, for ugly parents to give birth to a beautiful child. And as the historian W. E. H. Lecky has written, "That vice has often proved an emancipator of the mind is one of the most humiliating, but, at the same time, one of the most unquestionable facts in history."[27]

The vice of greed is not limited to material things. There is also what might be called moral greed, and its effects can be deadly, fatal to liberty, decency, self-restraint, and moderation. The alternative to the greedy pursuit of an unearthly perfection of protection of every right the modern imagination can generate for every person is a willingness to accept imperfection—because this earth is imperfect. We human beings are imperfect, and imperfection, incompleteness, and partial success mixed with partial failure are our proper lot in this earthly life.

Moral greed is one vice the authors of the Constitution of the United States did not suffer from or suffer in others. Their whole founding effort was a rejection of that vice and a search, instead, for principles and institutions that would build, as much as possible, on human frailties—frailties they thought were so prevalent that one might better turn them to the benefit of mankind rather than try to eradicate them. They knew from careful study of history and reflection on human nature that human weaknesses such as selfishness, cruelty, and greed can be totally eradicated only by suppressing all freedom and perhaps even eradicating great numbers of unoffending people. Instead of seeking to establish a heaven on earth, they sought to make life freer, more decent, more comfortable, more prosperous, safer, and, for most people, happier.

What, then, in sum, can be said about present-day novelties in the effort to secure rights? We can say that the demand for long lists of new economic and social rights is misguided and, by adding unnecessarily to the powers of government, will probably do more harm than good; that the emphasis on declarations of rights rather than on constitutions means focusing on the appendage rather than on the core of the problem; that we would do better in securing the rights of the people if we understood better what rights are and where they come from; and that we can benefit by a closer look at how rights are secured in those few nations that do the job relatively well.

The Constitution of the United States acknowledges the claim for protection of the rights of life, liberty, property, free speech, free press, free exercise of religion, peaceable assembly, petition, habeas corpus, public trial, and legal counsel; it prohibits self-incrimination, cruel and unusual punishments, *ex post facto* laws, and bills of attainder. Just as important for the security of rights, it also provides for the separation of powers, which prevents a concentration of power; a federal structure, which makes possible democratic government over an extended territory; a bicameral legislature, which promotes checks and balances and greater deliberation in the legislative process; an independent judiciary, to serve as a check on legislative or executive excesses; free, fair, and frequent elections; and all this designed to encourage a multiplicity of interests, in the end the best security for the rights of the people.

When we think of the millions of our fellow human beings who

164

suffer from officially sanctioned murders, kidnappings, torture, imprisonment without trial, secret trials, thought control, censorship, confiscation of property, and impoverishing economic deprivation, the task is clear for those who uphold the cause of human rights. How many ills of the world, how many crimes against the people would we not eradicate if these rights were established and enforced around the world? Does not securing these old rights take priority over the promulgation of scores of dubious, albeit fashionable, new generations of rights?

The most effective form the effort to secure the great rights of mankind could take in any country, and certainly in South Africa, would be a program that gives the highest priority to inculcating constitutionalism, rather than concentrating on the composition of a bill of rights, especially one that is expected to stand on its own. The reason should be evident. Rights are not perfectly secure anywhere, but they are relatively secure in countries so constituted that the powers of the government are both effective and effectively limited. If the government and the society are constituted in the right way, that is, with effective governmental powers and effective limits on those powers built into the constitutional scheme, rights will have a fighting chance—with or without a bill of rights. If the society and the government are badly constituted, with a maldistribution of powers or a concentration of unlimited or ineffectually limited powers, rights will be in constant jeopardy—with or without a bill of rights. The cause of constitutionalism and the cause of the rights of the people are but two names for the same thing.

10

Strengths and Limitations of a New National Government

Gretchen Carpenter

For many years the accent in South Africa has been on the supposed virtues of strong government, almost as if strong government and limited government were mutually exclusive. It is often said that one advantage of the Westminster system of government, which South Africa inherited from Britain, is its tendency to strong government. In keeping with this objective of strong government, the emphasis in South Africa has been on law and order rather than on justice, on effective government rather than on constitutionalism. (This is not to deny the value of law and order or of effective government by any means: it is a truism that order may be achieved without justice but that justice is impossible without order.)

The Westminster system was transplanted with some variations to virtually all the former British colonies when they became independent. The majoritarian structure of the system, coupled with the preeminence accorded to the will of Parliament, however, has not proved conducive to the growth of democracy in many of those former colonies. The majoritarianism and the parliamentary sovereignty took root, but the nuances and subtleties that mitigate the exercise of power in Britain were left behind. A system in which it is recognized that all governmental power needs to be limited and contained, no matter how democratically elected and legitimate the government, would appear to present a better solution. This is particularly true of states that cannot boast a centuries-old tradition of democracy. Even Britain's own unique brand of democracy is increasingly being weighed on the European scale and found wanting.

Modern constitutional thinking has progressed beyond the stage where governments have been invested with biblical powers; legitimate criticism of one's government is no longer seen as sinful at worst and unpatriotic at best (at any rate in more sophisticated societies able to distinguish between loyalty to the state and blind acceptance of the policies of the government of the day). It is recognized that there is a need for order and government in all societies, that the persons who exercise the powers of government should be authorized to do so by those whom they govern, but that these governors, being fallible human beings and therefore prone to folly, corruption, and the hunger for power, should also be subject to legal limits. The presence of restraints provides a more effective guarantee of good government than do traditional democratic measures such as periodic elections alone, for the simple reason that prevention is better than cure. Even more important, it has come to be realized that the imposition of constitutional restraints does not render a government powerless to act. Strong government is not irreconcilable with limited government: the limits merely ensure the proper exercise of government power.

Constitutional limits on governmental power can be imposed in a number of ways. The first and most fundamental of these is to be found in the institution of a representative legislature. The concept of representativeness implies, at the least, universal adult suffrage; free and periodic elections, with special measures to ensure that the voters are able to make an informed choice, as well as measures to prevent the intimidation and undue influencing of voters;[1] and, arguably, a system of representation that accurately reflects voter opinion.[2] Further refinements may be provided by the requirement of special majorities for certain categories of legislation or by the institution of a second legislative chamber; the latter possibility is discussed below.

A second constitutional principle, which is almost as universally revered, is the doctrine that the powers of government must be divided among the legislature, executive, and judiciary. The original doctrine, as espoused by Montesquieu and by John Locke before him, has been subjected to much adaptation, criticism, and analysis; the separation of powers also receives further attention presently.

The decentralization of power, whether in the form of full-blown federalism or in that of a system of more limited regional autonomy, is another potential means of diluting, if not invariably restraining, government power. This is one of the most vexed issues facing the framers of the new South African constitution. Because this is discussed elsewhere in this volume, I will not deal with this matter, except to say that there is general consensus among constitutional lawyers that some devolution or dispersal of political power is essential to the achievement of democratic government.

Justiciable declarations of human rights have become the vogue in recent decades. It is virtually inconceivable that any new constitution framed in the world today would not contain such an instrument. If nothing else, this is living proof of the confidence universally held in a bill of rights as the most effective means of protecting the individual citizens against both legislative and executive excesses. Certainly no bill of rights can claim unqualified success, but given the frailty of all human institutions, it outperforms the other available options for the protection of human rights. This issue is also dealt with elsewhere in this volume.

The specific issues addressed in this chapter are the following: First, should the powers of government be separated? Second, should the legislature be unicameral or bicameral? Third, what should the powers of the executive be?

Should the Powers of Government Be Separated?

Development of the Doctrine of Separation of Powers and Its Current Meaning. The French philosopher Montesquieu is usually regarded as the father of the doctrine of the separation of powers, but his work *L'Esprit des Lois* (1748) was based to a major extent on John Locke's *Treatise of Civil Government*, which appeared some fifty years earlier (in 1690).[3] While Locke had classified government functions as legislation, executive function (including the administration of justice), and the conduct of foreign relations, Montesquieu was responsible for the tripartite classification that has survived until today, namely, into the legislative, executive, and judicial branches of government. Just what Montesquieu understood by the separation of powers is not clear: apparently, his concept of the application of the doctrine in Britain may have been somewhat optimistic. His teachings nevertheless exerted an enormous influence on the framers of the American Constitution, with the result that there is a far greater degree of separation in the United States than in Britain and in countries such as South Africa, which followed the Westminster model closely in this regard.

It is generally taken for granted that some degree of separation of government powers is desirable not only to promote greater efficiency but also to prevent the excessive concentration of power in a single person or body. There is, however, considerable difference of opinion about the extent to which the separation of powers can limit government authority effectively.[4] (Little has been written about the doctrine in South Africa and even for that matter in Britain; in the United States, by contrast, entire volumes are devoted to the topic.)

While it must be conceded that, in the words of British writer Geoffrey Marshall, the concept of separation of powers is "notoriously susceptible to a variety of meanings,"[5] the current view is that the doctrine may imply the following: first, the formal division of state authority among the legislative, executive, and judiciary; second, the separation of personnel, so that one person or organ should not simultaneously perform in more than one branch of government; third, a separation of function so that one branch of government cannot usurp the functions and powers of another; and fourth, the principle of checks and balances, with each branch of government given specific powers to restrain the other branches and thus to achieve the desired equilibrium among the three components of government authority. The presence of checks and balances is a cardinal feature of the American constitutional system. The phrase *separation of powers* can also refer to the separation between the powers of the central government and the federal governments in a federation, but this is not the sense in which it is used here.

Even in the United States, there is no wholly consistent theory applied to cases of the separation of powers. The courts have, in recent years, moved from a formalist to a more functionalist approach.[6] The formalist approach emphasizes the demarcation of government powers and functions rather than the control that one branch of government may exercise over another. Undoubtedly, a rigid, or formalistic, division of powers reduces flexibility and, moreover, is neither essential nor even conducive to the curtailment of excessive government power. The idea of checks and balances is logically incompatible with an extreme interpretation of the concept of separation of powers. Conversely, the ideal of limited government is unattainable unless there is some measure of control by one organ of government over another. It would be difficult, if not impossible, to exercise effective control over three hermetically sealed organs of government functioning in total isolation from one another. The functionalist approach, therefore, appears to be a better option, even though it leads, according to Michael Yoder,[7] to judicial activism and to uncertainty.

Although the debate over the separation of powers has not been finally settled, a number of basic principles enjoy universal acceptance: the legislature should not be empowered to administer laws or to exercise judicial powers (except for internal disciplinary action, with legislation governing parliamentary privilege); the executive should not have legislative powers (except as specifically delegated by the legislature) or perform judicial functions; finally, the judiciary should not usurp the authority of either the legislature or the executive. But this is nothing more than a starting point, since a certain degree of multifunctionalism in government is inevitable and is, moreover, an essential element of the idea of checks and balances. Perhaps the somewhat simplistic rules stated above can be qualified by emphasizing that each of the three branches of government has certain primary functions. The relationships between the branches must be examined more closely.

Relationship between Legislature and Executive. It is a cardinal feature of the Westminster system that the members of the executive are also members of the legislature.[8] The rationale behind this arrangement is to ensure parliamentary control over the ministry. In theory, the members of the executive, being at the same time members of the legislature, are directly responsible to the legislature as a whole. But as we have seen in South Africa, this control is an illusion, particularly where the governing party in Parliament enjoys a large numerical majority. In most cases, the executive is directly responsible to the majority party in the legislature.

The principle that the legislature should be solely elected and that the executive should have no power to appoint any member of the legislature hardly needs argument. The appointment of an admittedly small number of members of Parliament by the state president under the 1983 constitution has understandably elicited criticism for this reason.[9] Likewise, the executive should have no power to convene or prorogue the legislature or to make decisions affecting the salaries, pensions, or tenures of the members of the legislature.

Since the state's revenue is in the hands of the legislature, the executive must answer fully to the legislature about any funds made available to it. To tolerate secret funds is to court corruption.

The phenomenon of delegated legislation is something to which careful attention must be given. It must be accepted that the conferment of some legislative powers on the executive is necessary. In many cases, the officials responsible for the drafting of subordinate legislation are the ones with the expertise needed to determine what is desirable or expedient. In any case, it is simply not practicable to burden the central legislature with every legislative measure imaginable. Certainly, it is not possible to run a modern state without making provision for delegated legislation.

The proliferation of measures whereby wide legislative powers are conferred on the executive is, however, cause for concern. In South Africa, we have seen this manifested in the emergency regulations promulgated in recent years. The Public Safety Act 3 of 1953 empowers the state president, acting in consultation with members of the cabinet, to exercise a subjectively worded discretion and to proclaim a state of emergency if he is of the opinion that the normal laws of the land cannot control a situation and to promulgate emergency regulations that may validly exclude the operation of the rules of natural justice and even oust the jurisdiction of the courts altogether. It is true that the courts have, in general, been reluctant to accept the intention to exclude the rules and to oust the courts,[10] but control over the exercise of emergency powers is slight.

Effective control over the exercise of delegated legislative powers is essential. Proper parliamentary control is the first of these: the delegated powers should be carefully circumscribed in the enabling legislation, and all such legislation should be tabled in Parliament, at the least. This procedure, at least, informs Parliament about the content of the legislation, even though it can hardly be said to constitute control.

There could also be a requirement that certain classes of subordinate legislation (by local and regional governments) must be ratified by Parliament or perhaps by a parliamentary committee. Furthermore, the authority delegated to subordinate legislatures should be carefully circumscribed and not couched in vague and general terms, particularly when individual rights and freedoms could be affected. The so-called Henry VIII clause (legislation that confers such wide powers on a subordinate legislature that even parliamentary legislation can be overruled or amended) is wholly unacceptable.[11] The members of the national legislature should take their responsibility in this regard seriously and ensure that adequate safeguards are built into the enabling statute and that they perform their control function meticulously. Finally, the requirement of publication and of notice and comment procedures may also serve an important control function by subjecting subordinate legislation to the scrutiny of public opinion.[12]

Relationship of the Legislature to the Executive and to the Judiciary. Legislative supremacy is perhaps the most striking feature of the Westminster system and, barring a few aberrations from the classical model, of the present South African system of government as well.[13]

For many years, the thought of substantive judicial review of legislation was anathema to the South African government. The main reasons given were that we have a tradition of parliamentary sovereignty, that a system of judicial supremacy is essentially undemocratic insofar as it negates the will of the people as represented in Parliament, and that a system of judicial supremacy would politicize the judiciary.[14] It is now generally accepted, however, that a supreme constitution with a judicially enforceable bill of fundamental rights is not only desirable but essential. The introduction of such a system would derogate from the supremacy of the legislature in certain respects: the most important, accepted principles are that no other body (including a court of law) is competent to express itself on the validity of legislation and that a sovereign parliament cannot be bound by any limitation imposed on it by its predecessors.[15] The legislature would nevertheless remain sovereign in the sense that no other legislature would be competent to make laws for the country. Moreover, the judiciary would not usurp the legislative function: it would not be competent to legislate except in the general sense that all judicial pronouncements make law.

Executive action should be fully subject to judicial scrutiny. This applies to legislative, judicial, and purely administrative acts by organs of the executive—including subordinate legislation, pronouncements of judicial administrative bodies such as the Publications Appeal Board, and administrative acts such as the issue and withdrawal of passports, disciplinary hearings by statutory bodies, and the issue of permits and licenses. The jurisdiction of the courts to examine the regularity of such action (as opposed to the merits or efficacy) must not in any circumstances be subject to being overruled. Judicial control should be guaranteed by more than a mere presumption that the legislature does not intend to supersede the jurisdiction of the courts. Clauses for such supersedure have no place in subordinate legislation.

As for the independence of the judiciary from the legislature, the question of who is to appoint and dismiss judges is a troubling one in South Africa (and elsewhere). It is generally agreed that the administration of justice in South Africa is experiencing a crisis of legitimacy. South African judges are appointed by the state president in consultation with the minister of justice but may be dismissed only by Parliament. This mode of appointment has been extensively criticized because there is no guarantee against political appointments.[16] The appointment of judges in the United States has also occasioned crises, the most recent incident being the furor around the nomination of Clarence Thomas to the Supreme Court. Thus, difficulties can arise even where both executive (president) and legislature (Senate) are involved in an appointment. Appointment and dismissal by the legislature are preferable to appointment and dismissal by the executive since the involvement of a representative body such as the legislature does lend legitimacy to the appointment.

Consideration should be given, however, to entrusting these powers to a wholly independent body, such as a judicial service commission in which professional lawyers would play a prominent part. (The Namibian Constitution provides for the appointment of judges by the president on the recommendation of the Judicial Service Commission. The commission is composed of the chief justice, another judge, the attorney-general, and representatives of the legal profession.)[17] Such an arrangement, however, holds the risk that the body may be seen as a "closed shop," leading once again to a lack of credibility and the perception, particularly in South Africa, that the establishment has a monopoly on judicial appointments, counter to the acknowledged need to democratize the judiciary. (Almost without exception, South African judges are white, male, and middle-class: only one woman and only one nonwhite have been appointed. Magistrates and public prosecutors are somewhat more representative of the community but are generally perceived to be public servants with one foot in the executive branch of government and one in the judicial branch.)

A Bicameral or Unicameral Legislature?

In keeping with the Westminster tradition, South Africa had a bicameral legislature from 1910 until the abolition of the Senate in 1980.[18] The present tricameral Parliament cannot be compared to the more common two-chamber parliaments, since all three chambers are lower houses, and they cannot be said to constitute a check on one another's powers, except perhaps concerning entrenched provisions.[19]

As a general rule, bicameral legislatures consist of one representative or lower chamber, which has the final say in the event of a conflict between it and the other chamber, and an upper house (more often than not called a senate), which often has a regional basis and gives subnational groups or regions more influence than they would otherwise have. (In the U.S. Senate, for example, each state is entitled to two members regardless of the state's population or relative wealth.) In addition, the second, upper chamber exerts—or is intended to exert—a moderating influence on the legislature as a whole and may (depending on its constitutional status) influence legislative policy and amend or revise draft legislation. In some cases, draft legislation may even be initiated in the second chamber. The status and role of the second chamber varies from system to system, one of the main factors being whether the constitutional system is federal or unitary.[20]

One point of disagreement at the Conference for a Democratic South Africa concerned the proposal by the South African government that the new parliament should consist of a representative lower house and a senate with representation favoring minorities and that this senate should possess a legislative veto. Not surprisingly, this found little favor with the predominantly black parties. At first, the African National Congress remained implacably opposed to a bicameral legislature in any form; it subsequently expressed qualified support for a regionally elected second chamber with a special mandate to oversee the implementation of the bill of rights.

Since a second legislative chamber adds materially to the cost of government, such a body must serve a real purpose. Options must therefore be carefully examined to ensure that the upper house does not become an expensive luxury.

Once a second chamber has been decided on, other important issues must be addressed: How the members are to be elected (or appointed); what the powers of the chamber will be, particularly vis-à-vis the first chamber. The South African Law Commission has commented on the poor record of second legislative chambers in unitary states. The British House of Lords, for example, cannot serve as a model for a second chamber elsewhere in the world because of its unique composition of members of the aristocracy, with a substantial proportion owing their membership to birth and privilege: it is in essence a most undemocratic institution and is regarded even in some British circles as an anachronism.[21] It is inconceivable that it could be transplanted anywhere else in this egalitarian age.

The Senate of the United States is generally regarded as one of the most successful second chambers, for possibly two reasons: the members are elected and not appointed, and one of the Senate's most important functions is to act as a check on the president and not merely to form part of the legislative process. It is certainly one of the most powerful second chambers and exerts considerable influence—some feel that it is indeed too powerful. The Canadian Senate, by contrast, is a body whose members are appointed by the executive; it has little real power and is not generally regarded as successful.

There seems to be little doubt that an elected second chamber is infinitely preferable to one appointed by the executive, which would be no more than an extension of the executive arm of government. Even an indirectly elected body (for example, the defunct South

African Senate, whose members were elected by members of Parliament and of provincial councils) is unsatisfactory. With both appointment and indirect election, the second chamber would be open to manipulation by the government of the day, thus rendering it useless. An upper house directly elected on a regional basis, like that of the United States (and Namibia, for that matter) appears to be the most sensible option. Apart from being representative, it has the advantage that a certain degree of constitutional protection may be given to minorities through regional autonomy and that it will not be a mirror image of the composition of the first chamber.

Determining the powers of the second chamber is more difficult. Consideration could certainly be given to making the body into a watchdog over the exercise of the chief executive or president's discretionary powers, if a powerful executive presidency is decided on. Vis-à-vis the first legislative chamber, it must be decided whether the second chamber is to have a veto over all legislation or over some legislation only, or no veto at all but only the power to delay legislation for, say, one session of Parliament. The last of these options would effectively turn the second chamber into an advisory body. Would it be worth the trouble and expense to have such a paper tiger? If, conversely, one opts for a true veto, the first question is whether the veto should apply to all legislation or only to certain classes of legislation, for example, laws affecting fundamental rights, emergency powers, and foreign affairs.

The next question is whether the second chamber's veto should signal the end of the matter or if some other constitutional means of resolving the deadlock should be considered. The requirement of a two-thirds majority in a joint sitting is a device with which South Africans are familiar. At first glance, it appears to be a sound solution, but the constitutional crisis of the 1950s showed that the government was able to circumvent the restriction by manipulating the constitution.[22] The Namibian solution, or something similar, may also be worth considering; for example, if legislation is vetoed by the second chamber, an increased majority will be required in the first chamber if the bill is reintroduced during the next sitting.[23] (The Swiss solution of referendums to decide important constitutional issues is undeniably democratic, but equally undeniably expensive and time-consuming.)

A combination of some of the possible solutions is also possible: a joint sitting in some cases and a reintroduction with special majorities in another, for example. The one solution unworthy of serious consideration is retention of the present South African President's Council, whether in its 1980 form (wholly nominated by the state

175

president) or in its 1983 form (partially nominated by the president and partially by members of Parliament). At least the 1980 council was a purely advisory body with no legislative role at all; a nonrepresentative body should not be entrusted with the resolution of parliamentary logjams in any circumstances.[24] The warning should be sounded here, as indeed in any issue involving constitutional restraints, that rigidity may appear the best means of guaranteeing democracy but excessive rigidity may prove counterproductive if it engenders so much frustration that a constitution is suspended or even jettisoned altogether.

The Powers of the Executive

With the emergence of the administrative state, the executive has become the most powerful of the three branches of government.[25] Control over the burgeoning powers of the executive in the modern administrative state is one of the most pressing constitutional issues facing any democracy.

In South Africa, with its powerful tradition of legislative supremacy, the insidious growth in executive might has prompted the commentator Johan van der Vyver to conclude that legislative supremacy has been superseded by executive supremacy.[26] His argument is based on the powerful role of the executive—the state president in particular—in the legislative sphere. As is customary in the Westminster system, most draft legislation is initiated by the cabinet, of which the president is the chairman. More significant, the president (acting in consultation not only with the speaker and the chairmen of the three houses of Parliament but also with the cabinet and possibly with the President's Council)[27] has the final say in determining whether legislation is classified as relating to own or general affairs, and the president has a discretion to refer a dispute among the houses to the President's Council[28] (which may be regarded as an extension of the executive arm of the government even though it is not structurally part of the executive). While one may argue about van der Vyver's finding that legislative supremacy has been supplanted altogether, there is no denying the disturbing growth in the influence of the bureaucracy at the expense of the other two branches of government. Nor is this trend confined to South Africa. It would be shortsighted (not to say naive) for the framers of the new constitution to imagine that if the powers of the legislature are carefully circumscribed, control over the executive will follow naturally.

Until the basic shape of the system has been agreed on, it is impossible to decide the best way to curb excessive executive power. At this stage, it is not even certain whether the new constitution will provide for a federation, a confederation, or a unitary system with a greater or lesser measure of regional autonomy.

Important issues relating to the executive include the following:

- whether a presidential, a parliamentary system, or a combination of the two should be opted for
- linked with the previous question, whether the head of state should be a figurehead with purely ceremonial functions or an executive president
- what the powers of the president should be, and whether these powers should be exercisable by him exclusively, in consultation with, or on the advice of the other members of the executive
- what control the legislature and the courts should have over the exercise of power by the executive in general and the president in particular
- whether the president should have the power to veto legislation, and if so, whether such a veto would be final or whether it can be overridden, for example, by a two-thirds majority vote in the legislature
- whether the president should be popularly elected or elected by Parliament or a parliamentary body
- whether the presidency should rotate
- whether the president should be eligible for reelection, and if so, for how many terms or successive terms
- whether the president's term of office should be linked with the life of the legislature, or be independent of it
- whether the cabinet should be composed only of members of the governing party or be a collegial cabinet in which all political parties (and possibly even other interest groups such as racial or language groups) are proportionally represented
- who should appoint the members of the cabinet, and whether such appointments should be subject to confirmation by any other body (such as the Senate if the appointment is made by the president)
- whether all cabinet ministers should be career politicians or whether some portfolios could be reserved for technocrats or persons with special expertise but no particular political affiliation
- how the public service, defense force, and police are to be composed, appointed, and controlled
- whether there should be a prime minister as well as a president, and if so, who should appoint him and what his functions and powers would be

• to whom the executive should be responsible, whether individually or collectively

• how control is to be exercised over the executive in all its ramifications (for example, whether an impeachment procedure could be instituted, and if so, what form it would take)

Some of the most important issues arising in this regard have been touched on already, mainly in the discussion of the doctrine of separation of powers. The South African Law Commission has suggested that the following factors will prove important in deciding how a future executive is to be structured: the legitimacy of the intended system; historical and traditional factors; ethnic diversity; the conflict potential of the system; and accepted democratic principles.[29]

A Final View

A few comments are in order here. First, clearly these factors overlap and influence one another. Legitimacy is perhaps the most important issue facing the framers of the new constitution, one that will have to be addressed when the structure of the legislature and the judiciary as well as that of the executive is decided. The link between legitimacy and historical factors is also obvious; there is bound to be a lack of confidence, particularly among black voters, in an executive based on traditional lines. Any advantage that familiarity with the existing system may offer is offset by its obvious flaws.

Ethnic diversity, also a historical factor, is another issue that needs to be addressed sensitively and intelligently. The law commission is of the opinion that a presidential system such as that of the United States has great potential for polarization and thus for conflict. A parliamentary system, conversely, can also lead to polarization (largely because it implies the kind of winner-takes-all majoritarianism that is a feature of the Westminster system and therefore makes little provision for the protection of minorities) and has a negative connotation in South Africa for historical reasons.

The commission suggests that a collegial cabinet similar to that in the Swiss system may provide the best solution for South Africa, mainly because the executive is less politicized in such a system. (It would be unwise to imagine that the Swiss system can be transplanted without further ado into other systems. Like the British—Westminster—system, its success depends on a unique political culture and particular political circumstances.)

The consocialism notion of Arend Lijphart[30] should also be mentioned in this context. Although the 1983 Constitution with its

tricameral Parliament was supposedly inspired by the idea of consocialism, it is a pale shadow of the real thing and manifests few
features of the genuine article. There is some semblance of segmental
autonomy in the dichotomy of own and general affairs but to such a
limited extent that it has had no impact on the realities of political life
in South Africa. Of the other elements of consocialism (mutual veto,
elite accommodation of political leaders, and proportionalism), there
is little sign at all.[31]

Whatever system is eventually adopted, the most important
points are that an extensive system of checks and balances must
apply and that the functions and powers of all three branches of
government and their organs must be provided for in the constitution
in some detail. Once again, it must be asked whether an extremely
generally formulated constitution such as that of the United States is
preferable to a more detailed one. All constitutions are broad to a
certain extent:[32] the last word has never been spoken in the interpretation of a constitution. (If the terminology of literary criticism is
used, according to the adherents of deconstruction theory, meaning
is indefinitely deferred.) But South Africa cannot afford a constitution
that is couched in such vague and general terms that racial and
gender discrimination, for example, could be construed as constitutional (as it was for many years under the American Constitution).

The importance of carefully circumscribing the constitutional
powers of the executive is aptly expressed in the following:

> The total power exercisable in the modern state is formida-
> ble. How to place controls upon it and to prevent its abuse
> by those in whom it is vested has been an intractable
> problem in the history of many countries. Even where des-
> potism does not prevail, societies have felt the need to place
> restraints upon the organs of the state, to ensure that the
> laws and the administration are responsive to the will of the
> people, and that justice is fairly dispensed.[33]

11

Solving the Problem
of Democracy

Walter Berns

What is government itself but the greatest of all reflections on human nature? If men were angels, no government would be necessary. If angels were to govern men, neither external nor internal controls on government would be necessary. In framing a government which is to be administered by men over men, the great difficulty lies in this: you must first enable the government to control the governed; and in the next place oblige it to control itself.

Federalist 51

Some years ago, before an audience of federal judges and law professors, I said that there was probably not a law school in the United States that did not offer a course in constitutional law or many that did not make it a part of the required curriculum but that, as far as I knew, none had a course on the Constitution itself. With a few conspicuous exceptions, the same was true of political science departments. There, as in the law schools, professors focused on the decisions handed down by the courts, mainly by the Supreme Court of the United States, differing from their law school colleagues only in their reasons for doing so.

The law professors were in the business of training practitioners who would need to know how to advise their clients (including, perhaps, government officials) and to try cases. Their emphasis, therefore, was on the law of those cases. The political scientists were interested in the factors that led, or might have led, to the decisions. As "scientists," they wanted to be able to predict the outcome of future cases. Their emphasis, therefore, was on judicial behavior, which they attempted to explain by quantifying the factors that might enter into it.

Lost in all this was any interest in constitutionalism. Those who ought to have been professionally concerned with it seemed to have taken it for granted. (The United States had lived under the Constitution for more than two hundred years: so what was the problem?) Pressed to define *constitutionalism*, they would have been nonplused; few made the effort, and fewer still studied it.

This indifference may have been inevitable; Tocqueville seems to have thought so. What is constitutionalism but formal government? And, as he points out, democrats—and American professors are surely democrats—are distrustful of forms and do not comprehend their utility. They aspire to easy and present gratifications, he says, and are exasperated by anything that stands in their way.

> Yet this objection which the men of democracies make to forms is the very thing which renders forms so useful to freedom; for their chief merit is to serve as a barrier between the strong and the weak, the ruler and the people, to retard the one and to give the other time to look about him. Forms become more necessary in proportion as the government becomes more active and more powerful. . . . Thus democratic nations naturally stand more in need of forms than other nations, and they naturally respect them less.

This problem, he concludes, "deserves most serious attention."[1]

That it received such attention at the beginning of the United States should be evident to anyone who takes the trouble to study the records of the convention that framed the Constitution and the debates (which were vigorous and extensive) surrounding its ratification. My task here is to explain the product of those deliberations and the problems it was intended to solve, in the opinion (an opinion emphatically confirmed by the situation of South Africa) that those problems were not, and are not, unique to America.

America's Good Fortune

Beginning in the autumn of 1787, Americans were asked to deliberate on a new constitution for the United States with a view to ratifying it. "The subject speaks its own importance," we read in *Federalist* 1, "comprehending in its consequences nothing less than the existence of the UNION, the safety and welfare of the parts of which it is

181

composed, the fate of an empire in many respects the most interesting in the world." Nor would these consequences be confined to America—not, at least, according to the authors of *The Federalist*:

> It has frequently been remarked that it seems to have been reserved to the people of this country, by their conduct and example, to decide the important question, whether societies of men are really capable or not of establishing good government from reflection and choice, or whether they are forever destined to depend for their political constitutions on accident and force.[2]

Now, some two hundred years later, we can say that America did set an example and that many, indeed most, countries have followed it. How many have profited from it is, however, another question. By my last reckoning (undertaken before the breakup of the Soviet Union and Yugoslavia), there were 164 countries in the world. All but 6 of them have written constitutions—Britain, New Zealand, Israel, Saudi Arabia, Oman, and Libya being the exceptions. But of those 158 written constitutions, more than half had been written since 1974, and during the period when America has had one constitution, France has had five. (And, as the old joke has the Paris taxi driver saying, "*Il y aura une sixième*" [there will be a sixth].) Although some may question how much the world has learned or, to be fair, can learn from the American example, without question Americans can stand to learn much from the experience of other peoples. They can, for example, learn to appreciate their Constitution and, incidentally, recognize how much its success is the product of the favorable circumstances that attended its birth.

This fact was acknowledged by Publius, the pseudonymous author of *The Federalist*.[3] The country was geographically united, he said, bound by navigable waters that facilitated communication and commerce and blessed with a variety of soils and productions watered "with innumerable streams for the delight and accommodation of its inhabitants" (*Federalist* 2). This passage comes to mind when we read of the drought and its attendant starvation in places such as Somalia.

Publius then points out that, in addition to its material blessings,

> providence [had] been pleased to give this one connected country to one united people—a people descended from the same ancestors, speaking the same language, professing the same religion, attached to the same principles of government, very similar in their manners and customs, and who, by their joint counsels, arms, and efforts, fighting side by

side throughout a long and bloody war, have nobly established their general liberty and independence.

I recall this passage whenever I read of the events in what was once Yugoslavia, where the Christian Serbs seem determined to annihilate the Muslims in Bosnia-Herzegovina; in Iraq where the government wages war on its own Kurds and Shiites; in what was once Czechoslovakia; in Nagorno-Karabakh, Georgia, and other parts of the once mighty Soviet Union; or in strife-ridden Cambodia.

Indeed, I have had occasion to recall it especially whenever I have, in one way or another, participated in discussions of constitutional matters in other countries:

• In Cyprus, for example, where some ten years ago Daniel Elazar and I were in Nicosia to discuss federalism in a country where Greeks and Turks were (and still are) separated by a line drawn across the breadth of the country, a line that was (and still is) being patrolled by a UN peace-keeping force.

• In Brazil, where in 1987, after listening to what I had to say on the subject of constitution making, a member of the audience denounced the organizer of the program for inviting an American to speak on that subject. "What," he asked, "can we learn from America? In two hundred years they've had only one constitution. Why not a Bolivian? They've had a hundred." (No doubt many factors have contributed to the longevity of our Constitution—not the least of them being the Union victory in our Civil War—but the good luck that attended its birth is surely one of them.)

• And, most recently, in South Africa, where the discussion of a new constitution necessarily involved the role of political parties. In this respect America was also fortunate. As Publius says, the convention that drafted the Constitution of the United States "must have enjoyed, in a very singular degree, an exemption from the pestilential influence of party animosities—the disease most incident to deliberative bodies and most apt to contaminate their proceedings" (*Federalist* 37).

Indeed, unlike South Africa and every other country that has attempted to write a constitution since America set the example in 1787, the question of who was to participate in the convention charged with writing it simply did not arise in the United States; it was not an issue. Contrary to the objection raised in my presence by that angry Brazilian, America has had two constitutions, and under the first of them—the so-called Articles of Confederation and Perpetual Union—the United States then consisted of thirteen quasi-sovereign states. Without question, then, the convention of 1787, if it were to meet, could be only a meeting of those states, each choosing its own representatives (and in whatever number it chose), with each state casting one vote. The importance of this should not be minimized. All the preliminary issues that have plagued the constitution-making process in other countries—who would be represented, and in what numbers, and with what authority, and where the convention should meet, and for how long, and in what language (or languages) the deliberations should take place, to say nothing of the question of whether they should be secret, closed to the press—were absent in the United States in 1787.

America was especially lucky—and again the comparison with South Africa is telling—in that its people were *one* people: one not only because they spoke the same language, professed the same religion, were attached to the same principles of government, and were similar in their manners and customs, but also, as Publius emphasizes, because they were united by a common enemy defeated in "a long and bloody war"—not just a common but a *foreign* enemy. Abraham Lincoln was to make much of this fact in the first of his major speeches. Speaking of the period immediately after the American Revolution, he pointed out that

> the deep rooted principles of *hate* and the powerful motive of *revenge*, instead of being turned against each other, were directed exclusively against the British nation. And thus, from the force of circumstances, the basest principles of our nature were either made to lie dormant, or to become the active agents in the advancement of the noblest of cause—that of establishing and maintaining civil and religious liberty.[4]

Americans should bear all this in mind (and be humbled by it) whenever they address the subject of constitution making in other countries, for no other country is now blessed as America was blessed at its beginning. In fact, it is no exaggeration to say that, among all the countries that have attempted to constitute (or, in the typical case, reconstitute) themselves, only the United States was given the opportunity to make a truly new beginning. Unlike France, for example, it did not continue to find itself with a sullen nobility, dispossessed by the revolution of its property and its privileges but not of its hopes for their recovery under a restoration of *un ancien régime*. Tocqueville acknowledged one aspect of this when he said that the "great advantage of the Americans is that they [had] arrived at a state of democracy without having to endure a democratic revolution, and that they [were] born equal instead of becoming so."[5]

Nor, unlike South Africa, was it faced with what Karl Marx would later call a proletariat nursing its legitimate grievances and thirsting for revenge. As Tocqueville said, there was no proletariat in America.[6] There were, of course, a large number of Africans enslaved under the laws of the states (almost exclusively the southern states), but unlike the Xhosas, Zulus, and certain other inhabitants of South Africa today who have some political power, they had neither political power nor, for well into the nineteenth century, a political voice.[7] As for the Indian tribes native to the North American continent, their presence, unlike that of the slaves, was noted in the Constitution but only as an alien people with whom the government might enter into treaties.[8] (These treaties had to be written and rewritten as the Indians were pushed ever further westward, even as the Xhosas were pushed back first beyond the Great Fish and then the Keiskamma and Great Kei rivers.)

Still, while America may owe the relatively easy adoption of the Constitution to those favorable circumstances, it owes its subsequent prosperity, security, and stability to that Constitution and to the handful of men who drafted it and secured its ratification. As I once wrote,

> Some were unknown (and remained so), but most of them came not as strangers to each other. The more distinguished among them especially had worked together in the Congress or army and, even when that was not the case, knew each other by reputation. They were a remarkably learned and talented group of men. Even Richard Henry Lee, who did his best to prevent the ratification of the Constitution, acknowledged that "America would probably never see an assembly of men of like number more respectable."[9]

They included James Madison, James Wilson, Benjamin Franklin, Alexander Hamilton, Gouverneur Morris, John Rutledge, Oliver Ellsworth, and, presiding over their deliberations, George Washington. (Thomas Jefferson, in Paris at the time, referred to the convention as "an assembly of demigods.")

Perhaps the most important consideration—and here again the contrast with South Africa is significant—they not only knew each other but, with few exceptions and despite the sharp divisions engendered especially by the slavery issue, trusted each other and had reason to do so. They understood the problems they faced and designed a government capable of dealing with them. These problems were not unique to the United States; indeed, they were similar to those now faced by South Africa.

Principles of Government

The framers of the Constitution had no illusions that their task was an easy one. The country's geographical isolation would not, by itself, protect it from foreign enemies; the Constitution would have to make provision for its defense. Thus, Congress was given the power "to declare war, grant Letters of Marque and Reprisal, and make Rules concerning Captures on Land and Water"; "to raise and support Armies"; "to provide and maintain a Navy"; and "to provide for calling forth the Militia to execute the Laws of the United States, suppress Insurrections and repel Invasions"; the president was made "Commander in Chief of the Army and Navy . . . and of the Militia of the several States, when called into the actual service of the United States."

In the event, these provisions proved adequate. Although sorely tested on occasion, especially during the Civil War, they allowed for the defense of the nation without—or only once—jeopardizing the liberties of the people.[10]

Then, although it was true that almost all Americans professed Christianity, the framers knew that this was no guarantee that America, unlike Britain, would be free of sectarian warfare. To guard against it, they consigned religion to the private sphere by separating church and state. They did this by providing that "no religious Test shall ever be required as a Qualification to any Office or public Trust under the United States" and by forbidding Congress "to make any law respecting an establishment of religion, or prohibiting the free exercise thereof." In this way, they hoped to take religion out of politics.

What is true respecting the problem of national defense is equally true respecting the problem of religion. Compared with other times and places, America has been remarkably free of religious strife— without (if the public opinion polls are to be believed) the people becoming irreligious.

The problem of most concern to the framers, and the one whose resolution required their greatest attention, had to do with the principles of government. In fact, even at the beginning, there were sharper differences respecting these principles than Publius would have us believe. He conveniently neglects to mention that at the time of the revolution about 20 percent of the population—approximately 500,000 persons—were Tories, who for one reason or another neither fought for independence nor were attached to its principles. Some were office holders under the Crown or soldiers or Anglican clergy; others, and the politically more interesting, were "throne and altar

Tories," dedicated monarchists loyal to the king as head of church and head of state. Most of them remained silent during the revolutionary struggle, but—and here again South Africa comes to mind—many chose to become political exiles. Some returned to England, and another 35,000 to 40,000 went to Nova Scotia. In 1784, they persuaded the British government to partition "New Scotland," thereby establishing for them another colony, New Brunswick, which later became (along with Nova Scotia) one of the ten Canadian provinces. Only the departure of the Tories made it possible for Publius to say that the Americans were attached to the same principles of government.

Those principles were set down in the Declaration of Independence of 1776, when Americans declared themselves to be a "new order of the ages," the first nation in all history to build itself on the self-evident truth that all men are created equal insofar as they are all endowed by Nature's God with the unalienable rights of life, liberty, and pursuit of happiness. The purpose of government, they then said, was to secure these rights. This was to be done—because, given their principles, it had to be done—only with the consent of the governed. With the Tories gone or silenced, there was no disagreement on this score.

But it was understood by the framers that, while Americans were attached to the idea of rights, they would not always agree on the definition of rights, or on how rights were to be secured, or on whose rights deserved to be secured or preferred. In fact, the framers expected the people to have sharply different views on these matters. Thus, the "one people" that declared its independence in 1776 and the "we, the people" that constituted a government in 1787–1788 to "secure these rights" would, as a matter of course, be divided into factions thereafter and, unless steps were taken to avoid it, warring factions. According to Publius (in number ten, the most frequently quoted and celebrated of *The Federalist*), "The latent causes of faction are . . . sown in the nature of man," and by definition these factions have interests "adverse to the rights of other citizens, or to the permanent and aggregate interests of the community." As the framers saw it, this was the principal problem the Constitution had to deal with.

What is more, nature, so equitable in its endowment of rights, was by no means equitable in its endowment or distribution of talents or faculties, particularly, as Publius puts it, the "faculties of acquiring property." Some men are naturally more intelligent, more enterprising, or more energetic, as well as healthier, stronger, or handsomer than others. Thus, by securing the equal rights of *un*equally endowed human beings, the society would be divided between "those who hold and those who are without property" or between the wealthy and the poor or between the relatively wealthy and the relatively poor. Still, Publius does not hesitate to say that protecting these "different and unequal faculties"—naturally different and naturally unequal—is "the first object of government."

Accomplishment of this object was made especially difficult because those without property, or with less property, would constitute a majority, and under a republican government the majority would rule. The task facing the framers was to design a Constitution making it less likely that this majority would misrule.

A Republican Government

There was no question but that the government would have to be republican in form. As Publius says in *Federalist* 39, "No other form would be reconcilable with the genius of the people of America; with that honorable determination which animates every votary of freedom to rest all our political experiments on the capacity of mankind for self-government."[11] Unfortunately, while there had been republics, none could serve as a model for America. For this reason, the framers of the Constitution had to devise a new form of republican government. As Harvey C. Mansfield, Jr., explains, there are important differences between the new republicanism and the old:

> [The new] republic is based on the presumption that *the problem of popular government comes from within the regime*—from factions and tyrannical majorities. So it provides a constitution through which the people chooses to limit itself not by preventing the majority from ruling as in oligarchy, or by retaining a privileged class to rule with the majority as in "mixed government," but [rather] by constructing a majority so that it will not be factious or tyrannical. This new kind of republic is contrasted (*Federalist* 9, 10, and 14) to the old kind found in the republican tradition, which is given the pejorative label *democracy*. In democracy, the presumption is that the danger comes from outside the regime—from monarchy and oligarchy. So the popular spirit must be aroused and kept in a state of vigilance against its enemies; and instead of a constitution providing self-chosen limited government, the main requirement is to cultivate this vigilant spirit in republican virtue. Republican virtue, in turn, requires a homogeneous people and a small territory so that citizens can know and trust one another.[12]

Publius's description of the earlier, classical republics—he mentions specifically the "petty republics of Greece and Italy"—is harsh indeed. They provided no barriers "against domestic faction and insurrection," he says; they were regularly overwhelmed by "tempestuous waves of sedition and party rage"; rather than serving as models for America, they were nothing so much as "the wretched nurseries of unceasing discord and the miserable objects of universal pity or contempt" (*Federalist* 9). Indeed, had it not been possible to devise models of a more perfect structure, "the enlightened friends to liberty would have been obliged to abandon the cause of [republicanism] as indefensible."

Fortunately, the science of politics had "devised models of a more perfect structure . . . which were either not known at all, or imperfectly known to the ancients": the regular distribution of power into distinct departments, the introduction of legislative balances and checks, the institution of courts composed of judges holding their offices during good behavior, and the representation of the people in the legislature by deputies of their own election. "These are means, and powerful means, by which the excellencies of republican government may be retained and its imperfections lessened or avoided" (*Federalist* 9). This "more perfect structure" provides the forms that, in Tocqueville's words, "serve as a barrier between the strong and the weak," and in so doing they serve as the means by which democracy is constitutionalized.

The Model of John Locke

Chief among the political scientists to whom the framers were indebted for this new model of republicanism was John Locke. Like that of Thomas Hobbes before him, Locke's political science begins with an analysis of the nonpolitical state of nature. Whereas, according to Hobbes, the state of nature was indistinguishable from the state of war wherein the life of man was "solitary, poor, nasty, brutish and short," Locke speaks rather of the "inconveniences of that condition."[13] But these "inconveniences" are such that, at a certain point, war becomes inevitable. Thus, "to avoid this state of war," as Locke puts it, "is one great reason of men's putting themselves into society and quitting the state of nature."[14] They do this by entering into a compact by which every man agrees to divest himself of "his natural liberty and puts on the bonds of civil society."

Hobbes, again, required men to yield their natural rights, or liberty, to a leviathan, but Locke finds this objectionable. Men are not so foolish, he says, to take care to avoid the mischiefs that may be

189

done them in the state of nature by "polecats or foxes," only to be "devoured by lions,"[15] which is to say, by leviathans, whose every act was to be considered law. To prevent this, he requires men to hand over their natural rights not to a leviathan but rather to the community with the understanding that the community be governed by laws made by a legislative body: "The great end of men's entering into society being the enjoyment of their properties in peace and safety, and the great instrument and means of that being the laws established in that society, the first and fundamental positive law [which is to say, constitutional law] is the establishing of the legislative power."[16] It is not by chance that Article I of the Constitution of the United States establishes the legislative power.

There is safety when the supreme power is exercised by the legislative rather than by the leviathan. As Locke says, the legislative rules not by "extemporary, arbitrary decrees" but by "promulgated, standing laws." In a well-ordered commonwealth,

> the legislative power is put into the hands of diverse persons who, duly assembled, have by themselves, or jointly with others, a power to make laws; which when they have done, being separated again, they are themselves subject to the laws they have made, which is a new and near tie upon them to take care that they make them for the public good.

There is safety, too, in the fact that the legislature will not be in constant session, which requires that there be another power to "see to the execution of the laws."[17]

With this, Locke lays the foundation for a separation of powers, one of the features of the "more perfect structure" that Publius speaks of in *Federalist 9*—and not merely one of the features, but the central feature, because it serves both "to control the governed" and to oblige the government "to control itself."

The obligation of the government to control itself should require little demonstration; it is certainly familiar to all students of American government. As Publius says in *Federalist 47*, "The accumulation of all powers, legislative, executive, and judiciary, in the same hands, whether of one, a few, or many, and whether hereditary, self-appointed, or elective, may justly be pronounced the very definition of tyranny." The separation of powers, combined with the innovation the framers learned from Montesquieu, namely, bicameralism, is one of the defining characteristics of the more perfectly structured republic.

It remains to describe how the separation of powers serves to control the governed. Traditionally, republicans were animated by a distrust of the executive, which in most cases meant the monarch. Thus, having declared their independence from George III, Americans proceeded to establish governments that, in the case of the Articles of Confederation, deliberately neglected to provide for an executive or, in the case of the early state constitutions, contained provisions "for reducing the executive to a position of complete subordination [to the legislature]." The Virginia Constitution of 1776 was typical in this respect: "[The governor] shall, with the advice of a Council of State, exercise the executive powers of the government, according to the laws of this Commonwealth; and shall not, under any pretence, exercise any power or prerogative, by virtue of any law, statute or custom of England."[18] The experience gained from this practice proved to be bitter, and the framers of the Constitution of 1787 were determined not to repeat it. Too frequently the laws had gone unenforced, taxes uncollected, and the common defense neglected. With this in mind, they separated the executive and the legislative powers and endowed the executive with powers derived from the Constitution itself.

Article II of the Constitution begins with this terse statement: "The executive Power shall be vested in a President of the United States of America." This executive was charged with the duty of executing the laws—as the Constitution puts it, "he shall take Care that the Laws be faithfully executed"—but, in addition, with responsibilities having little or nothing to do with the literal meaning of the word *execute*.

It was Locke, again, who first made the *republican* case for an independent executive. An executive was needed to execute the laws, and in this capacity he was subordinate to (even if not controlled by) the legislative power ("the supreme power of the commonwealth"). But Locke goes on to indicate that the well-being or, to be more precise, the safety of the commonwealth cannot be ensured by laws alone.

There is, in the first place, the problem of foreign affairs, which, he suggests, cannot be directed by "antecedent, standing, positive Laws." Foreign affairs belong to the "federative power," which Locke likens to the natural power every man had in the state of nature.[19] Since the exercise of this power—the power of "war and peace, leagues and alliances, and all the transactions with all persons and communities [outside] the commonwealth"—requires prudence, Locke puts it into the hands of the independent executive.

In addition to foreign affairs, however, the good of the society may require that some domestic matters "be left in the hands of him that has the executive power." There will be "cases where the

191

municipal law has given no direction," or where "a strict and rigid observation of the laws may do harm," or where it will be proper "to mitigate the severity of the law" by pardoning those who offend against it. Such cases require "prerogative," which Locke defines as the "power to act according to discretion for the public good, without the prescription of the law and sometimes even against it."[20]

One of the abiding questions of American constitutional law is whether "the executive power" vested in the president of the United States includes something like the prerogative as Locke defines it. Congress is inclined to deny that it does, but presidents, including the best of them, have ever claimed it.[21] And, if we accept the authority of *The Federalist*, the framers of the Constitution intended them to have it. The following passage from *Federalist* 28 might have been written by Locke:

> That there may happen cases in which the national gov-
> ernment may be necessitated to resort to force cannot be
> denied. Our own experience has corroborated the lessons
> taught by the examples of other nations; that emergencies of
> this sort will sometimes exist in all societies, however consti-
> tuted; that seditions and insurrections are, unhappily, mal-
> adies as inseparable from the body politic as tumors and
> eruptions from the natural body; that the idea of governing
> at all times by the simple force of law (which we have been
> told is the only admissible principle of republican govern-
> ment) has no place but in the reveries of those political
> doctors whose sagacity disdains the admonitions of experi-
> mental instruction.

As Locke says, emergencies cannot be dealt with by "antecedent, standing law"; they require the exercise of prerogative, which, to repeat, he defines as the power to act according to discretion for the public good, without the prescription of the law "and sometimes even against it." Locke's prerogative, then, is an extralegal power, extralegal because it exists by necessity, not by virtue of a constitution. But, according to Publius, this power to deal with emergencies is given a place in the Constitution; it is part of the executive power vested in the president of the United States. When exercising it, therefore, the president is not acting extralegally. For, according to *Federalist* 31, "a government ought to contain in itself every power requisite to the full accomplishment of the objects committed to its care, and to the complete execution of the trusts for which it is responsible, free from every other control but a regard to the public good and to the sense of the people."[22]

Among the objects committed to its care is "the preservation of the public peace" (*Federalist* 23), and as Publius makes clear, there will be times when this can best be done, in fact can only be done, by the president's exercising powers coming directly from the Constitution and "free from every other control but a regard to the public good and to the sense of the people."

Because he is not chosen by the legislature, and because he holds powers independently of the legislature, he can act without its consent. Because, unlike the numerous legislature, he is one, not many, he can act with dispatch. And because he is one, not many, it is easy to fix responsibility for what he does.[23]

To summarize, the separation of powers is a means of obliging the government to control itself; in this respect, it serves to limit government, which, in the American case, means the government of the democracy. It is also a means of controlling the governed by authorizing the president not only to enforce the law directly on the people but also, if necessary—for example, in times of "domestic insurrection" (*Federalist* 26)—to employ the extraordinary powers of his office. In this respect, the separation of powers serves to ensure an effective government, a government as strong as necessary. President Lincoln, who was faced with a massive insurrection, was to prove just how strong and effective this government could be.

The Role of the Judiciary

It is widely assumed, abroad as well as in the United States, that the most effective means of limiting government is the power exercised by the independent judiciary, the power of judicial review. With this power, the courts, ultimately the Supreme Court of the United States, may nullify the actions of the legislature and executive alike by declaring them unconstitutional. Indeed, with this in mind, Publius (in *Federalist* 9) speaks of the independence of the judiciary as one of the elements of the "more perfect structure" that makes republican government possible. And there is no question about that independence: once appointed (by the president with the advice and consent of the Senate), federal judges serve during good behavior, which in most cases means until they die or retire. (In fact, no Supreme Court justice has left the bench in any other manner.) In the 203 years of its existence, the Court has declared more than a thousand legislative enactments and executive actions unconstitutional (or, as the British would say, *ultra vires*).

Judicial review is thought to be especially important as a means of protecting those individual rights specified in the first ten amendments to the Constitution, popularly known as the Bill of Rights. It is sometimes said, for example, that Americans owe their freedom of speech, press, and religion primarily to judicial enforcement of the First Amendment (which forbids Congress to make any law "respecting an establishment of religion, or prohibiting the free exercise thereof; or abridging the freedom of speech, or of the press"). But judicial enforcement is only partly responsible for these freedoms, and the way in which it is not responsible should concern those South Africans who would rely on a judiciary for protection of their rights.

I have discussed this issue in great detail elsewhere.[24] Here, it is enough to point out that it was not until 1965 (and only once or twice since) that the Court declared an act of Congress a violation of the First Amendment. The record is much the same regarding the other provisions of the Bill of Rights. The Supreme Court, for example, has never declared a punishment imposed under federal law to be "cruel and unusual" in violation of the Eighth Amendment.

The judiciary has made a difference, however, in those cases where the states and localities have abridged rights. Hundreds of state statutes and local ordinances, as well as acts committed by local police, have been declared unconstitutional by the Supreme Court. That is, the courts have played their protective role within the federal system when they have been opposed by local (or, at most, regional) rather than national majorities. The local authorities are inclined to obey court orders, and, on those infrequent occasions when they refuse to do so, the courts can usually depend on the president to enforce them. After all, the Constitution requires the president to see to it that the laws are faithfully executed. (Thus, when Little Rock, Arkansas, backed by the governor of the state, refused to obey a court order requiring the racial integration of a local high school, President Eisenhower sent in elements of an airborne division; and that, as the saying goes, was that.) But enforcing an order against the president or Congress of the United States, while technically no different, is another matter, and sometimes proves to be impossible. (As legend has it, President Andrew Jackson once said, "John Marshall [the chief justice at the time] has issued his order, now let him enforce it.") A few examples will serve to illustrate the point.

• In 1857, the Supreme Court declared unconstitutional an act of Congress prohibiting slavery in the northern section of a federal territory. That decision was a major cause of the Civil War, and, the war having been won by the Union, it was reversed by a constitutional amendment in 1868.

• In 1870, by a vote of 4–3 the Court struck down a Civil War

194

statute making noninterest-bearing notes ("greenbacks") legal tender in payment of "all debts, public and private." Having been authorized by Congress to do so, the president proceeded to appoint two additional justices and, the following year, the enlarged Court—by a vote of 5–4—reversed the earlier decision.

• In 1895, the Court struck down a federal statute imposing a tax on incomes. Congress responded by proposing an amendment to the Constitution, which, when ratified in 1913, gave it the power "to lay and collect taxes on incomes, from whatever source derived, without apportionment among the several States, and without regard to any census or enumeration" (Sixteenth Amendment).

• Following a number of decisions striking down New Deal economic or commercial legislation, President Franklin D. Roosevelt proposed that Congress enlarge the Court from nine to as many as fifteen members. The Court, then, in its famous (or infamous) "switch in time that saved nine," reversed itself—indeed, not only reversed itself but also, in effect, announced that it would no longer question Congress's power to regulate interstate commerce.[25]

There are, of course, cases where judgments of unconstitutionality have been accepted by the Congress. In 1990, for a recent example, the Court struck down a federal statute prohibiting the burning of the American flag. Burning the flag, the Court said, is (or, in this case, was) a form of symbolic expression protected by the free speech provision of the First Amendment. But this was hardly a case where the Court succeeded in imposing its judgment on an obstinate Congress. That statute was enacted precisely to give the Court the opportunity to declare it unconstitutional. Declaring it unconstitutional was, to say the least, politically easy. When, however, during World War II President Roosevelt issued an executive order (subsequently ratified and confirmed by an act of Congress) empowering the secretary of war to round up thousands of Japanese-Americans and ship them off to detention centers, the Court acquiesced—not without a struggle, and not unanimously, but acquiesce it did.[26] The decision was greeted with dismay or disgust by many in the legal fraternity, but they ought not to have been surprised. As Publius said even in the beginning, "It would require an uncommon portion of fortitude in the judges to do their duty as faithful guardians of the Constitution, where legislative invasions of it had been instigated by the major voice of the community" (*Federalist* 78).

Fortunately, so far as the national legislature is concerned, such invasions are the exception, not the rule. In fact, they are rare—so rare that judicial action to protect rights is only rarely required—and they are rare largely because the Constitution, by devising a "more perfect" republican structure, makes it difficult for the "major voice of the community" to be expressed. As Publius says (and the emphasis is his), *"the people in their collective capacity"* are excluded from any share in the government (*Federalist* 63).

A Republican Constitution

The remarkable thing is that the framers were able to persuade the people to ratify this republican Constitution. Plainly, the framers made no effort to conceal the fact that they intended to put limits on democratic majorities; they said as much. They said that they intended the Constitution to exclude the people in their collective capacity from any share in the government; they said that the chief object of the government was to protect the diverse faculties of men, especially their "different and unequal faculties of acquiring property"; they took pride in the fact that their government was not a democracy but rather a republic that put some distance between the people and the levers of power:

• Their Constitution provided a president chosen not by the people but by electors who, having made their choice, would immediately disband.

• It provided a Senate chosen not by the people but by the state legislatures, each state, regardless of the size of its population, being entitled to choose two.

• It provided a House of Representatives chosen not by a majority of the whole people (*"the people in their collective capacity"*) but by majorities within each of the districts into which each state would be divided.

• It provided a Supreme Court with the power to veto popular legislation and with members who would, in effect, serve for life.

• Generally, it provided a system of divided power and checks and balances, and it was understood that what was most in need of being checked was popular majorities. Yet, these popular majorities gave it their consent.

The people were left in no doubt about the essential characteristics of the Constitution. Every aspect of it was subjected to intense scrutiny during the ratification debates. These debates, pitting Federalists (who favored ratification) against Anti-Federalists (who opposed ratification), were carried on in town meetings, in state conventions, and in the popular press. And for every Federalist paper, there was an Anti-Federalist paper; for every Publius, a Cato; for every

Cassius, a Brutus or Agrippa or Centinel or Hampden. The Anti-Federalists complained of the six-year terms for senators, of the reeligibility of the president, of the provision for a standing army (which they saw as a weapon to be used against the people), and, generally, of what they called the "aristocratic tendency of the Constitution." Patrick Henry, for example, who led the opposition in Virginia, said the Constitution "has an awful squinting; it squints towards monarchy." Yet, Virginia (albeit by a narrow margin) voted in favor of ratification, as did every other state. Under the circumstances, this was truly remarkable.

Publius recognized this and argued strenuously against Jefferson's suggestion that, in effect, the ratification process be repeated from time to time (*Federalist* 49). What Publius believed to be true then—namely, given another chance, the people would be likely to reject the Constitution because of the restrictions it imposed on popular majorities—would almost surely be true today. This judgment is strengthened by the changes that have been made since the Constitution was adopted. Senators are now chosen by popular vote of the people in the states,[27] and the right to vote, in state as well as in federal elections, has been extended not only to blacks and women but also to persons "eighteen years of age or older" and cannot be denied to persons by reason of their "failure to pay any poll tax or other tax."[28] Then, too, the early appearance of political parties had the effect of taking the choice of the president from the nominally independent electors and putting it in the hands of the people; and the day will surely come when the Electoral College itself will be abolished and replaced by a system of direct popular election.[29] (It will come when, as happened in 1888, the presidential candidate winning a majority of the popular votes fails to win an Electoral College majority.)

A Model Constitution

These changes in the direction of more democracy may satisfy the people, at least for the time being. They clearly do not satisfy many political scientists who, because of the positions they occupy, are capable of exerting an influence out of proportion to their numbers. The more radical among them (mostly Marxists) teach their students—and, thanks to a policy of open admissions and generous government subsidies, something approaching 50 percent of the people are, or have been, students—that the Constitution is an "elitist document" providing "democracy for the few."[30] Others, including a handful of the most illustrious, complain that, while not necessarily elitist, the Constitution still fails to provide government sufficiently (by which they mean immediately) responsive to the wishes of the people.

Of course, it was not intended to do this. By providing for the representation of the great variety of interests within the "extensive territory" of the United States, the Constitution was intended to prevent the formation of a majority with a common interest "adverse to the rights of other citizens, or to the permanent and aggregate interests of the community" (*Federalist* 10). In the United States, governing majorities would be (and still are) assembled not from among the people directly (not even when they are organized in or by political parties) but from among the representatives of the people. Because they represent different interests and because the legislative branch is separated from the executive and because the legislative branch is itself divided into House and Senate, assembling this majority is not a simple matter.

The political scientists find this division of interests exasperating; they write books complaining of the deadlock of democracy and propose to end that deadlock by instituting something like the British system. In a word, they want party government, in which party serves as the means by which majority opinion is readily translated into public policy.[31] For them, popular government means giving the people what they want (or what they say they want) as soon as they want it, which means a government unable to do anything unpopular.

Woodrow Wilson, a president of the American Political Science Association as well as of the United States, was one of the earliest proponents of party government in the United States. Writing in 1885, he complained that the Congress was too strong and the executive too weak, and the consequence of this was irresponsible government. How, he asked, can we identify whom to praise and whom to blame for what is done under this system? Indeed, who can be said to govern when power is divided between the executive and the Congress and, within the Congress, dispersed among the various standing committees? The cure for this was government by majority party. "The British system is perfected party government," he wrote, and among the features that make it perfect is that no effort is made in the House of Commons "to give the minority a share in law-making."[32] Nowhere does Wilson express any concern that a majority so organized and led might fit Publius's description of a faction.[33] Whereas the Constitution was intended to make democracy safe for the United States, Wilson's policy, which he embodied in a demagogic slogan, was to make the world safe for democracy. (Historians can decide whether, or to what extent, the world he helped to create provided the degree of safety he envisioned.)

Wilson's complaint and prescription were echoed in 1963 by James MacGregor Burns, another president of the American Political Science Association, and a few years earlier by an official committee of the association.[34] Indeed, there seems to be something about political scientists that leads them to favor efficient majority-rule government and to be oblivious of the forms (in Tocqueville's sense) that make it safe.

Writing from the Marxist perspective, still another president of the Political Science Association saw the Constitution as the product of a conspiracy among the holders of public securities, or personal as opposed to real property.[35] Other scholars have demonstrated that he was wrong about the conspiracy,[36] but there is no denying that the framers intended to lay the foundation for a commercial society: "By multiplying the means of gratification, by promoting the introduction and circulation of the precious metals, those darling objects of human avarice and enterprise, it serves to vivify and invigorate all the channels of industry and to make them flow with greater activity and copiousness" (*Federalist* 12). And there is no denying Publius's assertion that the protection of the diverse faculties of men, especially the "different and unequal faculties of acquiring property," was the "first object of government."

Yet what is this but the principle underlying the free market? And is not the free market the cause of the country's material prosperity, and is not that material prosperity widely shared, and is this not—as it was intended to be—one of the means of mitigating democratic envy and, therefore, a means of solving the problem of democracy? Those who complain of it are not, even now, the people. (What Tocqueville said 160 years ago remains true today: "As everyone has property of his own to defend, everyone recognizes the principle upon which he holds it.")[37] They are, instead, those without warrant and holding no public office who claim to speak in the name of the people: the Marxists and a handful of political scientists, to say nothing of those who have gone to school with Friedrich Nietzsche, Martin Heidegger, and their postmodernist epigones.[38]

They were not on the scene in 1787–1788, and their absence must be counted among those circumstances that favored the adoption of the Constitution. Without them, the framers were able to persuade the people to ratify a Constitution that establishes a government of the people and for the people but not immediately by the people. As Publius says, it is a government that derives all its powers directly or indirectly from the great body of the people and is administered by persons holding their offices during pleasure, or during good behavior, but from which *"the people in their collective capacity"* are excluded (*Federalist* 39, 63). By any fair reckoning, however, the people have not been excluded from its benefits.

For all these reasons, the Constitution of the United States can provide a model for South Africa.

12

A Comparative Perspective on Parties and Government

David Welsh

This chapter attempts to locate political parties within the operation of democratic political systems, and thereafter it speculates on the likely shape of a future South African party system in the light of the experience of other deeply divided societies.

Some General Considerations

A political party may be defined as an organization that seeks to aggregate voters and interest groups for the purpose of winning elections. Parties are, by definition, concerned with power: either by winning a sufficient number of seats or the principal executive office (the presidency) to constitute the government or at least by winning sufficient support to participate in a multiparty coalition government. Parties are, in theory, the transmission belt that converts voter preferences into representation in elected bodies.

Democratic government, at least as it is generally understood today, requires three fundamental institutional pillars:

- universal adult suffrage, enabling voters to vote in regular, free elections
- the upholding of civil liberties, including especially the freedom of expression and association
- an independent judiciary

These three requirements are individually and in combination necessary parts of a democratic order. The absence or serious infringement of any one removes a political system from the democratic category. Although even these formal requirements may be insufficient to ensure democratic government in societies characterized by deep and impermeable divisions, for purposes of the present discussion this definition will suffice.

This definition describes a *liberal* democracy, a species historically despised by a long tradition of Marxist thought that saw it as no more than *bourgeois* democracy, that is, a system in which the outer form of democratic government concealed an inner reality, rule by the bourgeoisie. In the aftermath of the astonishing collapse of Marxist-Leninist systems in all parts of the world, we hear little of the traditional critique, especially since, without exception, successor governments have chosen the liberal democratic form of government, even if many will be unlikely to sustain it. The one-party system characteristic of Marxist-Leninist states was thoroughly inimical to any credible conception of democracy, to say nothing of the utter lack of civil liberties. Much the same observation applies to the one-party system in vogue in postindependence Africa, although, to be sure, African one-party systems were never capable of matching the totalitarian scope of their Marxist-Leninist counterparts.

No less inimical to the concept of democracy was the symbiotic relationship between the single party and the formal organs of the state found in Marxist-Leninist systems and in African one-party systems. Liberal democracy does indeed imply "party government," but in general it is true to say that the dividing line between party and state (including bureaucracy, armed services, and police) is carefully maintained. The principle is an important one, even if it is often breached in practice by the political influence of civil servants and other state functionaries. (The famous BBC program "Yes, Prime Minister," whose theme is the manipulation of politicians by civil servants, is satire, but, like all good satire, it contains an important kernel of truth.)

In systems where political leaders come and go, as parties rotate in government, civil servants, especially senior ones, often enjoy continuity in office, as well as substantial security of tenure, which gives them a great advantage over the (relatively) temporary political heads of department, in knowledge of the particular portfolio, precedents, and awareness of the constraints, for example, on spending. Liberal democratic systems, by definition, imply that the voter has a choice of parties to support in elections. Competitive systems are the antithesis of the "one person–one vote–one candidate" elections characteristic of the former Soviet Union, where electoral choice, to the extent that it was permitted at all, was severely circumscribed. Adam Przeworski has written:

> Democracy is the realm of the indeterminate; the future is not written. Conflicts of values and of interests are inherent in all societies. Democracy is needed precisely because we cannot agree. Democracy is only a system for processing conflicts without killing one another; it is a system in which there are differences, conflicts, winners and losers. Conflicts are absent only in the authoritarian systems. No country in which a party wins 60 percent of the vote twice in a row is a democracy.[1]

Indeterminacy must be based on the principle of free electoral choice. The final sentence in the quotation above has important implications for the viability of democracy in deeply divided societies, but it also raises important questions about the quality of democracy in a number of states formally included in the democratic category. In Japan, for example, the Liberal Democratic party has governed since 1947, when a democratic constitution was established. Especially in recent times, moreover, the ruling party has been involved in corruption on a large scale. Can such a system be called "democratic"? Can India or Botswana, both of which have had long periods of rule by a hegemonic party, be called democratic? Or Italy, whose many governments from 1946 onward have all featured one constant—dominance in the coalitions by the Christian Democrats?

In no country cited above has a ruling party won 60 percent of the vote twice in a row (at least so far as this writer is aware), and, by all accounts, the electorates have had genuinely free choices and election outcomes have not been rigged. Przeworski's principle may not have been infringed, but in the spirit of his comments, in general long, unbroken periods of single-party dominance are hardly conducive to democratic health in any given political system.

The defining characteristics of democracy advanced in this chapter are capable of widely differing institutional expression. In the case of the suffrage criterion, for example, there is a wide variety of electoral systems. The type of electoral system may affect the party system and, in turn, the number of significant parties produced, as electoral outcomes will influence the form of government. As a rule of thumb, proportional representation tends toward multiparty systems and, in consequence, coalition government. Clearly, this is a major variable shaping the relationship between parties and government.

In this context, by my estimate of the approximately fifty political systems classified as stable liberal democracies, some 75 percent feature coalition government as an institutionalized norm. This figure excludes parties like the Indian National Congress, which has governed India for much of its postindependence period and which is in itself a broad-based coalition of relatively disparate forces. Likewise, although the American system does not lend itself to coalition government, its two major parties may not unreasonably be described as coalitions.

Another critical variable is the structure of government: the relationship between party and government in a Westminster system such as Britain's or New Zealand's is substantially different from that in a presidential system based on the doctrine of the separation of powers, as in the United States. In the Westminster system, where governments depend for survival on their continuing ability to command a majority in the lower house, parties are tightly disciplined and highly organized. In contrast, American parties in Congress are far less disciplined and more ideologically diffuse. In between these two different types, falls a wide range of intermediate party-government relationships. Whether a state is federal or unitary will also have an obvious impact on the relationship between parties and government. Federalism, by definition, establishes significant political arenas at regional, state, provincial, or cantonal level: the party governing at the central, or federal, level may not necessarily be the governing party in all the regional governments. It is precisely one of the attractive claims made for federalism that it can be conducive to political stability by allowing parties that lose out in federal elections the possibility of attaining power at the regional level. This may prevent or inhibit the alienation of such parties from the political system as a whole.

A further consequence of federalism is its impact on the internal dynamics of parties. By establishing subnational arenas of political competition and power, regional politicians acquire power bases that may make them relatively autonomous of the national party leadership. This is especially the case in a system such as the one in the United States, where presidentialism and the separation of powers already weaken the integration of parties as national institutions.

These introductory generalizations have stressed the key variables that shape the relationship between parties and government, and they have also sought to demonstrate the wide variety of institutions and practices consonant with liberal democracy as it was defined at the beginning of the chapter.

Democracy and the Divided Society

Let us consider further implications of the definition before exploring the possibilities of liberal democracy in deeply divided societies. The definition that was advanced, following the tradition in most Western political theory, is conceived in terms of individualism; that is, the right-bearing unit is implicitly assumed to be the individual, even though freedom of association, by permitting an aggregation of individual rights, may create all manner of groups, some of which may be recognized as having a legal or corporate personality of their own.

The definition's individualistic assumptions point to the major problem of organizing a democratic polity in circumstances of deep, crystallized, and continuing divisions in the society. Democracy presupposes competition for political office, and it presupposes that competing parties must enjoy the realistic possibility that they can obtain power, or a share of power. What is termed the Westminster model, for example, presupposes regular swings of the electoral pendulum so that defeated oppositions or ousted governing parties accept the fundamental fairness of the system because they do not regard themselves as having been shut out of power in perpetuity. They can live, reasonably contentedly, to fight another (electoral) day.

In divided societies—where groups, however composed or configured, endure through time and are relatively impervious either to losses of electoral support (by defection, for example) or to gains in support (by the recruitment of new strata or making new coalitions or alliances, for example)—the problem of the permanent minority may become an acute one, possibly leading to the minority's disaffection and certainly to a limitation on the political system's pretensions to democratic status. As Hans Daudt and Douglas W. Rae say,

> A democratic system with majority rule can only function in a satisfactory way if the conflicts that the system must deal with can be solved by compromises in such a way that everybody's interests are taken into account. Only in that case is it, theoretically at least, possible that there might be *unanimity* about the desirability of majority rule and only in that case will the system be experienced by anybody as coercive. If a person belongs to a minority that is permanently prejudiced by the system or harmed in what it considers its most fundamental rights, there cannot be any rational argument why he should consider the system as legitimate.[2]

Another recent theorist, Jane J. Mansbridge, writes:

> On its face, majority rule seems to protect interests equally because it gives each individual a vote of equal strength in the peaceful equivalent of a "fair fight." Yet despite the fairness implicit in tug of war and weights-in-the-scale analogies, majority rule does not always protect interests equally. As a winner-take-all system, it does not usually produce a proportional distribution of benefits, and it can create permanent minorities. If some minority is always on the losing side in every collective decision, few would say that the minority's interests were being protected, let alone that they were being protected equally. Majority rule ensures equality only in the procedure, not in the result.[3]

In the rise of democratic theory, majority rule has unquestionably been a principal theme. In his survey of America, Tocqueville begins his chapter "Unlimited Power of the Majority in the United States, and Its Consequences" with this statement: "The very essence of democratic government consists in the absolute sovereignty of the majority; for there is nothing in democratic States which is capable of resisting it."[4] But he was no less aware of the potential of majority tyranny.

The possibility of majority tyranny has also been an important issue in democratic theory. Both Tocqueville and John Stuart Mill, major nineteenth-century theorists, warned against such a tyranny, and the problem has been a recurrent one in scholarly debates. Few, if any, theorists of democracy would accord the description *democratic* to a regime that, even if elected by a large majority of the electorate, systematically persecuted and discriminated against minorities. The notion of democracy is centrally concerned with freedom. This concern, as it relates to the problem of majority tyranny, is captured by Lord Acton's famous dictum: "The most certain test by which we can judge whether a country is really free is the amount of security enjoyed by minorities."

Securing democracy in ethnically divided societies is difficult. Creating and sustaining an overarching sense of nationhood are major problems; protecting minorities against majority oppression and ensuring that they are enabled to participate effectively in the political system are others.

Ethnicity is a much-debated concept. In general, it refers to a politicized sense of identity derived from a common culture, including language and religion, and a putative claim to common ancestry. Often it focuses on a common territory, actually or supposedly the group's ancestral homeland. For purposes of this argument, race-based senses of identity or solidarity are conflated with those where the basis of solidarity is a cultural one. In some cases, ethnic antagonists are physically indistinguishable from each other: in Northern Ireland, for example, there are no significant phenotypic differences between Catholics and Protestants, who are in major respects culturally alike as well, except, of course, for the major denominational difference. In other cases, the ethnic markers may include visible physical differences, often color.

Little purpose would be served by reviewing the roots of ethnicity. Suffice it to say that while scholars have reached no consensus on this issue, many reject the view that ethnicity can be reduced to socioeconomic or classlike origins (without denying that socioeconomic inequalities can aggravate ethnic conflicts) but hold that its roots lie rather in the political, psychological, and social realm. Walker Connor, Anthony Smith, and Donald Horowitz are among the best-known theorists of this school.[5] Horowitz's *Ethnic Groups in Conflict* is widely regarded as the most comprehensive synthesis yet written of ethnic politics.

Horowitz shows, with massive empirical evidence, how in ethnically divided societies voters tend to support parties rooted in their respective ethnic groups. What he terms "ascriptive [meaning determined by birth or descent] party politics" has an inherent propensity toward rigidity. He illustrates his point by referring to a hypothetical model of a society with two ethnic groups, A and B, numbering 60 percent and 40 percent, respectively, of the population. Party A, rooted in Group A, will always win elections, but the process could hardly be termed democratic. Why?

> The election was democratically conducted. The results are in conformity with the principle of majority rule. But that is the sticking point. Majority rule in perpetuity is not what we mean by "majority rule." We assume the possibility of shifting majorities, of oppositions becoming governments, of an alterable public opinion. All this is foreclosed by the ascriptive character of the majority that voted for Party A. The election, intended to be a vehicle of choice, was no such thing and will be no such thing in the future; it registered, not choice, but birth affiliation. This was no election—it was a census.[6]

Horowitz's example is, of course, only a model, and, as he readily concedes, the political life of actual societies is more complex (although the model does bear an uncanny resemblance to the politics of Northern Ireland over the period 1921–1972, when the province had its own parliament). Commonly, there are more than two groups;

seldom do all ethnics vote for a single ethnic party, and the rules of the political system may require or encourage links that cut across ethnic divisions and thereby mitigate the potential conflict.

As a general rule, where the major lines of conflict are ethnic, and the major sources of political mobilization are ethnically based parties, voters tend to be far more tightly sewn into an ethnic party than would be the case of parties in more homogeneous societies where, for example, class is the principal base of parties. Characteristically, in ethnically divided societies, the floating vote is minuscule, if by "floating" one implies the transfer of political affiliations to parties based outside the voter's ethnic group. "Floating," in such circumstances, tends to occur between more moderate and more radical parties based within a single ethnic group. "Ethnic outbidding" is a common phenomenon. Moreover, interethnic parties do not generally prosper in ethnically divided societies—as the fates of the Alliance party in Northern Ireland and the Labour party in Malaysia show.

The problem of the permanent minority is a recurrent one in societies with significant ethnic divisions. Obviously, no two societies are alike, and the problem assumes various forms, depending on the particular context. In the universe of putatively democratic systems, the following examples illustrate the point.

Northern Ireland. Between 1921 and 1972, Northern Ireland possessed its own parliament, the Stormont, which enjoyed extensive powers of self-government. (In addition, Northern Ireland, as a province of the United Kingdom, was represented at Westminster.) For the entire duration of the Stormont's existence, however, the (Protestant-based) Unionist party possessed hegemonic de facto one-party control. The Catholics, although numbering more than one-third of the total Northern Irish population of one-and-a-half million, were a classic excluded minority, enjoying neither the prospect of winning a Stormont election nor even significant political leverage. John Darby writes:

> So comprehensive was the split in parliament that party votes applied to almost every branch of legislation. Few issues were trivial enough to create cross-party alignments. The only instance in the Northern Ireland parliament's history of the government supporting an opposition bill was the passage of the Wild Bird act of 1931, a measure which even the most ingenious argument could not make controversial. Stormont was an arena of conflict, not compromise.[7]

Israel. Let us assume for purposes of the argument that before 1967, the Arab minority represented 15 percent of Israel's total population. Israel's most distinctive feature is that it is a Jewish state, with Hebrew as its sole official language. Ian Lustick writes:

> Israel *is* both a Jewish state and a Zionist state, the character of the state having been determined by the ideological commitments that its major institutions have been designed to serve. Segmented from the Jewish community on the institutional as well as the structural level, Israeli Arabs are cut off from the mainstream of public power and purpose in Israeli society.[8]

As Sammy Smooha notes, Israel (excluding the occupied territories) qualifies as a political democracy on many counts: it has universal franchise (including Arabs), a multiparty system, fair elections, reasonably regular changes of government, civil rights, an independent judiciary, and a free press. While Arabs enjoy the vote, they are, nevertheless "second-class" citizens, who are in practice subject to various forms of discrimination. In terms of an unwritten rule, Arab, or preponderantly Arab, parties have never participated in a coalition government, and, given the present cast of Israeli politics, they are unlikely to do so. Smooha's conclusion is compelling: "The exclusion of the Arabs from national power and the unsettling fate of their representative organisations as permanent opposition parties present Israeli democracy with the severe problem of 'the tyranny of the majority.' "[9]

Sri Lanka. Sri Lanka is one of the few third world states with a regular alternation of government through the ballot box. While various authoritarian measures have flawed the quality of its democracy, the major infraction of its democratic credential has been the exclusion of Ceylon Tamils, a minority amounting to more than 11 percent of the population. Although parliamentary representation of the Ceylon Tamils has been nearly proportionate to their size, they have enjoyed little or no share in executive government, and their demands for autonomy, then for federalism, and, more recently, for secession have been resisted. Effective political competition occurs within the majority Sinhalese group, who account for 72 percent of the population. So the competition for power focuses on the Sinhalese vote, resulting in Tamil frustration with the political process.

Canada. The future of Canada as a federal state became moot in the 1990s, when Quebec's restiveness as a Francophone province in an

Anglophone-dominated state increased. French Canadians number more than 25 percent of the total Canadian population, and 83 percent of the population of Quebec. Since the "Quiet Revolution" of the 1960s, Quebec has emerged from its backwater status, and successive Quebec governments have striven for greater autonomy for Quebec within federal Canada. Although successive adjustments have been made to accede to Quebec's demand for greater autonomy, they have not caused the secessionist drive to abate. In the referendum of 1980, the secessionist option was decisively beaten, but since then a durable constitutional settlement has eluded the Canadians.

Canada has remained an impeccably democratic system, but the major complaint of Quebec leaders has been the "majoritarian" views of Anglophones that have made them resistant to Quebec's claims to be a distinct society. Kenneth McRae writes that in English Canada "majoritarian values are prominent in the political culture. . . . While Liberal ministries have had strong parliamentary representation from both linguistic sectors, they have had difficulty in persuading their English-speaking followers of the need for a restructuring of French-English relations."[10]

The United States. The effectiveness of blacks' political rights in the United States, especially in the South, was substantially enhanced by civil rights legislation in the 1960s, notably by the Voting Rights Act of 1965. Yet blacks, who number approximately 12 percent of the population, remain significantly underrepresented. Only 1.2 percent of elected offices at all levels of government were filled by blacks in 1989. A leading black American political scientist, Charles V. Hamilton, writes:

> It is still the case that most blacks are elected to office mainly when there is a sizable black constituency. . . . For the most part, white voters still prefer white candidates over black candidates. In the realm of analysis, one cannot say that blacks have reached political parity until a black candidate can run in an election in a majority white district and have an equal chance of being elected.[11]

Hamilton does note, however, that the federal system offers "several points of access," which facilitate a group's quest for empowerment by opening up optional routes.

Survey data published in 1989 show that more than 80 percent of blacks agreed that "all Americans do not have an equal chance"; 81 percent of blacks denied that they would automatically vote for a black candidate. How far this sentiment is actually translated into voting practice may be a matter of some doubt. It is at all events clear that the great majority of blacks continue to support the Democratic party.

South Africa. White politics of the past created a strong tendency for the ethnic determination of voting and minority exclusion in South Africa. The National Convention of 1908 generated a "convention spirit, a euphoric sense that at last white unity was attainable because Boer and Briton were prepared to put aside the intense conflicts of the recent past and together build "a new white nation." The two major architects of Union, Jan Smuts and John X. Merriman, confidently anticipated that South Africa's political evolution would produce a party system that cut across linguistic and cultural lines. Merriman, indeed, believed that "in race [the reference is to the two white linguistic groups] the people were essentially the same and experience proved to us that the race difference was superficial and would disappear."[12]

These overly optimistic assumptions were in due course belied by the pattern of mobilization. Afrikaners and English were substantially (though not completely) riven into separate political camps, breaking down somewhat between 1933 and 1939, but thereafter the divide reasserted itself. The government that assumed power in 1948 was rooted almost exclusively in the Afrikaans community, and consequent on the winner-take-all principle operating in the South African political system, the sizable English-speaking minority was excluded from any share in power at the national level. Only in the 1960s, when a significant minority of English-speakers began to support the National party, did this ethnic power monopoly begin to fray at the edges.

Nothing in the six case studies presented above should be construed as explicitly or implicitly applicable to the possible pattern of politics in a fully democratic South Africa. It has been said that although there are recurrent patterns in the politics of deeply divided societies, each case is sui generis. No simple extrapolations from any case can be made to the future experience of South Africa.

What political arrangements have succeeded in securing democracy in deeply divided societies? Before considering this question, we must examine further some implications of democracy. As one requirement, democracy *must* entail a minority party's ability at some future stage to become the majority party or, alternatively, to become part of a coalition with a majority in the legislature. Permanent or crystallized majority-minority party configurations vitiate a political system's democratic quality.

With hardly an exception, democratic governments in divided

societies have been either coalitions in which all or most of the most salient political actors have been represented or large aggregative parties ("catchall" parties) that accommodate the most prominent political segments. Of the countries with catchall parties, India is the most striking example. It is sometimes argued that its retention of democracy (with a two-year break in 1975–1977) for over forty years refutes the case for providing any special measures to ensure the genuine participation by political minorities however configured.

As the following brief account makes clear, the Indian political system does not operate on the winner-take-all principle.

• First, a major component of potential ethnic conflict was removed by the partition of Pakistan in 1947. (The fact that 2 million people died in the violence and 12 million refugees were created, while 10 percent—80 million people—of the remaining Indian population are Muslim should cause advocates of partition to think twice.)

• Second, the reorganization of the states in the 1950s on linguistic grounds paradoxically reduced (but did not eliminate) the importance of linguistic demands and enhanced unity by what has been called "coordinate mutuality" within a federal context.

• Third, the Indian National Congress, the dominant party for much of India's experience since independence, has operated as an interethnic coalition with strong consociational overtones. As Crawford Young says: "At the summit is a national political elite who are committed to reconciling differences through bargaining amongst themselves." India, in other words, is anything but a majoritarian democracy.

• Fourth, while India's extreme diversity has caused considerable tension and has left a number of troublesome issues unresolved (for example, Kashmir and Punjab), on the whole it has served as an integrative force. India's myriad criss-crossing lines of conflict have inhibited the development of a single axis of intense conflict that could polarize the entire society. Ainslee Embree remarks: "In a curious way, the bewildering complexities of Indian society that are so patently divisive have apparently worked in a countervailing fashion to create a pluralistic political society, with the structural strains . . . working to buttress each other."[13] Pluralism has been dispersed and substantially contained within state boundaries.

Democracies that survive twenty years and two changes of government are generally pronounced "stable" by political scientists. India meets these criteria, but it faces continuing threats from increasingly disaffected Muslims, especially in Kashmir; from Hindu militants, whose majoritarian aspirations threaten the delicate balance upon which Indian democracy has rested; and by Sikh separatist demands in the Punjab.

The more common basis of democracy in deeply divided societies has been the broad-based coalition, found in the classic European consociations—Netherlands, Belgium, Austria, Switzerland, and Luxembourg—and in some third world democracies, including Malaysia (whose democratic credentials are seriously flawed) and Lebanon (1944–1975). To be sure, there have been serious failures: Cyprus, Surinam, Nigeria, Sudan, Fiji, and, obviously, Lebanon. The sources of the failure in some cases have had less to do with the actual workings of the system than the destabilizing effect of outside forces (Cyprus and Lebanon). Consociationalism's protagonists claim some limited success in structuring democracies in inauspicious conditions, but it is no magic formula. Consociationalism is in any case a matter of degree: particular systems can be semiconsociational or may embrace certain elements of consociationalism (usually the principle of coalition).

Its critics may validly point out the failures and shortcomings of consociationalism, but they would surely have to recognize that majoritarian systems would have caused even more intense conflict (assuming, which one cannot, that majoritarian systems could have been instituted in the first place) than the failed effort at consociation and its variants. However states like Lebanon, Sudan, or Nigeria attempt to restructure democracy, one thing can be confidently predicted: majoritarian systems that exclude significant political players from a share of power in the national government have no chance of succeeding.

In a survey of independent African states after twenty-five years (written in 1985), a leading student of African politics, Donald Rothchild, says:

> Where a single ethnic group (and its allies) appear to have captured control of state institutions . . . the costs in terms of intense interethnic conflict have proved high. Other ethnic peoples feel excluded from the decision-making process and conclude, rightly or wrongly, that public policies are biased in favour of the dominant political group. Their feelings of powerlessness and comparative disadvantage contribute to a decline in the legitimacy of the state itself, provoking ill-feeling, negative group memories, and even military coups and attempts at ethno-regional secession. An alternative to the dominance of a single group is some form of ethnic-based political coalition. Where all major ethnic groups are assured of at least minimal participation in the governing

process—whether by formal political rules . . . or by informal rules . . . collaboration replaces group competition.[14]

The case of Mauritius is instructive in this respect. It is a small island state (1 million people) with a Hindu majority of 52 percent (who have always constituted the decisive group in determining which party, or parties, constituted the government), Creoles, Muslims, whites, and Chinese. Its politics have usually been conducted largely along ethnic lines. How has it succeeded in maintaining a vigorous parliamentary democracy? According to the Zimbabwean political scientist Eliphas G. Mukonoweshuro,

> Mauritian politicians, over the years, have managed to turn their potentially explosive diversity into a political strength. Out of this poly-ethnic plethora, they have woven a political spoils system which has ensured that each ethnic group has an established stake in the system. This has resulted in the emergence of rules of the political game whose legitimacy and legality is accepted by all the dominant political forces on the island.[15]

So far as is known, no state with an ethnically diverse citizenry has been able to sustain democracy on the basis of simple majoritarianism. Similarly, no state has been able to overcome ethnic divisiveness by outlawing it.

Overwhelmingly, the evidence from the third world is that no state has been able to inculcate a sense of nationhood in its citizenry by "hot-house" methods of nation building. Switzerland is virtually unique in being, in the correct sense, a nation-state whose sense of nationhood transcends ethnic differences. It is unlikely, however, that the Swiss experience could be exported. A further striking feature of ethnically divided societies is that in no single case has a transformation into a "nonethnic" situation occurred (excluded, of course, are the horrific cases of genocide, mass expulsion, and forced assimilation). Most South African political movements are committed to the creation of a nonracial democracy. As a statement of commitment to a wholly nondiscriminatory system, it is an attainable ideal. If it refers to an attitudinal predisposition that animates ordinary individuals on a large scale and penetrates the warp and woof of political and social life, it will be a long time in the making. The evidence cited from the United States, with the most powerful economy in the world and a remarkable history of absorbing immigrants, is far from being nonracial in the attitudinal sense.

The evidence assembled in this section of the chapter has included brief sketches of a wide variety of ethnically divided societies.

These observations demonstrate that, with rare exceptions, parties in such societies are rooted in particular segments of the population so that many of the assumptions held to operate in less diverse societies do not apply. Party government may become synonymous with government by a dominant ethnic group, and parties based in minorities may be excluded from any realistic prospect of a share in power in national government. Such an outcome is profoundly antithetical to the democratic ideal discussed in the introduction.

It is beyond the scope of this chapter to discuss techniques of promoting democratic government in deeply divided societies, although several possible institutional mechanisms, such as federalism and coalition government, have been mentioned in passing. The problem is too deep-seated to be contained by constitutional design, indispensable though this is. Ultimately, serious questions have to be raised about the appropriateness of the nation-state model in states with sharp ethnic conflicts. In a striking analysis of African circumstances, Basil Davidson has described the "generalized collapse of the nation-statist project."[16] As the examples of Canada, Belgium, and the recent separation of Czechoslovakia show, the lack of fit between "nation" and "state" is not a problem confined to developing states.

Some Implications for South Africa

South African voters in a hypothetical future democratic election will almost certainly reflect the long legacy of conflict in their preferences. What may loosely be called "racial memories" will be powerful spurs. Attitudinal nonracialism will prove elusive, but this need not preclude amicable and cooperative relationships and the growth of a South Africanism based on a common recognition that despite their diversity South Africans are united by more than what divides them and that their essential interdependence is the basis of cooperation.

Przeworski stresses that the hallmark of democracy is its "uncertainty."[17] This chapter, accordingly, makes no attempt to predict a configuration of political parties after a democratic election. Constitutions, however, must try to anticipate as many political contingencies as possible, even though they will never be able to anticipate all.

Two assumptions underpin this analysis: first, that South Africa has a strongly entrenched "zero-sum" political culture, deriving from both its long history of conflict and the distinctive operation of its Westminster-derived political institutions; second, that the major parties, the African National Congress and the National party, will have their principal support bases in the black and the white popula-

tions, respectively. The "intermediate" Coloured and Indian categories are likely to distribute their votes, according to survey data,
between both the major parties, as well as others. The Democratic
party may well pick up significant support from them, as well as from
its traditional constituency and among blacks. An important constraint on the excessive racialization of politics could be found in the
mediating effect of the Coloured and Indian categories and, if it is
reasonably successful, the Democratic party. Another constraint will
be the aspiration of all parties to attract support from all groups. It is
inconceivable that the broad racial groups will confront one another
as monolithic blocs. Although this probability will smooth the edges
of racial conflict, it is most unlikely to alter the racial basis of the
major parties.

While the emergence of a dominant, broad-based, aggregative
(catchall) party seems unlikely, it is distinctly possible that the ANC,
with overwhelming black support, fair Coloured and Indian support,
but minuscule white support, could (like SWAPO in Namibia, though
not on the scale of ZANU in Zimbabwe) win a majority. If the winner-
take-all precept were to prevail, perhaps majorities of nonblack categories and a significant minority of blacks might go unrepresented in
the cabinet at the national level. All of this is highly conjectural and
is not offered as a prediction, merely as a possibility that political
engineers should take note of.

What is the likely trajectory of politics? This is even less amenable
to prediction, but there would seem to be at least three possibilities:
(1) the crystallization of the outcome mooted in the preceding paragraph; (2) the fractionalization of the dominant party and the intensification of intrablack political rivalries, including subnational ethnic-
ities; (3) the intensification of "ethnic outbidding," for example, gains
by the Pan-Africanist Congress (PAC), accusing the ANC of "going
soft," "selling out," or the like. The second and third possibilities, it
should be noted, are not mutually exclusive.

It is likely that racial voting will continue to predominate in the
two major population categories. The comparative analysis of divided
societies lends no support to the optimistic view that alternative,
nonethnic bases of mobilization will eliminate, eclipse, or even significantly change rival ethnic voting. (But it should be stressed that
voting that largely follows ethnic lines does not guarantee that all
voters from a particular group will support a single, ethnically based
party.) Possible alternative bases of mobilization would be class
(which is largely encapsulated by ethnicity), religion (not a serious
source of division in South Africa—on the contrary, a potentially
significant bedrock of common values and cross-cutting ties), region,

and ideology (almost certainly likely to be subsumed under ethnicity).

The highly tentative nature of these possibilities makes it clear that they are not projections. They do, however, call to mind Przeworski's comment that "constitutions that are observed and last for a long time are those that reduce the stakes of political battles."[18] Even if South African constitution makers cannot predict political configurations with anything remotely like accuracy, they should surely recognize that our future democracy will be a tender plant: reduced stakes are likely to be in the interests of all contenders. In our context that implies, at the least, that political minorities (however composed or configured) should feel included, not shut out. Coalition government will be a minimum requirement, at least until the tender plant is stronger.

13

Constitutionalism and a Semiparty System in the United States

James W. Ceaser

This examination of the political process in the United States, specifically the party system and representation, will begin with a discussion of an apparently distant and unrelated topic: the character of American constitutionalism. The reason for this detour is that, without an understanding of the connection between the political process and constitutionalism in America, the American political process is unlikely to hold much interest for South Africans engaged in the task of constitution making. The American political process is an eminently practical and empirical subject, and the experience of the United States in this area differs so dramatically from that of South Africa that no simple account of American politics can offer a basis for dialogue or instruction. But when the link between the American political process and constitutionalism is made clear, the American case might help to promote fruitful reflection on some of the constitutional issues that face South Africa.

The object of such an exercise is obviously not to suggest a transfer of American laws or institutions to South Africa. It is rather to encourage consideration of certain basic constitutional principles. If some of these principles should prove interesting, their implementation in a different context would necessarily assume a different institutional form. It is an axiom of comparative politics that general principles translate into different societies in quite dissimilar ways. Such was the starting point of the most perceptive of all foreign observers of America, Alexis de Tocqueville, when he undertook his famous study, *Democracy in America*. "Let us not turn to America," he counseled his French readers, "in order slavishly to copy the institutions she has fashioned for herself, but in order that we may better understand what suits us; let us look there for instruction rather than models."[1]

American Constitutionalism and the Political Process

The American Model. South African scholars of comparative politics today show a pronounced tendency to identify American constitutionalism with the related concepts of a written constitution and judicial review. South Africans appear to be heavily influenced in this view by recent German legal scholarship, where judicial review of a written constitution, particularly respecting the protection of constitutionally sanctioned rights, has been referred to as the American model. This model has increasingly become the practice in Germany under the Basic Law, and German scholars have embraced judicial review as a fundamental element of modern constitutionalism.

There is another reason, however, why this aspect of America's political system should be of great interest today in South Africa. The current South African system is based on a Westminster model of parliamentary sovereignty, without a written constitution or constitutional adjudication. As the discussions to establish a new constitution have proceeded, a consensus has emerged among all the major parties to abandon the Westminster system and to adopt the American model of an "entrenched" constitution with review by an independent judiciary.

Sound reasons connect these elements of constitutionalism with the American tradition. Americans, after all, proudly proclaim themselves to be the first to create governments by written constitutions and then to make governments subject to them. Referring to the early attempts of the states to construct their governments after the American Revolution in 1776, Thomas Jefferson wrote, "Virginia . . . was not only the first of the States, but, I believe I may say, the first of the nations of the earth . . . to form a fundamental constitution, to commit it to writing, and to place it . . . where everyone should be free to appeal to its text."[2]

The importance of this innovation was never thereafter in doubt in America. Written constitutions helped establish a new relationship between the people and their government. Sovereignty was no longer understood to be vested in the government but in a constitution that is a creation of the people. Government acts legitimately only as it

219

acts pursuant to the constitution. Government is thus made subservient to the people, whose will is expressed through the solemn and deliberative decisions that have gone into ratifying a constitution.

America's founders developed this theoretical argument further by giving it a practical, institutional foundation. If the primacy of the written constitution over government was to be respected, the constitution could not be considered as being on the same plane as ordinary law or be changed by the same process employed to enact normal legislation. On this point again, America's founders counted themselves innovators. As James Madison noted in *The Federalist*, "The important distinction so well understood in America between a Constitution established by the people and unalterable by the government, and a law established by the government and alterable by the government, seems to have been little understood and less observed in any other country."[3]

Indeed, it was the failure of the British, or Westminster, model to observe this distinction that led to the founders' specific criticism of that system. In words that might as well have been penned by any South African constitutional scholar today, the founders objected that under the British system "it is maintained that the authority of the Parliament is transcendent and uncontrollable as well with regard to the Constitution as the ordinary objects of legislative provision."[4] A constitution must have the status of "fundamental law," and there must accordingly be a distinct process for making constitutional changes.

Finally, the American founders were the first to entrust the protection of the Constitution, at least in some degree, to an independent judiciary. Although the original Constitution ratified in 1789 did not contain a full bill of rights, it did have several important rights guaranteed in it. The protection of these rights, Alexander Hamilton argued in *The Federalist*, "can be preserved in practice no other way than through the medium of courts of justice, whose duty it must be to declare all acts contrary to the manifest tenor of the Constitution void."[5]

Hamilton's essay was the first important statement of the doctrine we know today as judicial review. The proponents of a bill of rights sought to extend this argument to apply to a fuller list of particular rights. Some of the founders considered this step unwise, not because they did not favor the protection of rights but because they thought it impossible to encode many of them in meaningful legal terms that could be enforced, without exception, as genuine articles of law.

Proponents contended, however, that listing rights in the Constitution, besides having an educative value for the people, would also provide greater security for these rights by allowing for court action through judicial review. A Bill of Rights was added to the U.S. Constitution two years later, in 1791.

No one, therefore, does a disservice to America's contribution to constitutionalism by pointing to the great innovations of a written constitution with judicial review. Nevertheless, there is a danger in identifying these features as the core of the U.S. Constitution or the essence of the American model of constitutionalism. Not only does this view distort the traditional American understanding of constitutionalism; it is also apt to lead scholars to downplay or ignore aspects of America's constitutional experience that are equally important to the protection of rights. After all, if judicial review of a written constitution is taken to be the American model, then in adopting this feature, one has taken quite enough from America. For the rest, it would be better to shop elsewhere.

For this reason, preliminary to an investigation of any other aspect of America's political experience, it is essential to revisit briefly the American understanding of constitutionalism. This analysis should help make clear the importance of the political process, as sketched in part by the U.S. Constitution, to the American understanding of constitutionalism.

The American Model Reconsidered. Virtually all agree that the fundamental aim of the American constitutional system is the protection of basic rights under a government that is democratic and effective. Effective or energetic government refers broadly to one able to provide for defense and security and to carry out its own policies in a reasonably efficient manner. Let us, for the sake of this investigation, consider the goal of the protection of rights in isolation, even though this goal obviously cannot be secured in the real world in the absence of an effective government. Restricting our focus to this question, we find that—contrary to the view implied by purveyors of the American model—the protection of basic rights has not been conceived in America as the exclusive, or even the primary, domain of judges interpreting constitutional provisions. Rather, at least until quite recently, it has been seen largely as the responsibility of the political process.

America's founders assigned so much of this responsibility to the political process for two reasons. The first relates to what the founders called the "natural feebleness of the judiciary [which] is in continual jeopardy of being overpowered, awed, or influenced by its co-ordinate branches."[6] Writing in 1788 before the establishment of

221

judicial review, the founders probably exaggerated the weakness of the judiciary as a way of building a stronger case for its independence. But their analysis is not without merit. Where there is a strong will on the part of the political bodies to disregard rights, it is difficult for courts and judges, no matter how independent they may be in theory, to hold out for a long time. Courts lack a base in direct popular support, the strongest force in a democratic system.

To be sure, with the development over time of a strong tradition of judicial independence, as has occurred in the United States, courts can win a measure of general support and thus can begin to operate with considerable confidence. But the historical record of courts should caution against inflated expectations. Even in the United States, often courts either have failed to make a stand or have been effectively overridden.

Taking into account, therefore, the inherent limitations of the judicial power in a democratic system, the founders argued that it was necessary for the political process to be so arranged as to make a violation of rights less likely. Such arrangements should be instituted, they maintained, even if it meant making government somewhat less energetic in implementing legislative policies. Security and defense were a different matter and allowed for quick action by the executive.

Accordingly, we find the institutional devices in the American system—separation of powers, checks and balances, and a "semiparty system"—that I will describe below. Moreover, the ability of the Supreme Court to maintain its independence and confidence has depended in part on these same institutional devices. The division of power among different political bodies has allowed the Court at critical points to find an active ally inside the political process, so that it has not been left to stand entirely alone. At some moments in American history, this was the president, at other moments the Congress.

The second reason why the political process holds a large share of the responsibility for protecting rights has been widely overlooked. The protection and implementation of many fundamental rights, including such important "first generation" rights as property and privacy, cannot be fully achieved by the simple mechanism of listing rights and making them subject to legal adjudication. Rights in substantial measure can be protected and implemented only through the general policies adopted by government. They are of necessity embedded in a network of laws and statutes. It is accordingly impossible to separate the realm of rights from the realm of ordinary law.

Consider, for example, the fundamental right to acquire and hold property. To be sure, courts of law, working from bills of rights and various constitutional provisions, can provide important protection for certain basic aspects of property rights, such as an injunction against taking property for public use without just compensation (the Fifth Amendment). Yet it is clear that one's right to property can be undermined by ordinary legislative acts that fall within the powers of what any legislature can do. Property, we know, can be effectively destroyed by an excessive tax rate, by regulations that make conducting business impossible, by zoning laws, by inflationary policies, and so on. There is no limit in a modern economy to the ways in which "ordinary" legislative acts may impinge on a right to acquire property.

Nevertheless, when one speaks of the implementation of a right, as in a right to *acquire* property, it is evident that positive legislation is often required. Without such legislation, for example, there could be no corporations, which require laws of limited liability, and different forms of intellectual property would have scant protection. Modern property in many aspects scarcely exists without certain laws, and these laws must be enacted and adjusted as circumstances change. The need for legislation in the protection of property applies as well to certain other fundamental rights, such as a right to a zone of privacy.

Summarizing the founders' argument, then, we can say that while courts relying on bills of rights can do much to protect basic rights, a major part of the responsibility for implementing rights lies with the political process. This understanding has been a central theme of traditional American constitutionalism. Thus, the modern view that teaches a disjunction between rights and politics not only is misleading but also offers a dangerous departure from a sound understanding of constitutionalism. The identification of rights with things that courts alone deal with—protecting "trumps" that are absolute—perpetuates the false notion that the political process is concerned with mere interests, while only courts and judges deal in the sacred realm of protecting rights. This view reduces politics to a lowly and secondary activity, while it inflates the role of legal processes far beyond what anyone could have imagined—and far beyond what courts are competent to do. The consequence is to foster political irresponsibility on the one hand and judicial highhandedness on the other.

It is beyond my purpose here to discuss the origins of this misunderstanding. Suffice it to say that while this view is foreign to the original tradition of American constitutionalism, American scholars in this generation bear much of the responsibility for spreading it. This view has won the acclaim of American legal scholars and has become the standard view in American law schools. From this bastion, it has expanded, with the assistance of innumerable international conferences, into the world's legal community, where it has become reified as the American model. Notwithstanding America's own reluctance to enter into certain international human rights conventions, the American model has served as an intellectual inspiration to the burgeoning enterprise of international human rights commissions and tribunals.

The American model, so conceived and misnamed, has led to repeated misinterpretations of one of the most famous arguments about the character of American constitutionalism—the argument for pluralism developed by James Madison in *Federalists* 10 and 51. The details of this argument need not be rehearsed here. The important point at issue for Madison in these essays is how the political process can be arranged, through the character of representation and the dispersion of power among different institutions, to protect and implement important rights and maintain a constitutional system.

Yet despite Madison's own presentation of his argument, a number of modern scholars have contended that his whole line of reasoning is confused. For, they say, if Madison were really talking about *rights*, he clearly could not have gone on as he did to discuss representation and legislation. Rights, after all, are absolutes that are supposed to be guaranteed by courts, not subject to adjustment by legislators. What Madison was really talking about, then, was not rights, but interests.

It is a measure of the hold of the American model on America's and the world's thinkers today that so tortured an interpretation should have gained such wide currency. If Madison was "guilty" of anything, it was only of having the subtlety to conceive of the problem of rights and of how they are protected in terms broader than the modern institution of judicial review. For Madison, the content of many rights is fleshed out and protected in and through a political process. "What are many of the most important acts of legislation," he asked, "but so many judicial determinations, not indeed concerning the rights of single persons, but concerning the rights of large bodies of citizens?"

The protection of rights is not just a function of courts wielding their trumps, but the contingent task of making proximate adjustments of general principles to changing sets of circumstances. The protection of rights so conceived involves the ability of groups and interests to acquire, at the end of the day, a reasonable and fair result from a whole array of public policies. The prospect for achieving such a result depends on the practical characteristics of the political process, such as the way in which political power is allocated and dispersed and the prevailing views of political representation.

Nothing in this understanding of constitutionalism, I should emphasize, is intended to diminish a proper regard for the role of judges or courts. On the contrary, as America's founders emphasized, the protection of rights indeed often involves near-absolute claims that individuals can take into courts of law and that courts can protect. But it does not follow from this claim that courts are the only protector of rights or that the question of rights ends where politics begins. Politics is also a process for realizing and protecting rights.

We should now be in a position to appreciate that a substantial part of American constitutionalism, both in establishing a democratic and effective government and in protecting and implementing rights, is found in the political process. With this argument in mind, it is possible to return to an earlier point of contrast and make the following assertion: the difference between the American and the Westminster systems inheres as much in the different characters of their political processes as in the existence of judicial review.

A Semiparty System

Certain linguists have said that many of the rules of grammar of any language can be extrapolated from a careful analysis of a single sentence. Perhaps the same can be said of the "grammar" of an electoral system. To test this idea, I pulled the first "sentence" from the record of the 1988 election returns. It consists of the electoral returns from the small state of Maine, which for reasons of geography happens to be listed first in the table of electoral data in the *United States Statistical Abstract*.

Recall, first, a few basic facts about the American electoral system. Elections in America are set by the calendar—not, as often happens under parliamentary systems, by the fall of a government or by the decision of the government to hold an election. Presidential elections in the United States are held every fourth year.

Citizens vote for two other federal offices. One is for members of the House of Representatives, a body of 435 persons elected from single-member geographic districts of roughly equal population and serving a term of two years. Second, citizens vote for members of the Senate, a body of 100 members; two senators are elected from each of the fifty states to serve six-year terms. To ensure stability and continuity, elections to the Senate are staggered, and only one-third of the body is renewed in each election.

Thus, federal elections are held every two years. In the year of a

225

TABLE 13–1
Results of Federal Elections in Maine, 1988

	No. of Votes	% of Vote
President–Vice president		
Bush–Quayle (Republican)	304,087	56
Dukakis–Bentsen (Democrat)	240,508	44
Senate		
Wyman (Republican)	104,009	19
Mitchell (Democrat)	446,520	81
House District 1		
O'Meara (Republican)	115,549	37
Brennan (Democrat)	189,161	63
House District 2		
Snowe (Republican)	164,597	66
Hayes (Democrat)	85,576	34

NOTE: Minority party candidates have been omitted, and percentages have been rounded off.
SOURCE: *United States Statistical Abstract.*

presidential election—for example, 1988, 1992, and 1996—citizens vote for a president, a member of the House, and in about one-third of the states for a senator. In an election year when a president is not being chosen—for example, 1986, 1990, and 1994—referred to as "midterm" or "off-year" elections, citizens vote for members of the House and in a third of the states for a senator. Citizens cast their vote for these different offices at the same elections—that is, on the same day at the same time.[7] But the election for each office is quite distinct. Citizens today make a separate choice on their ballot for the president, for senator, and for a member of the House of Representatives.

In the election in Maine in 1988, citizens voted for three different federal offices—for president, for a senator, and in two districts for members of the House of Representatives. The results are listed in table 13–1.

Anyone from a parliamentary system scanning these results is apt to view them with bewilderment, if not downright disbelief. They appear to make no sense and to reflect a totally different grammar, as different as Afrikaner or English is from Hungarian. The point that causes perplexity is the radical swing in the party scores among the

226

elections. The same citizens who gave a twelve percentage point victory to Mr. Bush (a Republican) gave a sixty-two–point victory in the Senate race to Mr. Mitchell (a Democrat). This picture grows more perplexing when one looks at the two House districts. In district 1, the voters gave the Republican (Ms. Snowe) a huge victory, while also giving a huge margin to Mr. Mitchell.

Two slight qualifications should be stated about this analysis. First, the large point difference in the party scores between the presidential and the senatorial votes does not mean all the voters ignored the party label. Survey results would probably show that virtually all those who voted for the Republican for the Senate or the House also voted for President Bush. This does leave a huge group of citizens, however, who were voting for candidates from different parties. Second, although this example from Maine was selected randomly (because it appeared first), it represents a fairly extreme case. But it is extreme in degree only; much the same was happening in a less pronounced form in many states and districts.

The great difference in the character of the parliamentary and the American systems with regard to representation may be captured by a simple cultural observation. Whereas a citizen from a parliamentary system would demand an explanation for the oddity of the results in Maine, an American observer would likely see no need for special comment; the results would appear more or less normal. Obviously, the grammatical rules of these two systems are quite different.

What is going on? There are two logical possibilities. First, the voters are thinking chiefly in terms of parties, but they are schizophrenic—perhaps deliberately so. A voter might be reasoning along the following lines: I am voting for a Republican for president, but I want to make sure that the whole of the government is not under the control of the Republican party. I will therefore seek to introduce a kind of check by putting a different party in control of the other institutions.

As strange as this thinking might appear to a South African, at least it presupposes a voter who thinks primarily in terms of party, the characteristic logic among voters in a parliamentary system. Not so, however, with the second possibility. Here the citizens cast their votes not on the basis of party but on the merits of the individual candidate or on how well that individual might serve the interests of the congressional district or the state. According to this possibility, nothing schizophrenic has occurred in the results in Maine. The outcome of the election reflects the citizens' choice about which individuals they preferred for the specific offices. While the party label appears on the ballot, it is just not that important to the voter.

Voting studies can help us to know which of these two possibilities is more important. While evidence suggests that some voters in recent years deliberately acted to split their choice between the parties, by far the greater part of the deviation from a party vote occurs because many voters base their choice *not* on political party but rather on a judgment about the persons running.

This point is confirmed not just from what we know about the voters but from what we can observe of the candidates in the course of their campaigns. Candidates in the United States often present themselves to the electorate chiefly not on the basis of which party they belong to but rather on the basis of who they are, what they as individuals stand for, what they would do in office, and how they would serve the interests of the district or state. Foreign observers who study American electoral campaigns for Congress are surprised to find that in some cases the candidates may hardly even mention their party affiliation. The party element, in short, is not always important, either to the voters or to the candidates.

Let us, then, attach a name to the system we have begun to describe. The United States is, and for more than 150 years has been, a semiparty system. As this label suggests, both party and nonparty influences are at work in the system, even though up to now, in order to explain the contrast with the Westminster system, I have stressed the nonparty elements. The concept of the political party is neither absent from the American system nor dominant, as it is in a parliamentary system. This fact accounts for the oddity of American elections.

Some have argued that the limited role for the party in the American system places it "behind" other democratic systems, which have supposedly developed beyond ours. But the notion that a putative historical trend can supply the criterion for judging what is choiceworthy in politics has been exploded in recent years, along with many other historicist myths. Nor is it clear any longer where "history" in the area of parties and representation seems to be taking us. For many years it was an article of faith among political scientists, based on the writings of Maurice Duverger, that the collectivist parties, with their programmatic ideas of representation, were replacing the more individualist, "bourgeois" parties.[8] Yet the bourgeois type of party has emerged as the prominent survivor, at least in Europe. Let us, then, dismiss any simple idea that history has conveniently decided for us the character of modern parties and representation. These matters are determined by local circumstances and by the choices of those who fashion laws and constitutions.

A semiparty system rests on a pluridimensional view of representation. In America today, three basic notions of representation coexist, sometimes in an uneasy relationship. The first two views are associated with the American founding and together constitute the classical view of representation. The third is the party view, which developed shortly after the American founding and has been added to the American system in the actual practice of politics.

The first view of representation is that the representative be selected for a capacity to act for the good of the nation. The representatives ideally constitute a "chosen body of citizens, whose wisdom may best discern the true interests of their country and whose patriotism and love of justice will be least likely to sacrifice it to temporary or partial considerations."[9] This idea is connected to the concept of deliberation in politics, especially with regard to the legislative branch. A representative goes to Congress and makes up his mind, having reasoned on the merits of the arguments presented for discussion. Essential to this concept is the idea that each individual representative must not be bound in his legislative vote, either by his constituents or by an association with the president or fellow members of Congress. Each member of Congress has the right, nay the duty, to decide how to vote at his discretion with respect to every individual question that faces the legislature.[10]

The second view of representation is that the representative acts to promote the interests of his geographic constituency, be it the state or the congressional district. The representative is a kind of ambassador of the state or district in the national councils, at least where the interests of his constituents are involved. The representative makes sure that the views of the constituency are presented and that in any national policy enacted the special concerns of the district are not overlooked—indeed, that they are well taken care of. The representative remains unbound in his vote under this view, but the object of his attention and concern is narrower. And much of the legislative activity is taken up with bargaining and logrolling rather than pure deliberation.

These two ideas of representation are at some level in tension, and in the eighteenth century they were sometimes presented as the two dominant, rival theories of representation. Edmund Burke's "Speech to the Electors of Bristol" (1774) is the most famous exposition of these two views and of the tension between them. America's founders appeared to have taken a more pragmatic view of this tension. They made provisions to foster the first idea of representa-

229

tion, which remained their ideal and standard, even as they realized that the second idea must inevitably play a substantial role in a democratic system that spanned a large territory. For the founders, then, these two views shaded in practice into each other, and a sharp distinction between them was not always possible. For our purposes, the two views make up variants of a classical or preparty understanding of representation, characterized by the idea that the representative acts individually as a free agent and is not bound by the program of a national party.

The third view of representation is the modern party view. The representative here represents the positions of a national party, where the party stakes out a program or at least embodies a certain distinguishable set of principles about the basic idea of where to take the nation. In selecting a representative, the citizen votes primarily for the general party view, with the qualities of the individual representative being, if not irrelevant, then generally not decisive. The expectation in this vote is that the representative will work with the rest of the team, subordinating any personal views to the collective wisdom and will of the party. Local interests are subordinated to the party view. An election, in this general understanding, does more than choose a set of individuals. It indicates a national direction and expresses a will of where the majority, should there be one, wishes to go.

This idea of representation, though not part of the original American founding, was invented within the first decade of the nation's existence. Thomas Jefferson, one of the founders of the Democratic party (which is the oldest political party in the world today), wrote as follows about the election of 1800: "The nation declared its will by dismissing functionaries of one principle and electing those of another, in the two branches, executive and legislature, submitted to their election."[11] After virtually dying out by 1816, parties were revived in the 1820s and became a fully accepted part of the American political system by the 1830s. In terms of comparative political development, it therefore can be said that Americans gave birth to the modern, mass-based political party and to the idea of party representation in a democratic context.

Americans thus have had long experience with parties and with the party understanding of representation. The party rests on top of the original system as a kind of sedimentary overlay that has modified but never replaced the system. It would be a mistake, however, to conceive of a semiparty regime as a system that has assigned a fixed and unchanging weight to the different ideas of representation. The real characteristic of this system is the fluid and dynamic relationship

230

between the classical and the party ideas. In some eras, the party idea has been stronger than in others, and within the same era it has expanded or contracted according to the prevailing political circumstances. Some national elections find the party idea operating in little more than name; in others, either the public decides or circumstances dictate that party should "count" considerably.

No single, frozen formula, then, dictates the weight of the different representative principles in America's semiparty system. Not only does that weight vary according to shifts in political circumstances, but it has also changed in response to certain defects attached to an excessive reliance on one or the other idea of representation. As one idea gains ascendancy and reveals some of its problems—for example, a sense of being oppressed that is connected with the rigidity of too much party discipline on the one hand, or a sense of drift or policy fragmentation connected with individual, classical representation on the other—an adjustment can be made. A mechanism of checks and balances operates among the different ideas of representation inside the electoral process itself.

We can now state more clearly the difference between the American system and most other democratic systems. In modern parliamentary systems the party theory has eclipsed the classical idea of representation, while in the United States the classical idea has always been quite strong. Even this characterization, of course, is an oversimplification. As anyone who studies modern parliamentary systems will testify, important nonparty elements are often at work just beneath the surface, not to mention the many parties or blocs that represent local geographic or nationalist sentiments. Indeed, an indepth analysis of parliamentary regimes today would almost certainly show an increase in nonparty pressures over the past quarter-century. But for the time being at least, the large difference in degree between parliamentary systems and the United States constitutes a difference in kind.

Another, more striking comparison illustrates the difference between the American semiparty system and the parliamentary systems. In every major parliamentary regime, a system of election by proportional representation has been either seriously considered or actually put into operation. In the United States, proportional representation would be nonsense. This is not because of the existence of single-member districts, though they are a contributory factor. It is because of the governing concept of representation. Proportional representation is based on the idea of proportions, which assumes a common denominator. That common denominator is the party vote, of which the proportion is a share. If the voters are not voting principally for parties, however, but for individuals, no common denominator exists.

One final expression of the difference between elections in a parliamentary system and in America's semiparty system is that, by and large, an election in a parliamentary system can be conceived of as one event. The essence of that event is captured in the answer to the question, How many seats did each party win? In the United States, an election is simultaneously one event and some five hundred separate events. People will generally want to know how the parties did. But perhaps even more, they will want to know which individuals won certain races of importance to them. That is much of the "meaning" of an election.

The Causes of a Semiparty System

What are the causes for the existence of the semiparty system in the United States? Since it is a hybrid—part nonparty and part party—one must look at both sides of the equation to understand its causes.

On the classical or nonparty side of the equation, first is the fact that this view of representation is part of the spirit of the Constitution, even if it was never written into that document. America is still governed by the Constitution, with only a modest number of formal modifications. Some of the best statements in political theory of the classical view of representation are found in *The Federalist*, and that view remains both the traditional and the preferred one in America.

A second reason for the persistence of the classical element in American politics is the structure of the government itself. Under a separation-of-powers system, Congress does not choose the president, and the government does not fall if the Congress and president are in disagreement. Indeed, there is no "government" to fall. The government is nothing more nor less than the existing set of elected officials, who must live with each other until the calendar brings the next election. Without a government that can fall, the ultimate incentive for party discipline does not exist. If members of the president's party desert him in a vote in Congress, nothing really "happens." Indeed, sometimes a president can win with more support from members of the opposition party than from his own. In any event, if the president's view does not prevail, one simply goes on to the next question.

The system of representation is not just a logical consequence of this structural arrangement, but also a cause for its existence and continuance. As the voters in choosing a president and members of Congress vote in large degree for individuals and hold them accountable as individuals, each elected official has his own independent relationship with his constituents that is not controlled by the party. This electoral connection ensures that there will be a separation of powers not only in theory, but in reality as well.

The third factor that maintains the nonparty element of representation in the United States is the system of nomination of the candidates within the parties. Although the parties loosely nominate the candidates, in fact it is the citizens in each state or district who identify with the party that made this decision. As a consequence, there is no central party control over the nomination of the candidates, and the classical idea of representation prevails to a large extent even in the nomination of the candidates inside the parties.

Still, the United States is a semiparty system, which means there is some element of party in the system. Occasionally, that element can be surprisingly strong, even with all the nonparty influences at work. The party element is caused, first, by the idea of party representation in the United States, which has its own long and honorable tradition. This idea has been called on at certain moments, by Jefferson in 1800 and by other leaders thereafter, to insist on a collective sense of purpose attached to a national party principle or program.

Another cause of the party element is, paradoxically, the very system of separating the powers of the president from those of Congress that works in favor of the classical theory of representation. Because these two institutions are so independent of each other yet so require each other's cooperation, a mechanism of some kind is needed to provide coordination. The political party has been one of the instruments filling that role. There used to be a saying, or perhaps a prayer, in American politics: What the Constitution separates, party unites. To be accurate, however, one would have to add, Only some of the time and only in some measure.

The Characteristics of a Semiparty System

What are some of the characteristics of a semiparty system? The party element that operates as a subtext is already comprehensible to those in a parliamentary system; it is the consequences that flow from the nonparty influences that merit attention here.

First, there is no necessity for—and often no such thing as—the majority, at least as that term is understood in a parliamentary system. In America, no group of representatives are virtually bound to vote together or to function as a unified team. The party may supply a certain element of this sentiment, but it does not monopolize the American process. Indeed, since American politics frequently

TABLE 13–2

Two Key Congressional Votes during the Presidency of George Bush

(A yes vote supported the position of President Bush, a Republican)

Final Budget Reconciliation, October 26, 1990[a]

House of Representatives		Senate	
Yes	No	Yes	No
228	200	54	45
47 Republicans	126 Republicans	19 Republicans	25 Republicans
181 Democrats	74 Democrats	35 Democrats	20 Democrats

Authorization to Use Force for the Persian Gulf War, January 12, 1991[a]

House of Representatives		Senate	
Yes	No	Yes	No
250	183	52	47
164 Republicans	3 Republicans	42 Republicans	2 Republicans
86 Democrats	179 Democrats	10 Democrats	45 Democrats
	1 Independent		

a. The first vote took place before the 1990 elections and the second vote after, which accounts for the difference in the number of Republicans and Democrats between the two votes. Not all members voted.
Source: Author.

functions with different parties in control of the presidency and the Congress, a strict party majority would make governing impossible. But even when the same party controls all the branches of the government, it does not function as a party or a majority in the parliamentary sense.

Governing in the United States therefore does not consist of calling forth the preexisting majority, the members of which are known in advance. Rather, majority formation is an iterative process. *Majorities must be built on each issue, each question, and each policy.* Whether a majority will exist usually cannot be known in advance; and who will be in that majority, should it form, also cannot be known. The exception occurs when party sentiment is running very high and when the same party controls the presidency and both houses of the Congress. Each issue must produce its own majority.

An example of the curious pattern of voting in Congress is found in table 13–2, which records the votes on the two most important questions during the presidency of George Bush. On the first vote on the budget bill in 1990, when the president abandoned his promise not to raise taxes, the position favored by President Bush managed to prevail even with a majority of his own party members voting against it. Of course, this position was adopted by the president after consulting with various members of the opposite party. The second vote, on the Persian Gulf War, more closely resembles a parliamentary division, especially in the Senate. Still, as the president's party did not hold a majority, he needed support from some Democrats to prevail.

More generally speaking, as one moves from vote to vote in Congress, the majority changes in composition. Because the individual members of Congress decide on their own, each majority is different. In terms of parliamentary voting, every vote is virtually a conscience vote, with some pressure from the party.

Second, and as a consequence of this system, almost every legislative issue involves a process of deliberation and bargaining. Often this process involves individuals working together from different parties. Each session of Congress is filled with instances of members working together on issues where they share common ground, while opposing each other on issues where they are deeply divided. Inveterate foes on some issues, they may be staunch allies on others. There is therefore no simple line dividing friends and foes in Congress but a complex network of contacts that crosses the aisle and forces individuals to explore relationships with other members. To be in the minority party is not necessarily to be without power or influence, for the votes are usually not strict party votes.

Finally, as each individual congressman and senator—and of course, the president—is his own free agent, power is remarkably dispersed on domestic issues in the United States. As the party or majority does not control the game, power often lies in the many congressional committees and ultimately with each individual elected official. Scores of elected officials are thus important in Washington, and hundreds hold at least a piece of power and exercise it at their own discretion. Not only does this system work to satisfy the ambitions of many elected officials and to enlist their energies in legislating and policy making, but it provides multiple points of access for different interests and groups. The individual representative is the window or entry point through which groups press their claims and seek to protect their interests and rights. This system obviously can lack discipline and coherence, but it does satisfy a sense of sharing power and openness to the major interests of society.

Conclusion

These last three points are important enough to be reformulated as a conclusion, as they pose a series of basic questions that have been largely ignored in modern liberal democratic theory. They have been ignored, on the one hand, because they do not even occur in the logic of parliamentary regimes, and on the other hand, because treatments of American democratic theory generally stress as significant only the legal aspects of the so-called American model. The theoretical implications of America's political process have thus been forgotten or shunted to the side, as curiosities irrelevant to the great issues of democracy and constitutionalism.

The first question to be asked is whether modern democratic representation must be attached exclusively to the idea of party. Almost everyone assumes today that there is only one idea of representation—the party idea. Modern democratic government is party government. Nonparty elements of representation are regarded as quaint vestiges of a bygone era, which are either discouraged or, in some cases, placed incoherently into a second chamber of parliament.

Yet it is not at all certain that democratic theory so conceived is doing a good job of accounting for practice, let alone guiding it. Even in parliamentary systems we are finding more pressures emerging from other notions of representation besides that of the political party. Sometimes these new ideas deviate from democratic standards of democracy and preach corporatist or ascriptive principles. The classical principle, while it may allow for a good deal of informal weight from such elements, is fully compatible with the democratic idea. It may be wondered, therefore, to what extent it is wise today to lock a particular idea of representation into an entrenched constitution. May not this be an area in which we are likely to see some important changes, where room should be left, at least at lower levels of government, to experiment with other concepts of genuinely democratic representation?

The second forgotten question is whether democratic theory can be indifferent to the number of persons who hold some part of the active, formal power in the political system. This question has been hidden under the currently reigning assumption that as long as those holding power are subject to election, the system is democratic and any remaining differences are negligible. Yet observation of the American political process indicates that it matters greatly whether immediate, effective power is in the hands of a tiny handful of persons, even if they are subject ultimately to some kind of democratic check, or whether it is placed into scores of hands. The dispersion of political power inside the American system constitutes one of its chief points of differentiation from the Westminster system.

Finally comes the question of how majorities are formed in a democratic political system. This question, too, has been ignored under the dominant assumption that a democratic system must always have—or be in search of—a majority. America's political system, however, is based on an iterative process of forming discrete majorities, which are not by necessity based on a party majority. This system is arguably at the crux of the protection of rights and liberty through the political process. It is through this process that various groups, representing large numbers of individuals, have often been able to protect their interests and rights.

Of course, institutional solutions never work perfectly. Their criterion of success is not whether they succeed all the time but whether they operate to set in motion a certain desired and beneficial tendency. For this reason, incidentally, analysts of a legalistic bent often fail to appreciate institutional solutions, for legalistic analysts reason in absolute terms. It does not constitute a contradiction, therefore, to note that the iterative process of forming discrete majorities has not only been associated with egregious failures in American history but has also contributed directly to the inability to protect rights. Nevertheless, this process has contributed to the maintenance of rights and the cause of constitutionalism.

To a far greater extent than is commonly realized, then, the genius of the American system lies in its political process and not exclusively in the legal model of judicial review. By considering some of these political principles—not with a view to copying them but with a view to finding what Tocqueville called instruction—those preparing to write a new constitution for a great country may find something helpful in the American experience.

Notes

CHAPTER 2: CONSTITUTIONALISM IN SOUTH AFRICA, *Pierre J. J. Olivier*

1. Willie Esterhuyse, "The Normative Dimension of Future South African Political Development," in D. J. van Vuuren et al., *South Africa in the Nineties* (Pretoria: HSRC Publishers, 1991), pp. 19–38.

2. Louis Henkin, *Constitutionalism, Democracy, and Foreign Affairs* (New York: Columbia University Press, 1990), p. 6.

3. John E. Finn, *Constitutions in Crisis—Political Violence and the Rule of Law* (New York: Oxford University Press, 1991), p. 28.

4. Ibid., p. 29.

5. See Charles H. McIlwain, *Constitutionalism: Ancient and Modern*, rev. ed. (Ithaca, N.Y.: Cornell University Press, 1947), pp. 21–22; Jethro K. Lieberman, *The Enduring Constitution* (St. Paul: West Publishing Co., 1987), p. 10; Henkin, *Constitutionalism, Democracy, and Foreign Affairs*, pp. 6–7; Boulle, Harris, and Hoexter, *Constitutional and Administrative Law* (Cape Town: Juta, 1989), p. 20.

6. Finn, *Constitutions in Crisis*, p. 29.

7. Lieberman, *The Enduring Constitution*, p. 10.

8. John Locke, *Civil Government*, book 2, chap. 2.

9. Henkin, *Constitutionalism, Democracy, and Foreign Affairs*, p. 6.

10. Graham Walker, *Moral Foundations of Constitutional Thought* (Princeton: Princeton University Press, 1990), p. 4.

11. Ronald Dworkin, *Taking Rights Seriously* (Cambridge, Mass.: Harvard University Press, 1977), pp. vii–viii, 1–13, 131–49; *A Matter of Principle* (Cambridge, Mass.: Harvard University Press, 1985), p. 34; and Finn, *Constitutions in Crisis*, pp. 28 and following.

12. See ibid.

13. Ibid., p. 29.

14. Carl J. Friedrich, *Transcendent Justice* (Durham, N.C.: Duke University Press, 1964), p. 3.

15. Finn, *Constitutions in Crisis*, p. 36.

16. Ibid.

17. Walter F. Murphy, "An Ordering of Constitutional Values," *Southern California Law Review*, vol. 53 (1980): 706–7.

18. Austin, *The Province of Jurisprudence Determined*, ed. 1954: 254; and Dicey, *Introduction to the Study of the Law of the Constitution*, 9th ed: 68.

19. 1937 AD 229 at 237.

20. *Principes de politique applicables à tous les gouvernements représentatifs*, Paris 1815, pp. 38–39, as quoted by Ghita Ionescu, "The Theory of Liberal Constitutionalism," in Vernon Bogdanor, ed., *Constitutions in Democratic Politics* (Vermont: Gower Press, 1988), pp. 33 at 35 and following.

21. Laurence J. Boulle, *South Africa and the Consociational Option* (Cape Town: Juta & Co., 1984), pp. 1–3.

22. Finn, *Constitutions in Crisis*, p. 30.

23. Sotirios Barber, *On What the Constitution Means* (Baltimore: Johns Hopkins University Press, 1984), p. 103.

24. Finn, *Constitutions in Crisis*, pp. 40–41.

25. McIlwain, *Constitutionalism*, p. 144.

26. See Boulle, Harris, and Hoexter, *Constitutional and Administrative Law*, pp. 38–41.

27. Ibid., p. 48.

28. D. H. van Wyk, "Persoonlike status in die Suid-Afrikaanse Publiek-reg," (LLD thesis, Unisa, 1979), p. 77.

29. Dion Basson and Henning Viljoen, *South African Constitutional Law* (Cape Town: Juta, 1988), p. 220.

30. Ibid., p. 224.

31. Boulle, Harris, and Hoexter, *Constitutional and Administrative Law*, p. 89.

32. Ibid., pp. 49–51.

33. Richard Luyt, "African Constitutionalism: Constitutions in the Context of Decolonization," in John Benyon, ed., *Constitutional Change in South Africa* (Pietermaritzburg: University of Natal Press, 1978), p. 16.

34. Issa G. Shivji, "State and Constitutionalism in Africa: A New Democratic Perspective," in African Regional Institute on Comparative Constitutionalism, Working Papers of the American Council of Learned Societies, 1989, p. 23.

35. Published in *Policy Guide*, vol. 1, no. 9 (1992), June 1992, p. 1.

36. Ibid., clause B 1.1.

37. Ibid., clause B 1.3.

38. Ibid., clause B 2.2.

39. Ibid., clause B 5.1.

40. Ibid., clause B 8.

41. See *Sowetan*, February 8, 1990, p. 6.

42. Bertus de Villiers, *Pitfalls for Negotiations and Democracy* (Pretoria: H.S.R.C. Publications, 1992), p. 4.

CHAPTER 4: FEDERALISM AND THE POLITICAL PARTIES, *Kader Asmal*

1. National Party, *Constitutional Rule in a Participatory Democracy* (Pretoria: 1990), p. 9.

2. Ibid., p. 10.

3. Ibid., par. 2.6.1.

4. British Royal Commission on the Constitution 1969–1973, par. 531.

5. Ibid., par. 526.
6. *Star*, September 4, 1991.

CHAPTER 5: CAN AMERICAN FEDERALISM HELP? *Daniel J. Elazar*

1. Donald Lutz, *Popular Consent and Popular Control: Whig Political Theory in the Early State Constitutions* (Baton Rouge: Louisiana State University Press, 1980).
2. Daniel J. Elazar, *The American Constitutional Tradition* (Lincoln: University of Nebraska Press, 1988), pp. 97–98.
3. Martin Landau, "Federalism, Redundancy, and System Reliability," *Publius*, vol. 3, no. 2 (1973), pp. 173–96.

CHAPTER 6: LIBERTY, COMMERCE, AND PROSPERITY, *Dennis Davis*

1. Robert Dahl, "Why Free Markets Are Not Enough," *1992 Journal of Democracy*, vol. 15 (1982).
2. Sunstein, *After the Rights Revolution* (Cambridge: Harvard University Press, 1990), pp. 40–41.
3. Charles Simpkins, in P. Hugo, ed., *Redistribution and Affirmative Action: Working on South Africa's Political Economy* (Johannesburg: Southern Book Publishers, 1992), p. 126.
4. S. Archer and P. Moll, in I. Abedian and B. Standish, eds., *Economic Growth in South Africa: Selected Policy Issues* (Cape Town: Oxford University Press, 1992), p. 150.
5. Sunstein, p. 41.
6. Arblaster, *Democracy* (1987), p. 80.
7. *Interim Report on Group and Individual Rights* (Pretoria: South African Law Commission, 1991).
8. Law Commission, *Interim Report*, p. 364.
9. David Dyzenhaus, *South African Journal on Human Rights* (SAJHR), vol. 24 (1991).
10. Law Commission, *Interim Report*, p. 535.
11. Ibid., p. 536.
12. John Rawls, *Theory of Justice* (Oxford: Oxford University Press, 1971), p. 182.
13. Geoff Budlender, *SAJHR*, vol. 8 (1992), p. 302.
14. See, for example, Lochner v. New York 1905 (198), U.S. 45; Coppage v. Kansas 1914 (236) U.S. 1; Pennsylvania Coal Company v. Mahon 1922 (260) U.S. 393.
15. Richard W. Bauman, *SAJHR*, vol. 8 (1992), p. 355.
16. L. H. Tribe, *American Constitutional Law* (Westbury: Foundation Press, 1988), p. 571.
17. Law Commission, working paper no. 25, project 58: Group and Human Rights, 1989, pp. 464–65.
18. J. Murphy, *SAJHR*, vol. 8 (1992), p. 385.

19. (1967)(2) SCR 762.

20. (1977) Supp. SCR1.

21. See *Yale Law Journal*, vol. 10 (1991), p. 527.

22. Robert Nozick, *Anarchy, State and Utopia* (Oxford: Blackwell, 1975).

23. Jennifer Nedelsky, *Private Property and the Limits of American Constitutionalisers: The Madisonian Framework and Its Legacy* (Chicago: University of Chicago Press, 1990), p. 1.

24. Cappelletti, "The Future of Legal Education: A Comparative Perspective," *SAJHR*, vol. 8 (1992), p. 10.

25. See the Draft Article 3 of the Law Commission's proposed bill.

CHAPTER 7: DEMOCRACY AND THE ACQUISITIVE SPIRIT,
Marc F. Plattner

1. Arthur Okun, *Equality and Efficiency* (Washington, D.C.: The Brookings Institution, 1975), p. 1.

2. Richard de Lone, *Small Futures*, a report of the Carnegie Council on Children (New York: Harcourt Brace Jovanovich, 1979), pp. xi, 28.

3. Quoted in Martin Diamond, "The Federalist," in Morton Frisch and Richard Stevens, eds., *American Political Thought* (New York: Charles Scribner's Sons, 1971), p. 52. My understanding of *The Federalist* has been profoundly influenced by Diamond's writings. See also Martin Diamond, "The Federalist," in Leo Strauss and Joseph Cropsey, eds., *History of Political Philosophy*, 2d ed. (Chicago: Rand McNally, 1972).

4. Publius was the pseudonym used by all three authors of *The Federalist*, Alexander Hamilton, James Madison, and John Jay. I refer generally to Publius here rather than to the individual authors of particular numbers of *The Federalist* because I believe that the work as a whole expresses a consistent viewpoint on the issues I am addressing.

5. Alexander Hamilton, James Madison, and John Jay, *The Federalist*, with an introduction by Clinton Rossiter (New York: New American Library, 1961), No. 10, p. 78.

6. Ibid., No. 10, p. 78.

7. Baron de Montesquieu, *The Spirit of the Laws*, trans. Thomas Nugent (New York: Hafner Publishing Company, 1949). *The Spirit of the Laws* is discussed at length in *Federalist* 9 and 47, and cited in 43 and 78. My analysis of Montesquieu owes a great deal to Thomas L. Pangle's superb study, *Montesquieu's Philosophy of Liberalism* (Chicago: University of Chicago Press, 1973).

8. Montesquieu, *Spirit of the Laws*, bk. 4, sect. 5; bk. 5, sect. 3; bk. 8, sect. 16; cf. bk. 4, sect. 7.

9. *Federalist* No. 9, p. 73; No. 6, p. 57; No. 10, p. 81.

10. Montesquieu, *Spirit of the Laws*, bk. 11, sects. 2, 6.

11. Ibid., bk. 11, sect. 5; bk. 19, sect. 27; bk. 20, sect. 7; bk. 11, sects. 4, 6. At one point, Montesquieu refers to England as "a nation that may be justly called a republic, disguised under the form of monarchy" (bk. 5, sect. 19).

12. *Federalist* No. 9, p. 72; No. 47, pp. 301–8.

13. Ibid., No. 10, p. 81.

14. James Madison to Thomas Jefferson, 24 October 1787, in Gaillard Hunt, ed., *The Writings of James Madison*, 9 vols. (New York: G. P. Putnam's Sons, 1900), 5:31.

15. *Federalist* No. 10, p. 83; No. 51, p. 324; No. 10, p. 84 (see also No. 14, pp. 100–101; No. 37, p. 227); No. 56, p. 349.

16. Thomas Jefferson, *Notes on the State of Virginia*, in Adrienne Koch and William Peden, eds., *The Life and Selected Writings of Thomas Jefferson* (New York: Modern Library, 1944), p. 280.

17. *Federalist* No. 12, p. 91.

18. Ibid., No. 24, p. 161. Publius elaborates on this point in No. 28, pp. 184–85. That he was aware of the departure this view represented from the classical republican ideal of the citizen-soldier is revealed in No. 8, p. 69: "The industrious habits of the people of the present day, absorbed in the pursuits of gain and devoted to the improvements of agriculture and commerce, are incompatible with the condition of a nation of soldiers, which was the true condition of the people of those [that is, the ancient Greek] republics."

19. Ibid., No. 10, p. 81; No. 51, p. 325.

20. Ibid., No. 51, p. 322.

21. Adam Smith, *The Wealth of Nations*, ed. Edwin Cannan (Chicago: University of Chicago Press, 1976), IV, ii, p. 475.

22. Cf. *Federalist* No. 44, pp. 281–83.

23. Alexis de Tocqueville, *Democracy in America*, ed. Phillips Bradley, trans. Henry Reeve, rev. by Francis Bowen, 2 vols. (New York: Vintage Books, 1945), vol. 2, bk. 2, ch. 14, p. 151 (cf. *Federalist* No. 62, pp. 382–83). The explicit discussion of "self-interest rightly understood" is in Tocqueville, vol. 2, bk. 2, chs. 8–9. I have borrowed the phrase "regularity of morals," used at the beginning of this paragraph, from vol. 2, bk. 2, ch. 11, p. 140. Indeed, the series of chs. 8–20 of vol. 2, bk. 2 of *Democracy in America* provides a marvelously illuminating discussion of the commercial character of the American regime.

24. *Federalist* No. 10, p. 81.

25. At several places in *The Federalist* Publius does acknowledge that republican government must be based on moral qualities and attachments that go beyond self-interest—see especially No. 49, pp. 314–15, and No. 55, p. 346. Very little is said about how these qualities and attachments may be fostered, however, and their development is certainly not regarded as the goal of the constitutional republic.

26. Ibid., No. 1, p. 36; No. 3, p. 42; No. 10, p. 78; No. 37, pp. 226–27; No. 85, pp. 521–22.

27. Ibid., No. 43, p. 279; No. 28, p. 180; No. 51, pp. 324–25.

28. John Locke, *Second Treatise*, in Peter Laslett, ed., *Two Treatises of Government* (New York: New American Library, 1965), ch. 9, sect. 124. In the sentence immediately preceding the one quoted here, Locke states that he understands the term "property" to include men's "lives" and "liberties" as

well as their "estates"; this hardly diminishes, however, the extraordinary political importance Locke gives to property in its ordinary sense of material possessions.

29. John Locke, *A Letter Concerning Toleration*, ed. Patrick Romanell (New York: Bobbs-Merrill, 1950), p. 46.

30. Ibid., pp. 47–48.

31. John Locke, *First Treatise*, in Laslett, *Two Treatises of Government*, ch. 4, sect. 42. Consider the following remarks of Montesquieu on the understanding of justice characteristic of commercial societies: "The spirit of trade produces in the mind of a man a certain sense of exact justice, opposite, on the one hand, to robbery, and on the other to those moral virtues which forbid our always adhering rigidly to the rules of private interest, and suffer us to neglect this for the advantage of others.

The total privation of trade, on the contrary, produces robbery, which Aristotle ranks in the means of acquiring; yet it is not at all inconsistent with certain moral virtues. Hospitality, for instance, is most rare in trading countries, while it is found in the most admirable perfection among nations of vagabonds." *Spirit of the Laws*, 20:2.

32. John Locke, *Second Treatise*, ch. 5, sects. 37, 41.

33. Madison to Jefferson, in Hunt, *Madison*, 5:27.

34. In addition to the passages cited in notes 35 and 36 below, see *Federalist*, no. 37, p. 227; no. 44, pp. 282–83.

35. Ibid., no. 7, p. 65; no. 44, pp. 281–82; no. 85; pp. 521–22; no. 10, p. 84.

36. Ibid., no. 10, pp. 77–78, 79.

37. Ibid., no. 35, pp. 214–15; no. 10, pp. 82–83.

38. See Cecelia Kenyon, ed., *The Antifederalists* (Indianapolis: Bobbs Merrill, 1966), p. xxvii, and E. A. J. Johnson, *The Foundations of American Economic Freedom* (Minneapolis: University of Minnesota Press, 1973), pp. 191–92.

39. Thomas Jefferson, "Second Inaugural Address," in Koch and Peden, *Jefferson*, p. 344.

40. Thomas Jefferson to Joseph Milligan, April 6, 1816, in Albert Bergh, ed., *The Writings of Thomas Jefferson*, 20 vols. (Washington, D.C., 1907), 14:466.

41. See Johnson, *American Economic Freedom*, pp. 310–11. James Madison (in Hunt, *Madison*, 6:86) asserts that republicanism is strengthened "by the *silent* operation of laws, which, *without violating the rights of property*, reduce extreme wealth towards a state of mediocrity, and raise extreme indigence toward a state of comfort" (italics added). The founders' desire to reduce economic inequality is always mitigated by their concern to preserve the legitimate rights of property. Hence they never advocate direct redistributive measures, but seek indirect and unobtrusive—that is, "silent"—means to this end.

42. Thomas Jefferson to Rev. James Madison, October 28, 1785, in Koch and Peden, *Jefferson*, p. 390. Progressive taxation is endorsed by Montesquieu in *Spirit of the Laws*, 13:7, and by Adam Smith in *Wealth of Nations*, V, ii, Part II, Article 1.

43. Thomas Jefferson, *Autobiography*, in Koch and Peden, *Jefferson*, pp. 38–39.

44. Tocqueville, *Democracy in America*, vol. 1, ch. 3, pp. 49–55.

45. Arthur Okun, *Equality and Efficiency*, pp. 42–50; John Rawls, *A Theory of Justice* (Cambridge: Harvard University Press, 1971), pp. 15, 74.

46. For a more extended critique of the redistributionist view, see Marc F. Plattner, "The Welfare State vs. the Redistributive State," in *The Public Interest*, no. 55 (Spring 1979), pp. 28–48.

47. *Federalist* No. 14, p. 104.

CHAPTER 8: HUMAN RIGHTS AND RULE OF LAW, *John Dugard*

1. See John Dugard, "Toward Racial Justice in South Africa," in L. Henkin and A. Rosenthal, eds., *Constitutionalism and Rights: The Influence of the United States Constitution Abroad* (New York: Columbia University Press, 1990), p. 349.

2. John Dugard, *Human Rights and the South African Legal Order* (Princeton: Princeton University Press, 1978), pp. 14–25, 393–97; Edward S. Corwin, *The Higher Law Background of American Constitutional Law* (Ithaca: Cornell University Press, 1955); A. E. Dick Howard, *The Road from Runnymede: Magna Carta and Constitutionalism in America* (Charlottesville: University of Virginia Press, 1968); Philip B. Kurland and Ralph Lerner, eds., *The Founders' Constitution*, 5 vols. (Chicago: University of Chicago Press, 1987).

3. See the Declaration of Independence of July 4, 1776, which enumerates the colonists' grievances against British rule.

4. See Dugard, "Toward Racial Justice," pp. 16–24, 393–94.

5. John Dugard, "Grotius, the Jurist and International Lawyer: Four Hundred Years On," *South African Law Journal*, vol. 100 (1983), p. 213.

6. Sir John Wessels, *History of the Roman-Dutch Law* (Grahamstown, South Africa: African Book Company, 1908), pp. 291–93.

7. I. G. Kotzé, *Memoirs and Reminiscences*, vol. 2 (Cape Town: Maskew Miller, 1949), pp. xli–xlii; John Dugard, "Chief Justice versus President: Does the Ghost of *Brown v. Leyds NO* Still Haunt Our Judges?" *De Rebus*, no. 165, 1981, p. 421.

8. Dugard, "Toward Racial Justice," pp. 42–43.

9. L. M. Thompson, *The Unification of South Africa 1902–1910* (Oxford: Clarendon Press, 1960), pp. 99–101.

10. E. Kahn, *The New Constitution* (Cape Town: Juta & Co., 1962), p. 2.

11. South Africa, *House of Assembly Debates*, vol. 108, cols. 11481–94, 11191–93, 11345, 11177, 11367, 11491, 11385–88, 11445–46 (August 15–17, 1983).

12. See, generally, on this subject John Dugard, "The Jurisprudential Foundation of the Apartheid Legal Order," *Philosophical Forum*, vol. 18 (1987), p. 115.

13. See Francois Venter (currently one of the National party's principal constitutional advisers), "The Withering of the Rule of Law," vol. 8 (1973),

Speculum Juris, n. 69 at pp. 86–88. See, too, the *Second Report of the Constitutional Committee of the President's Council PC4/1982*, par. 9.10.

14. See, further on this subject, John Dugard, "A Bill of Rights for South Africa?" *Cornell International Law Journal*, vol. 23 (1990), p. 441.

15. See n. 10.

16. Establishment and Powers of Legislative and Executive Authority for Territory of South West Africa, Proc. R.101, *Government Gazette* 9790 of June 17, 1985.

17. South Africa, *House of Assembly Debates*, vol. 8, cols. 4014–15 (April 23, 1986).

18. The South African Law Commission is established by the South African Law Commission Act 19 of 1973. The law commission consists of seven members from the ranks of the bench, legal profession, government, and universities.

19. The text of these guidelines appears as Appendix D (p. 167), in John Dugard, ed., *The Last Years of Apartheid: Civil Liberties in South Africa*, South African Update series (New York: Ford Foundation—Foreign Policy Association, 1992). See, too, *South African Journal on Human Rights*, vol. 5 (1989), p. 129.

20. See A. Sachs, *Protecting Human Rights in a New South Africa* (Cape Town: Oxford University Press, 1990); A. Sachs, "A Bill of Rights for South Africa: Areas of Agreement and Disagreement," vol. 21 (1989), *Columbia Journal of Human Rights Law Review*, p. 3; N. Masemola, "Rights and a Future South African Constitution," vol. 21 (1989), *Columbia Journal of Human Rights Law*, p. 45; Penuel M. Maduna, "Judicial Review and Protection of Human Rights under a New Constitutional Order in South Africa," vol. 21 (1989), *Columbia Journal of Human Rights*, p. 73.

21. South African Law Commission, *Working Paper on Group and Human Rights*, no. 25, project 58 (Pretoria, March 1989). This report is generally known as the *Olivier Report* because of the dominant role played by Justice P. J. J. Olivier in this compilation.

22. South African Law Commission, *Olivier Report*, Draft bill of rights, art. 20, p. 474.

23. Ibid., p. 383.

24. See the equivocal statement of the state president, F. W. de Klerk, February 2, 1990, on this subject: *Debates of Parliament (Hansard)* (February 2, 1990).

25. See F. W. de Klerk's speech at the federal congress of the National party held on September 4, 1991, reported in Dugard, *Last Years of Apartheid*, Appendix G, p. 189.

26. ANC, Constitutional Committee, *A Bill of Rights for a New South Africa* (working document) (Cape Town: Centre for Developmental Studies, University of the Western Cape, 1990).

27. Published in Dugard, *Last Years of Apartheid*, Appendix F, p. 176.

28. South African Law Commission, Government Printer, Pretoria, *Interim Report on Group and Human Rights*, project 58 (August 1991).

29. Cited in Dugard, *Last Years of Apartheid*, Appendix G, p. 195.

30. Ibid., p. iii.

31. In the United States, it was the successful revolution that gave legitimacy to the constitutional enterprise. The Bill of Rights served no such purpose: hence the absence of a bill of rights from the original constitutional compact. In South Africa, the absence of a clear victory for the liberation forces has compelled the principal liberation movement—the ANC—to search for legitimating instruments in the constitutional field.

32. This reads: "State parties particularly condemn racial segregation and apartheid and undertake to prevent, prohibit and eradicate all practices of this nature in territories under their jurisdiction." Alternatively, such a condemnation could be included in a preambular paragraph.

33. Art. 1.

34. Art. 7(2).

35. Art. 15(2). This paragraph provides that the prohibition on retrospective penal laws contained in art. 15(1) shall not "prejudice the trial and punishment of any person for any act or omission which, at the time it was committed, was criminal according to the general principles of law recognized by the community of nations."

36. See Maduna, "Judicial Review."

37. Ibid., pp. 2–13.

38. This philosophy is expressed in art. 1, which describes the rights contained in its Draft Bill as "fundamental rights to which every individual . . . is entitled." Dugard, *Last Years of Apartheid*, Appendix F, p. 176.

39. Ibid., p. iii.

40. This is the formulation employed by the International Covenant on Civil and Political Rights. See, too, the preamble of the Universal Declaration of Human Rights.

41. Establishment and Powers of Legislative and Executive Authority for Territory of South West Africa.

42. Dugard, *Last Years of Apartheid*, pp. 10–12.

43. Art. 18 of the 1991 interim report; Dugard, *Last Years of Apartheid*, p. 75. See, too, art. 5 of the ANC Constitutional Committee's document on a bill of rights; ibid., Appendix G, p. 189.

44. South African Law Commission, *Olivier Report*.

45. Thomas Emerson, *The System of Freedom of Expression* (New York: Random House, 1970).

46. 341 US 494 (1951). See, too, the dictum of Justice Oliver Wendell Holmes in Abrams v. United States 250 US 616 (1919).

47. The South African Law Commission places no specific restriction on its formulation of free speech in art. 12; Dugard, *Last Years of Apartheid*, Appendix F. It accepts, however, that this right may be curtailed in circumstances that are "reasonably necessary" for reasons of state security, good morals, public health, the administration of justice, the rights of others, or the combating of crime (art. 34).

48. Raymond Suttner, "Freedom of Speech," in *South African Journal on Human Rights*, vol. 6 (1990), p. 372; Albie Sachs, "Towards a Bill of Rights in a Democratic South Africa," *South African Journal on Human Rights*, vol. 6 (1990), pp. 13, 22.

49. Art. 14(4).

50. Art. 4(a) of the International Convention on the Elimination of All Forms of Racial Discrimination.

51. Art. 23(1).

52. "No Platform for Racists. What Should the View of Those on the Left Be?" *South African Journal on Human Rights*, vol. 6 (1990), pp. 374, 397–98.

53. See, for example, Burton v. Wilmington Parking Authority 365 US 715 (1961); Petersen v. City of Greenville 373 US 244 (1963). For a survey of these cases, see Philip B. Kurland, "Egalitarianism and the Warren Court," *Michigan Law Review*, vol. 68 (1970), pp. 629f., 649ff.

54. Sec. 201(a).

55. Art. 14(3)(9).

56. Art. 17. The law commission's assertion that art. 17 is qualified by art. 34 (par. 7.258, p. 367) is not convincing.

57. 198 US 45, 75 (1905).

58. South African Law Commission, *Interim Report*, p. 356.

59. Art. 23.

60. Dugard, *Last Years of Apartheid*, Appendix D, pp. 167–71.

61. Neither the International Covenant on Civil and Political Rights nor the International Covenant on Economic, Social or Cultural Rights contains such a right.

62. Sachs, "Towards a Bill of Rights in a Democratic South Africa" (1990), p. 13.

63. See its working document, *A Bill of Rights for a New South Africa*, pp. xii–xiii.

64. Art. 11.

65. South African Law Commission, *Interim Report*, par. 7.251, pp. 364–65.

66. See, for example, Nicholas Smith, "Affirmative Action: Its Origin and Point," *South African Journal on Human Rights*, vol. 8 (1992), p. 234; Heinz Klug, "Rethinking Affirmative Action in a Non-Racial Democracy," *South African Journal on Human Rights*, vol. 7 (1991), p. 317.

67. South African Law Commission, *Interim Report*, pp. 289–95.

68. Art. 3(b) in ibid.

69. See Albie Sachs, *Protecting Human Rights in a New South Africa* (Cape Town: Oxford University Press, 1990), pp. 19, 30.

70. Art. 13, in ANC, *Bill of Rights*. Italics added.

71. See the comments of the South African Law Commission, in Dugard, *Last Years of Apartheid*, par. 7.96, p. 302.

72. See, generally, on this theme, Sachs, *Protecting Human Rights*.

73. See, too, the European Social Charter (1961) and the African Charter on Human and Peoples Rights (1981).

74. See C. R. M. Dlamini, "The South African Law Commission's Working Paper on Group and Human Rights: Towards a Bill of Rights for South Africa?" *South African Public Law*, vol. 91 (1990), p. 96.

75. J. M. Didcott, "Practical Workings of a Bill of Rights," in J. van der Westhuizen and H. Viljoen, eds., *A Bill of Rights for South Africa* (Durban: Butterworths, 1988), p. 58.

76. See the Indian Constitution of 1949. For an examination of the application of these directives, see Bertus de Villiers, "Directive Principles of State Policy and Fundamental Rights: The Indian Experience," *South African Journal on Human Rights*, vol. 8 (1992), p. 29, and "The Socio-Economic Consequences of Directive Principles of State Policy: Limitation on Fundamental Rights," *South African Journal on Human Rights*, vol. 8 (1992), p. 188.

77. Namibian Constitution of 1990, arts. 95–101.

78. ANC, *Bill of Rights*, pp. viii–ix. See, too, art. 10.

79. South African Law Commission, *Interim Report*, pp. 537, 664.

80. Etienne Mureinik, "Constitutionalizing Economic Rights," *South African Journal on Human Rights*, vol. 8 (1992). See, too, the discussion and criticism of Mureinik's views in that journal.

81. International Covenant on Civil and Political Rights (art. 1); International Covenant on Economic, Social and Cultural Rights (art. 1); and African Charter on Human and Peoples' Rights (art. 20). See, too, the Charter of the United Nations (arts. 1(2), 55) and the Final Act of the Helsinki Conference (1975, p. viii).

82. See John Dugard, *Recognition and the United Nations* (Cambridge: Grotius, 1987), p. 158ff.

83. Ibid., pp. 104, 161–62.

84. South African Law Commission, *Interim Report*, p. 60.

85. See Lea Brilmayer, "Secession and Self-Determination: A Territorial Interpretation," *Yale Journal of International Law*, vol. 16 (1991), p. 177.

86. South African Law Commission, *Interim Report*, p. 80.

87. There is considerable writing on this subject. See, for example, John Dugard, *Human Rights and the South African Legal Order* (Princeton: Princeton University Press, 1978), p. 4.

88. Ibid.

89. South African Law Commission, *Olivier Report*, pp. 411–12.

90. Dugard, *Last Years of Apartheid*, p. vi.

91. Brown v. Board of Education 347 US 483 (1954).

92. Brandenburg v. Ohio 395 US 444 (1969).

93. See, for example, Miranda v. Arizona 384 US 436 (1966); Gideon v. Wainwright 372 US 335 (1963).

94. Dred Scott v. Sandford 60 US 19 (How) 393 (1857).

95. Plessy v. Ferguson 163 US 537 (1896).

96. Lochner v. New York 198 US 45 (1905).

97. Korematsu v. United States 323 US 214 (1944).

98. Dennis v. United States 341 US 494 (1951).

99. For a survey of judicial behavior on this subject, see M. Rothenbühler,

"The Vietnam War and the American Judiciary: An Appraisal of the Role of Domestic Courts in the Field of Foreign Affairs," *Zeitschrift für Auslandisches Offentliches Recht und Volkerrecht*, vol. 33 (1973), p. 312; L. Henkin, "Vietnam in the Courts of the United States: Political Questions," *American Journal of International Law*, vol. 63 (1969), p. 284.

100. Stanford v. Kentucky 492 US 361 (1989).

101. Bowers v. Hardwick 106 478 US 186 (1985).

102. United States v. Alvarez-Machain (1992) 31; International Legal Materials 900. Cf. the decision of the South African Appeal Court in S v. Ebrahim 1991 (2) SA 553 (A).

103. Justice Oliver Wendell Holmes in Southern Pacific Co v. Jensen 244 US 205 at 221 (1916).

104. The European Convention on Human Rights, which these bodies apply, is substantially similar to the International Covenant on Civil and Political Rights.

105. See William A. Schabas, *International Human Rights Law and the Canadian Charter* (Toronto: Carswell, 1991).

106. See, generally, on this subject, Richard Kluger, *Simple Justice: The History of* Brown v. Board of Education *and Black America's Struggle for Equality* (New York: Alfred A. Knopf, 1976); Jack Bass, *Unlikely Heroes: The Dramatic Story of the Southern Judges of the Fifth Circuit Who Translated the Supreme Court's Brown Decision into a Revolution for Equality* (New York: Simon and Schuster, 1981).

107. The pre-Republican Constitution (as amended, Act 9 of 1956), the 1961 Constitution (sec. 59 of Act 32 of 1961), and the 1983 Constitution (secs. 18[2] and 34[3] of Act 110 of 1983) all expressly denied the courts the power to review Acts of Parliament.

108. Dugard, "Toward Racial Justice," pp. 28–33, 64–65.

109. Ibid., part 4; C. Forsyth, *In Danger of Their Talents: A Study of the Appellate Division of the Supreme Court of South Africa from 1950 to 1980* (Cape Town: Juta & Co., 1985).

110. See A. van Blerk, *Judge and Be Judged* (Cape Town: Juta & Co., 1988).

111. R. Wacks, "Judges and Injustice," *South African Law Journal*, vol. 101 (1984), p. 266.

112. For example, in Rossouw v. Sachs 1964 (2) SA 551 (C); Minister of the Interior v. Lockhart 1961 (2) SA 587 (A).

113. See art. 16 of the draft bill of rights, in Dugard, *Last Years of Apartheid*, and *Constitutional Principles for a Democratic South Africa*, Appendix F, in Dugard, ibid., p. 181. The latter document stresses that such a court should be representative, independent and be "accountable only to the principles of the Constitution."

114. In 1990, the Committee for Constitutional Affairs of the National party–controlled President's Council endorsed the establishment of a constitutional court; President's Council, *Constitutional Systems*, PC 1/1990 (Government Printer, 1990).

115. Project 77, pp. 1165–1220. See, too, N. R. L. Haysom, *Constitutional*

Court for South Africa, Occasional Paper 14 (Johannesburg Centre for Applied Legal Studies, November 1991).

116. Ibid., p. 1,218.

117. Criminal Law Amendment Bill, 1992. See the *Star*, June 15, 1992, p. 5.

118. See on this subject *State Crimes, Punishment or Pardon* (Queenstown, Md.: Justice and Society Program, Aspen Institute, 1989).

CHAPTER 9: WHAT IS A BILL OF RIGHTS? *Robert A. Goldwin*

1. James Madison, letter to Thomas Jefferson, October 17, 1788.

2. Ibid.

3. In the sections that follow, I have drawn liberally from my essay, "Droits, structure et modération: La filière traditionelle américaine pour assurer les droits," in Terence Marshall, ed., *Théorie et Pratique du Gouvernement Constitutionnel: La France et les États-Unis* (Paris: Éditions de l'Espace Europeén, 1992).

4. Machiavelli, *The Prince*, chap. 15, "On Those Things for Which Men, and Especially Princes, Are Praised or Blamed."

5. John Locke, *Second Treatise of Government*, chap. 8, "Of the Beginning of Political Societies."

6. Alexander Hamilton, John Jay, and James Madison, *Federalist* 9.

7. This was the most remarked sentence in Senator Barry Goldwater's speech accepting the nomination of the Republican National Convention in San Francisco in 1964.

8. On the difference between the right of resistance to tyranny and the right of revolution, see my essay "Is There an American Right of Revolution?" in *Why Blacks, Women, and Jews Are Not Mentioned in the Constitution, and Other Unorthodox Views* (Washington, D.C.: AEI Press, 1990), pp. 46–54.

9. See Robert A. Goldwin, Art Kaufman, and William A. Schambra, eds., *Forging Unity out of Diversity: The Approaches of Eight Nations* (Washington, D.C.: American Enterprise Institute, 1989), for discussions of the constitutional efforts to cope with the problems presented by diversity in India, the United States, Belgium, Canada, Switzerland, Spain, Malaysia, and Yugoslavia.

10. Art. I, sec. 2, clause 3, as amended by the Fourteenth Amendment. For the present citizenship status of the American Indians, see chapter 10 by Walter Berns in this volume.

11. When the Nineteenth Amendment was added in 1920, providing that "the right of citizens of the United States to vote shall not be denied or abridged by the United States or by any State on account of sex," no provision of the Constitution of the United States had to be revised or deleted, for there had never been in it any barrier to voting by women. The barriers had all been in state legislation or state constitutions.

12. Art. VI, clause 3.

13. Letter to James Madison, November 18, 1788.

14. Art. I, sec. 8, clause 8: "The Congress shall have power . . . to promote the progress of science and useful arts, by securing for limited times to

authors and inventors the exclusive right to their respective writings and discoveries." This provision is the constitutional basis of all copyright and patent legislation, but it is notable that the words *copyright* and *patent* do not occur.

15. The absence of emphasis on rights in a constitution need not suggest inattention to them. A number of civil rights are protected in the original, unamended Constitution, including, among many others, the right to a trial by jury in all criminal cases, the right to the privilege of the writ of *habeas corpus*, the right to be free from the danger of *ex post facto* laws, and the right not to be exposed to a religious test to hold public office. But, significantly, in all of these unemphatic constitutional provisions, the word *right* was not used. See Joseph Bessette, "Guarding the Constitution from Legislative Tyranny," in Robert A. Licht, ed., *Is the Supreme Court the Guardian of the Constitution?* (Washington, D.C.: AEI Press, 1993).

16. *Federalist* 51.

17. "Congress shall make no law respecting an establishment of religion, or prohibiting the free exercise thereof; or abridging the freedom of speech, or of the press, or the right of the people peaceably to assemble, and to petition the Government for a redress of grievances."

For an account of Madison's role, see Herbert J. Storing, "The Constitution and the Bill of Rights," in Robert A. Goldwin and William A. Schambra, eds., *How Does the Constitution Secure Rights?* (Washington, D.C.: American Enterprise Institute, 1986), pp. 15–35.

18. *Federalist* 10.

19. Letter to Thomas Jefferson, October 17, 1788.

20. *Federalist* 51.

21. This phrase was used often by Madison; it appears in his letter to Jefferson, October 17, 1788, as well as in *Federalist* 40.

22. *Federalist* 51.

23. *Federalist* 84.

24. Art. IV, sec. 4.

25. See Bernard Schwartz, *The Bill of Rights: A Documentary History* (New York: Chelsea House Publishers, 1971), p. 527.

26. See Carl Becker, *The Declaration of Independence: A Study in the History of Political Ideas* (New York: Knopf, 1948).

27. Cited in Leo Strauss, *Persecution and the Art of Writing* (Glencoe, Ill.: Free Press, 1952), p. 22.

CHAPTER 10: LIMITATIONS OF A NEW NATIONAL GOVERNMENT, *Gretchen Carpenter*

1. The British constitutional author, Sir Ivor Jennings, in *The Law and the Constitution* (London: University of London Press, 5th ed., 1959), p. 62, holds the view that free elections, freedom of expression of public opinion, and the recognition of the status of the parliamentary opposition provide the best guarantees of freedom, regardless of the form of government and the presence of formal constraints on the legislature. Lively and free expression

of public opinion depends to a major extent on the right to receive and to disseminate information, a right until now not duly recognized in South Africa. Truly free and fair elections cannot be guaranteed purely by legislation prohibiting the intimidation or undue influencing of voters. If the government of the day is in a position to suppress information that may sway voter opinion, the fact that the electorate is "free" to vote as it chooses means little.

2. There appears to be consensus today that systems of proportional representation reflect voter opinion more accurately than systems of territorial representation. Territorial representation is a cardinal feature of the Westminster system and has been described by H. W. R. Wade in *Constitutional Fundamentals* (London: Stevens, 1980), p. 5, as a system of misrepresentation rather than one of representation. W. H. Olivier, "Party Systems and Electoral Systems," in D. J. van Vuuren and D. J. Kriek, eds., *Political Alternatives for South Africa: Principles and Perspectives* (Durban: Butterworths, 1983), pp. 341–42, by using statistics also illustrates the way in which political reality has been distorted by the system of territorial representation in both Britain and South Africa. A more sophisticated system of territorial representation, such as one requiring an absolute majority rather than a simple first-past-the-post majority or some other variation on the basic theme, however, could certainly serve to eliminate some weaknesses of the system as we know it (see Olivier, "Party Systems and Electoral Systems," pp. 342–45). While it would therefore be too sweeping to state that only a system of proportional representation is truly democratic, clearly a good deal of thought needs to be given to the electoral system when a new constitution is being drafted.

3. Some authorities would have it that the idea of a dispersal of government powers can be traced back as far as Plato and Aristotle and that the concept of separation of functions among the monarch, House of Lords, and House of Commons predated Locke. Both Locke and Montesquieu accepted the principle that the monarch should have a legislative veto. See in this regard J. P. verLoren van Themaat, *Staatsreg*, 3rd ed., by M. Wiechers (Durban: Butterworths, 1981), p. 48, n. 69; O. Hood Phillips, *Constitutional and Administrative Law*, 6th ed. (London: Sweet & Maxwell, 1978), p. 12; M. Hough, "Die Ontwikkeling en Kontemporêre Betekenis van die Leerstelling van Verdeling van Staatsgesag," *De Jure*, vol. 11 (1978), no. 2, pp. 346–48.

4. Among those who regard the doctrine as overrated are British writers such as Walter Bagehot, *The English Constitution* (Ithaca, N.Y.: Cornell University Press, 1933); O. Hood Phillips, "A Constitutional Myth: Separation of Powers," *Law Quarterly Review* (1977), vol. 77, no. 1, p. 11; and W. A. Robson, *Justice and Administrative Law: A Study of the British Constitution* (London: Stevens, 1928), who described the doctrine as "an antique and rickety chariot." Conversely, see Colin Munro, "The Separation of Powers: Not Such a Myth," *Public Law* (Spring 1981), p. 19, and the vast literature on the topic in American legal literature.

5. G. Marshall, *Constitutional Theory* (Oxford: Clarendon Press, 1971), chap. 5, cited by Munro, "Separation of Powers," p. 21.

6. See Michael Yoder, "Separation of Powers: No Longer Simply Hanging in the Balance," *Georgetown Law Journal* (1990), vol. 80, p. 173.

7. Ibid., p. 174. Yoder favors what he calls the public citizen standard, so named because it reflects the approach by Justice Kennedy in Public Citizen v. U.S. Department of Justice 109 S. Ct. 2558 (1989). This approach lies somewhere between the two extremes of formalism and functionalism.

8. See, for example, Gretchen Carpenter, *Introduction to South African Constitutional Law* (Durban: Butterworths, 1987), pp. 75–76; D. H. van Wyk, "The Westminster System," in D. J. Van Vuuren and D. J. Kriek, eds., *Political Alternatives for South Africa: Principles and Perspectives*, 1983, pp. 259–73; L. J. Boulle, "The Second Republic—Its Constitutional Lineage," *Comparative and International Law Journal of Southern Africa* (1980), vol. 13, p. 1.

9. He nominates four members, one from each province, to the House of Assembly, sec. 41(1)(b) of the Republic of South Africa Constitution Act 110 of 1983, and two each to the House of Representatives, sec. 42(1)(b), and the House of Delegates, sec. 43(1)(b). For criticism of this provision, see Harold Rudolph, "Nominated Members of Parliament and the Demise of the Entrenched Sections," *South African Law Journal* (1981), vol. 98, p. 346.

10. See, for example, State President v. Tsenoli; Kerchoff v. Minister of Law and Order (1986) 4 SA 1150(A); Radebe v. Minister of Law and Order (1987) 1 SA 586(W); Nqumba v. State President (1987) 1 SA 456(E). In general, see also Marinus Wiechers, *Administrative Law* (Durban: Butterworths, 1985), pp. 282–85, where he explains that an ouster clause is inoperative when an administrative act is so manifestly defective that it is not merely voidable but void. Although the act has been performed and therefore cannot be said to be a factual nullity (the person concerned has indeed been arrested or detained), it is deemed to be a legal nullity because the administrative organ has grossly exceeded the powers conferred on it. Steyn Uitleg van Wette, 5th ed., 1981, p. 288, lists seven grounds on which an ouster clause may be found to be inoperative: (1) excess of power, or *ultra vires*; (2) fraud, or *mala fides*; (3) a refusal or failure by the administrative organ to exercise its discretion at all; (4) unauthorized delegation; (5) ulterior (unauthorized) purpose; (6) irredeemable vagueness or uncertainty; and (7) failure to comply with provisions relating to the exercise of the power conferred.

11. Examples of such wide conferment of power are found in the powers that the state president previously possessed from sec. 25 of the Black Administration Act 38 of 1927 (repealed by sec. 5 of Act 108 of 1991) by virtue of his constitutional position as supreme chief of the black population of South Africa (sec. 93 of the Constitution Act). An example worth considering in this regard is the Model State Administrative Procedure Act of the United States, which contains model rules that must be adhered to by subordinate legislatures.

12. One of the few praiseworthy features of the Provincial Government Act 69 of 1986 is that sec. 16 requires the administrator to give interested parties an opportunity to state their views before promulgating subordinate legislation in terms of the act.

13. See A. V. Dicey, *Introduction to the Study of the Law of the Constitution*, 10th ed. (Johannesburg: Macmillan, 1975), p. 70, who refers to the sover-

eignty of Parliament as the keystone of English constitutional law; and see the oft-quoted statement by Jennings, *Law and Constitution*, p. 147: "Thus Parliament may remodel the Constitution, prolong its own life, legislate ex post facto, legalise irregularities, provide for individual cases, interfere with contracts and authorise the seizure of property, give dictatorial powers to the Government, dissolve the United Kingdom or the British Commonwealth, introduce communism or socialism, or individualism or fascism, entirely without legal restriction"; G. N. Barrie, "Die Soewereiniteit van die Parlement" LL.D. thesis, University of South Africa, 1968; L. J. Boulle, B. Harris, and C. Hoexter, *Constitutional and Administrative Law* (Cape Town: Juta & Co., 1989), p. 117.

14. See the *Interim Report* of the South African Law Commission on Group and Human Rights, Project 58, Pretoria 1991, p. 302 et seq. In particular, see the article written by the present minister of justice, H. J. Coetsee, "Hoekom nie 'n Akte van Menseregte vir Suid-Afrika," *Tydskrif vir Regswetenskap* (1984), vol. 9, p. 5.

15. The question whether procedural limitations imposed on a sovereign parliament derogate from its sovereignty was answered in the negative in the famous South African case Harris v. Minister of the Interior (1952) 2 SA 428(A). The court held that such restraints related only to manner and form and not to the area of power and therefore did not affect the essence of parliamentary sovereignty in any way. Such an issue could not really arise in Britain itself because of the absence of any statute providing for entrenched provisions such as secs. 35, 137, and 152 of the South Africa Act. In Britain, the debate about a sovereign parliament's powers to limit itself (and thus its successors) crystallized into an enquiry whether the sovereignty of the British Parliament is continuing (in which case no limitation is possible) or self-embracing (which permits of some effective abdication of power); see Carpenter, *Introduction*, pp. 149–55, and the authority cited there.

16. See J. J. Gauntlett, "Appointing and Promoting Judges: Which Way Now?" *Consultus* (1990), vol. 3, p. 24; South African Law Commission, *Report on Constitutional Models Project 77* (1991), Pretoria, p. 1101 et seq.

17. Articles 82 and 85 of the Namibian Constitution.

18. The Senate was abolished by sec. 13 of Act 101 of 1980.

19. See Carpenter, *Introduction*, p. 287. The houses have an effective veto only for the entrenched provisions (listed in sec. 99). All other legislation dealing with general affairs could previously be referred to the President's Council (abolished during 1993) for its decision in a dispute among the houses: see sec. 78 of the Constitution Act, read with sec. 32.

20. See the South African Law Commission, *Report on Constitutional Models Project 77*, chap. 16, p. 837 et seq.

21. See, for example, G. Winterton, "Is the House of Lords Immortal?" *Law Quarterly Review* (1979), vol. 95, p. 386; South African Law Commission, *Report on Constitutional Models*, chap. 16, pp. 842–43.

22. See Carpenter, *Introduction*, pp. 141–47, for an account of the constitutional crisis that ended with the judgment in Collins v. Minister of the Interior (1957) 1 SA 552(A).

23. Sec. 75 of the Namibian Constitution.

24. See Carpenter, *Introduction*, pp. 369–70.

25. See C. F. Strong, *Modern Constitutions* (London: Sidgwick & Jackson, 1972), p. 209.

26. J. D. van der Vyver, "Political Sovereignty," in C. F. Visser, ed., *Essays in Honour of Ellison Kahn* (Cape Town: Juta & Co., 1989), p. 328.

27. Sec. 16 of the Constitution Act, read with section 19(1)(b).

28. Sec. 32 of the Constitution Act.

29. South African Law Commission, *Report on Constitutional Models*, chap. 21, p. 1071.

30. See the discussion of Lijphart's theories in L. J. Boulle, *South Africa and the Consociational Option* (Cape Town: Juta & Co., 1984).

31. See Carpenter, *Introduction*, pp. 14–16.

32. See Harry H. Wellington, *Interpreting the Constitution* (New Haven: Yale University Press, 1990), p. 43.

33. Patrick J. Dalton and Robina S. Dexter, *Constitutional Law* (London: Oyez, 1976), p. 29.

CHAPTER 11: THE PROBLEM OF DEMOCRACY, *Walter Berns*

1. Alexis de Tocqueville, *Democracy in America*, vol. 2, bk. 4, chap. 7.

2. *Federalist 1*.

3. *The Federalist* (or *Federalist Papers*) began as a series of letters, eighty-five in number, written by Alexander Hamilton, James Madison, and John Jay, under the pseudonym of Publius, and published in New York City newspapers to persuade the people of the state of New York to ratify the Constitution drafted in Philadelphia during the summer of 1787. "Written with a haste that often bordered on the frantic," as the editor of a modern edition of the work says, and "printed and published as if it were the most perishable kind of daily news," *The Federalist* is, nevertheless, "the most important work in political science that has ever been written, or is likely ever to be written, in the United States." In addition to its importance in the realm of political science or theory, it is understood to be the most authoritative commentary on the Constitution. As a result, it is widely used as a college text and is probably one of the few books that can be found in every American library, including those located overseas.

4. Abraham Lincoln, "Address to the Young Men's Lyceum of Springfield, Illinois," January 27, 1838, in *Lincoln: Speech and Writings*, vol. 1 (New York: Library of America, 1989), p. 35.

5. *"Le grand advantage des Américains est d'être arrivés a la démocratie sans avoir a souffrir de revolutions démocratiques, et d'être nés egaux au lieu de le devinir."* Tocqueville, *Democracy in America*, vol. 2, pt. 2, chap. 3.

6. *"Pourquoi en Amérique, pays de démocratie par excellence, personne en fait-il entende contre la propriété en general ces plaintes qui souvent retentissent en Europe? Est-il besoin de le dire? c'est qu'en Amérique il n'y a point de prolétaires"* (Ibid., vol. 1, pt. 2, chap. 6, sec. 3 [*"De L'Idée Des Droits Aux Etats-Unis"*]).

7. See Robert A. Goldwin, *Why Blacks, Women, and Jews Are Not Mentioned*

in the Constitution, and Other Unorthodox Views (Washington, D.C.: AEI Press, 1990).

8. Interestingly enough, while the slaves were freed by the Thirteenth Amendment to the Constitution and made citizens of the United States by the Fourteenth, it was not until 1924 that Congress enacted a statute declaring all Indians "born within the territorial limits of the United States . . . to be citizens of the United States" (43 *Statutes at Large* 253).

9. There is no question but that the liberties of Japanese-Americans were jeopardized during World War II. See "The Role of the Judiciary." On the question of civil liberties during the Civil War, see Mark Neely, *The Fate of Liberty: Abraham Lincoln and Civil Liberties* (New York: Oxford University Press, 1991).

10. Walter Berns, *Taking the Constitution Seriously* (New York: Simon and Schuster, 1987), pp. 93–94.

11. Some years later, James McHenry, a delegate to the Constitutional Convention from Delaware, recorded the following entry in his *Anecdotes*: "A lady asked Dr. Franklin Well Doctor what have we got a republic or a monarchy—a republic replied the Doctor if you can keep it." See Max Ferrand, ed., *The Records of the Federal Convention of 1787*, vol. 3 (New Haven: Yale University Press, 1937), p. 85.

12. Harvey C. Mansfield, Jr., *America's Constitutional Soul* (Baltimore: Johns Hopkins University Press, 1991), p. 211.

13. Hobbes, *Leviathan*, pt. 1, chap. 13; Locke, *Two Treatises of Government*, 2, secs. 101, 123.

14. Locke, *Treatises*, 2, sec. 21.

15. Ibid., sec. 93.

16. Ibid., sec. 134.

17. Ibid., secs. 143, 144.

18. Charles C. Thach, Jr., *The Creation of the Presidency, 1775–1798* (Baltimore: Johns Hopkins University Press, 1923, 1969), pp. 28, 29.

19. Locke wrote,

> There is another power in every commonwealth which one may call natural, because it is that which answers to the power every man naturally had before he entered into society; for though in a commonwealth the members of it are distinct persons still in reference to one another, and as such are governed by the laws of the society, yet, in reference to the rest of mankind, they make one body which is, as every member of it before was, still in the state of nature with the rest of mankind. Hence it is that the controversies that happen between any man of the society with those that are out of it are managed by the public, and an injury done to a member of their body engages the whole in the reparation of it. So that, under this consideration, the whole community is one body in the state of nature in respect of all other states or persons out of its community.
>
> This, therefore, contains the power of war and peace, leagues and alliances, and all the transactions with all persons and communities without the commonwealth, and may be called "federative," if

anyone pleases. So the thing is understood, I am indifferent as to the name (*Treatises*, 2, secs. 145, 146).

20. Ibid., sec. 160.

21. Abraham Lincoln, for example, suspended the privilege of habeas corpus, a power that, from its place in the Constitution, would seem to belong to the Congress; acting in his capacity as commander in chief, he freed the slaves, which, he had argued when first taking the presidential oath of office, the Congress had no authority to do. To mention one more example, Franklin D. Roosevelt, without any authority from Congress, traded fifty of the Navy's warships to the British in exchange for ninety-nine-year leases on some naval bases.

22. As one might expect, this is a recipe for conflict between the legislative and the executive branches. Depending on the circumstances, each exercises the supreme power, and there is no rule—and in the nature of the case, there cannot be a rule—for determining those circumstances. Whether the executive has exceeded his authority is sometimes (but not always) determined by the Supreme Court, usually the final arbiter of constitutional questions. But if the executive defies the Court (as Abraham Lincoln did), the question of whether he exceeded his authority is determined, in principle, by the people and, in practice, by a court of impeachment, which under the Constitution is the Senate of the United States, with the chief justice of the United States presiding.

23. The importance of this principle was demonstrated when it was violated by President Ronald Reagan in the so-called Iran-Contra affair. He pleaded ignorance of the extraordinary actions undertaken by his subordinates, chiefly Colonel Oliver North and Admiral John Poindexter, and the country has not yet seen the end of the controversy this provoked.

24. Walter Berns, "The Constitution as Bill of Rights," in Robert A. Goldwin and William A. Schambra, eds., *How Does the Constitution Secure Rights?* (Washington, D.C.: American Enterprise Institute, 1985), pp. 50–73.

25. Dred Scott v. Sandford, 19 How. (60 U.S.) 393 (1857); Hepburn v. Griswold, 8 Wall., (75 U.S.) 603 (1870); Knox v. Lee, 12 Wall. (79 U.S.) 457 (1871); Pollock v. Farmers' Loan & Trust Co., 157 U.S. 429 (1895); National Labor Relations Board v. Jones and Laughlin Steel Corp., 301 U.S. 1 (1937).

26. Eichman v. United States, 110 S.Ct. 2404 (1990); Korematsu v. United States, 323 U.S. 214 (1944).

27. Seventeenth Amendment.

28. Fifteenth, Nineteenth, Twenty-fourth, and Twenty-sixth Amendments.

29. The advent of political parties ensured that presidential electors would be chosen by popular vote of the people; this became evident as early as 1800. Nevertheless, because these popular votes are aggregated at the state rather than at the national level, because each state is given a number of electors equal to "the whole number of Senators and Representatives to which [it] may be entitled in the Congress," and because each state, regardless of the size of its population, is entitled to two senators, it is always

possible that the person who wins a majority of the electoral votes will not have won a majority of the popular votes.

30. Michael Parenti, *Democracy for the Few*, 3d ed. (New York: St. Martin's Press, 1980).

31. Party government would be possible in the United States only by amending the Constitution in fundamental respects. See, James Ceaser, ". . . . . ."

32. Woodrow Wilson, *Congressional Government* (1885; reprint, New York: Meridian Books, 1956), p. 91.

33. "We have in this country," Wilson complained (ibid., p. 142), "no real leadership." But real leadership, especially charismatic leadership, was precisely what the framers sought to prevent (see *Federalist* 10). What is interesting here is the way Americans speak, or refuse to speak, of government. Whereas the British speak of the Major (Thatcher, Wilson, Churchill, Chamberlain, Disraeli, etc.) government and the Canadians of the Mulroney (Trudeau, Diefenbaker, Mackenzie King, etc.) government, Americans speak of the Bush (Reagan, Carter, Roosevelt, Lincoln, Jackson, Washington) administration. This, I think, is not by chance; rather, it derives from the Constitution.

34. James MacGregor Burns, *The Deadlock of Democracy: Four Party Politics in America* (Englewood Cliffs, N.J.: Prentice-Hall, 1963); Committee on Political Parties, American Political Science Association, *Toward a More Responsible Two-Party System* (New York: Rinehart, 1950).

35. Charles A. Beard, *An Economic Interpretation of the Constitution of the United States* (New York: Macmillan, 1936).

36. Robert E. Brown, *Charles Beard and the American Constitution* (Princeton, N.J.: Princeton University Press, 1956); Forrest McDonald, *We the People—The Economic Origins of the Constitution* (Chicago: University of Chicago Press, 1958).

37. "*Chacun ayant un bien particulier à défendre, reconnaît en principe le droit de propriété.*" Tocqueville, *Democracy in America*, vol. 1, pt. 2, chap. 6, sec. 3 ("*De l'idée des droits aux Etats-Unis*").

38. See Allan Bloom, ed., *Confronting the Constitution: The Challenge to Locke, Montesquieu, Jefferson, and the Federalists from Utilitarianism, Historicism, Marxism, Freudianism, Pragmatism, Existentialism* . . . (Washington, D.C.: AEI Press, 1990), especially chaps. 10, 12, and 15.

CHAPTER 12: PARTIES AND GOVERNMENT, *David Welsh*

1. Adam Przeworski, *Democracy and the Market: Political and Economic Reforms in Eastern Europe and Latin America* (Cambridge: Cambridge University Press, 1991), p. 95.

2. Hans Daudt and Douglas W. Rae, "Social Contract and the Limits of Majority Rule," in Pierre Birnbaum, Jack Lively, and Geraint Perry, eds., *Democracy, Consensus, and Social Contract* (London: Sage Publications, 1978), p. 335.

3. Jane J. Mansbridge, *Beyond Adversarial Democracy* (New York: Basic Books, 1980), p. 266.

4. Alexis de Tocqueville, *Democracy in America*, ed. Henry Steele Commager (London: Oxford University Press, 1946), chap. 14.

5. See Walker Conner, "Eco- or Ethno-nationalism?" in *Ethnic and Racial Studies*, vol. 7, no. 3 (1979); Anthony D. Smith, *The Ethnic Revival* (Cambridge: Cambridge University Press, 1981); and Donald L. Horowitz, *Ethnic Groups in Conflict* (Berkeley: University of California Press, 1985).

6. Horowitz, *Ethnic Groups in Conflict*, p. 86.

7. John Darby, *Conflict in Northern Ireland: The Development of a Polarised Community* (Dublin: Gill and Macmillan, 1976), p. 112.

8. Ian Lustick, *Arabs in the Jewish State: Israel's Control of a National Minority* (Austin: University of Texas Press, 1980), p. 90.

9. Sammy Smooha, "Minority Status in an Ethnic Democracy: The Status of the Arab Minority in Israel," in *Ethnic and Racial Studies*, vol. 13, no. 3 (1990), p. 407.

10. K. D. McRae, "Constitutionalism and the Canadian Political System," in Kenneth McRae, ed., *Consociational Democracy: Political Accommodation in Segmented Societies* (Toronto: McClelland and Stewart, 1974), p. 252.

11. Charles V. Hamilton, "On Parity and Political Empowerment," in Janet Dewart, ed., *The State of Black America 1989* (New York: National Urban League, 1989), pp. 114–15.

12. David Welsh, "Federalism and the Problem of South Africa," in Murray Forsyth, ed., *Federalism and Nationalism* (Leicester: Leicester University Press, 1989), pp. 253–54.

13. Ainslie T. Embree, "Pluralism and National Integration: The Indian Experience," *Journal of International Affairs*, vol. 27, no. 1 (1973), p. 46.

14. Donald Rothchild, "State-ethnic relations in Middle Africa," in Gwendolen M. Carter and Patrick O'Meara, eds., *African Independence: The First Twenty-five Years* (Bloomington: Indiana University Press, 1985), pp. 82–83.

15. Eliphas G. Mukonoweshuro, "Containing Political Instability in a Poly-ethnic society: The Case of Mauritius," *Ethnic and Racial Studies*, vol. 14, no. 2 (1991), p. 200.

16. Basil Davidson, *The Black Man's Burden* (London: James Currey, 1992).

17. Przeworski, *Democracy and the Market*, pp. 12–13.

18. Ibid., p. 36.

CHAPTER 13: CONSTITUTIONALISM AND A SEMIPARTY SYSTEM, *James W. Ceaser*

1. Alexis de Tocqueville, *Democracy in America*, preface to the 12th ed., J. P. Mayer edition (New York: Doubleday, 1969), p. xiv.

2. Thomas Jefferson to Major John Cartwright, June 5, 1824.

3. *Federalist* 53, p. 331.

4. Ibid.

5. *Federalist* 78.

6. Ibid.

7. Because of the federal character of the American system, there are a few exceptions to all of the rules and generalizations that I am making here. They have no material bearing, however, on the direction of the argument.

8. See the argument in Duverger's well-known work, *Political Parties*, trans. Barbara and Robert North (New York: Wiley and Sons, 1954).

9. *Federalist* 10.

10. For a treatment of this theme, see Joseph Bessette's "Deliberative Democracy," in Robert A. Goldwin and William A. Schambra, eds., *How Democratic Is the Constitution?* (Washington, D.C.: American Enterprise Institute, 1980), and the forthcoming work by the same author, *The Mild Voice of Reason: Deliberative Democracy and American National Government* (Chicago: University of Chicago Press).

11. Letter to Spencer Roane, September 6, 1819.

A NOTE ON THE BOOK

This book was edited by
Cheryl Weissman, Dana Lane, and Ann Petty
of the staff of the AEI Press.
The text was set in Palatino, a typeface designed by
the twentieth-century Swiss designer Hermann Zapf.
Coghill Composition, of Richmond, Virginia,
set the type, and Data Reproductions Corporation,
of Rochester Hills, Michigan, printed and bound the book,
using permanent acid-free paper.

The AEI Press is the publisher for the American Enterprise Institute for Public Policy Research, 1150 17th Street, N.W., Washington, D.C. 20036; *Christopher C. DeMuth*, publisher; *Edward Styles*, director; *Dana Lane*, assistant director; *Ann Petty*, editor; *Cheryl Weissman*, editor; *Mary Cristina Delaney*, editorial assistant (rights and permissions).

www.ingramcontent.com/pod-product-compliance
Lightning Source LLC
Jackson TN
JSHW011933131224
75386JS00041B/1354